# Surviving and Prospering
# in a
# Business Partnership

By Jay Jacobsen

Published by The Oasis Press®

Grants Pass, Oregon

Published by The Oasis Press*
300 North Valley Drive
Grants Pass, OR   97526
 503/479-9464

International Standard Book Number 1-55571-041-7 (binder)
                                   1-55571-072-7 (paper)

The publisher does not assume and hereby disclaims any
liability to any party for any loss or damage caused by
errors or omissions in **Surviving and Prospering in a
Business Partnership**, whether such errors or omissions
result from negligence, accident, or any other cause.

Printed in the United States of America

First edition

6 5 4 3 2 1

Revision Code: AA

*The Oasis Press is a Registered Trademark of Publishing Services, Inc.,
 a Texas corporation doing business in Oregon as PSI Research.

To Mickey—the best partner ever!

# TABLE OF CONTENTS

# Introduction

This is a guide to surviving and prospering in a business partnership. It is designed to give you a practical basis for the decisions you will need to make in getting your partnership started on the right foot (or to help your existing partnership become even more successful).

Starting a successful business venture is a tough proposition, and it often makes sense to approach it through a partnership to give yourself a better shot at success. Here are some of the reasons:

o **Complementary skills.** Ideally, you and your partners will each bring a different skill base to the business. One of you may be the outgoing, sales-and-marketing type, while another may be best at the administrative and financial areas of the business.

o **Friendship and support.** Starting and operating a business involves a lot of dedication and hard work. For many of us, it is comforting to know that we will have the constant support and friendship of partners. This has the additional benefit of reducing stress.

o **Make more money.** With partners, it is possible to increase your business to a larger size than you could ever reach on your own.

o **Lower risk.** The increased skills and resources that a team brings to the business will lower your risk of failure. In addition, the investment and credit that are required will be shared among all of you.

o **Challenge and satisfaction of team approach.** With the right partners, you will operate in an environment where everyone will be challenged to perform at their best level of performance. You will have the satisfaction of knowing that key decisions have been made after the give-and-take of discussion between partners.

o **More time off.** With shared responsibility for management, you and your partners will be able to fill in for each other. One of the biggest complaints of sole proprietors is that they can never take time off from the business.

o **Fun.** Good partners will enjoy working with each other. Many entrepreneurs include having fun as one of their objectives for the business, and it seems to be a key to success.

o **Synergy.** This is the principle that one plus one can equal three. In a good partnership, you may find that one plus one can equal four or five!

o **It just feels right.** All of the theories on decision-making have this element. The best decisions, even after detailed analysis and quantifications, are based on a subjective or gut feeling that they are right.

Thousands of partnerships are formed every day. Joining forces with partners can be a profitable and pleasant experience, or can turn into a nightmare. A partnership is really a business marriage, and there is nothing in most people's training and background that prepares them for the commitment they are undertaking when they exchange business vows. We all enter into the relationship with enthusiasm and hope. The keys to sustaining this enthusiasm, as well as sustaining the life of the partnership, are planning and communication.

Your planning should start with an understanding of how a partnership compares with the other forms of business that are available. These comparisons are outlined in the first chapter. Once you are sure that a partnership makes the most sense for your business, see chapter 2 which looks at the the legal and practical requirements for setting up your partnership.

"Choosing Your Partners" is the subject of chapter 3. This section is designed to help you step back and review the people with whom you are about to enter into a long-term business relationship. Use the "Partner Scorecard" on page 27 as a quick way to think about and rate your partners, and take a moment to review the skills and experience of each partner to make sure they complement one another.

Chapter 4 contains a complete review of a partnership agreement. (A partnership agreement for your own use is included in the Appendix A.) By reviewing the provisions of the agreement and the accompanying comments, you will begin to understand the issues facing you as you set up and operate your partnership. You will get a feel for the serious problems that can be avoided by advance planning and agreement.

A discussion of everyone's favorite topic—income taxes—follows in chapter 5. Partnership income taxes are one of the most complicated areas of tax law; therefore, a basic understanding of how they work is essential to the success of your business.

Chapter 6 covers the "Limited Partnership," which is a form of partnership set up to accommodate investors. In return for relinquishing control of the business to the general partner, limited partners receive limited liability and the pass-through of tax advantages, while participating in the profits. Like the discussion on tax laws, this chapter is designed to give you a basic familiarity with a complex subject.

Chapter 7, "Partnership Problems," gives you illustrations of the problems that can develop no matter how well you plan. Use experience as your instructor so that you will be prepared for all the possibilities.

Finally, chapter 8 provides you with "Partnership Lessons" based on years of experience. These lessons are summed up with a checklist, so that you can quickly review your own partners. It should come as no surprise that partners can be cunning, manipulative, devious and grabby. Learn some of the signs to watch for, so that you can spend your time on more productive pursuits.

There are many long-standing successful partnerships. The most notable are in professions where you see large accounting, law, engineering, architectural, and other firms that have been commercial successes for many years. If you think about some of the outstanding firms in you local area, they are probably partnerships. The key to a successful partnership is choosing the right partners and defining the way you will work together to reach your company's objectives.

It is my hope that your partnership will be a prosperous and enjoyable experience. **Go forth and succeed!**

# Chapter One
# The Nature of Partnership

*"Once the people begin to reason, all is lost."*

Voltaire (1694-1778)
Letter - 1766

### 1.1 Choosing the Legal Form of Business

There are two ways to own a business: by yourself, or in combination with other persons. Owning a business alone is referred to in legal terms as a *sole proprietorship.* (A sole proprietorship can be a business that is owned and operated by both spouses.)

When you combine your efforts with those of others, there are several forms of business that you can choose, such as general partnership, limited partnership, joint venture, and corporation. Let's look at a brief definition of each of these entities.

### A. General Partnership

Under the Uniform Partnership Act (UPA), which has been adopted by every state except Louisiana, a *partnership* is defined as "an association of two or more persons to carry on as co-owners of a business for profit" (UPA, Section 6(1)). The key word is profit. Joint tenancy or combined ownership of property does not, in and of itself, create a partnership. But if the owners endeavor to share profits, there is a presumption that a partnership exists.

Partners are not necessarily individuals. A partnership can be formed among individuals, partnerships, corporations, and other associations where there is an intention or express agreement to conduct business as co-owners.

For federal tax purposes, a *partnership* is defined more broadly as "a syndicate, group, pool, joint venture, or other unincorporated organiza- tion through and by means of which any business, financial operation, or venture is carried on and which is not a corporation, trust, or estate" (Internal Revenue Code (IRC) Section 761). The tax treatment of partnerships is discussed in more detail in chapter 5, "Partnership Income Taxes."

Perhaps the biggest area of confusion concerning partnerships is the partnership agreement. No formal written partnership agreement is necessary for a partnership to exist. In fact, most partnerships do not have any sort of written agreement. Working without an agreement is fine until there is a disagreement among partners that cannot be settled amicably. When a disagreement does occur, the partners must turn to the laws adopted by their state legislature and courts for guidance. It is much wiser, however, to draft a written agreement that covers as much as possible of the relationship among partners, since state laws do not usually reflect the understandings that partners believe they have among themselves.

Unless modified by agreement, the existence of a partnership is personal to the partners. If any one of them dies, becomes permanently disabled, or withdraws for any reason, the partnership dissolves automatically by operation of law.

## B. Joint Venture

A *joint venture* is a general partnership that is formed for the purpose of engaging in one particular business transaction or conducting business for a certain limited period of time. Examples of a joint venture would be a concert, festival, or play. Legally, joint ventures are treated as partnerships. Thus, the distinction is more one of definition and custom, than one of any practical significance.

Since a joint venture is a form of partnership, it should be treated in the same way for legal purposes. The partners are always best advised to have a written partnership agreement that covers the terms of their joint venture.

## C. Limited Partnership

The *limited partnership* is a partnership in which there are one or more general partners and one or more limited partners. *Limited partners* are usually investors only. They are not active participants in the business of the partnership and they are not liable for the partnership's obligations.

Unlike a general partnership, a limited partnership must have a written agreement and record a certificate of limited partnership with the state, so that its existence is a matter of public record.

If there are enough investors and enough money involved, extensive state and federal securities laws for the protection of investors will apply. Always check with an attorney who is knowledgeable in this area of the law if you are forming a limited partnership. **Failure to comply with securities law requirements may be a criminal offense.**

One of the primary advantages for an investor in a limited partnership is potential tax benefits. Although investors' liability is limited, profits and losses are passed through to them without first being taxed at the partnership level. This is an important distinction from a corporation, wherein profits are first taxed at the corporate level and then dividend distributions to investors are taxed again. Corporate losses cannot be passed through to investors.

## D.  Corporation

Under legal definition, a *corporation* is a business entity which becomes a "legal" or "fictitious" person in and of itself. It is owned by its shareholders, who have limited liability for its debts and obligations. Because it is a legal entity, a corporation has perpetual life. If any of the shareholders die or transfer their stock for any reason, the corporation continues to exist.

Although smaller corporations are generally managed by their shareholders, who also serve as directors and officers, it is possible for the shareholders to elect a board of directors which can then hire and fire management for the company.

## E.  S Corporation

Certain small corporations may be taxed like partnerships if they elect *S corporation* status. Briefly, the requirements that a corporation must meet to qualify for S corporation status, are the following:

o   It must be a domestic (U.S.) corporation;

o   It cannot have more than 35 shareholders;

o   It can only have shareholders who are only individuals or estates and are not nonresident aliens;

o   It cannot have more than one class of stock; and

o   It cannot have any subsidiaries of which it owns 80% or more.

The primary advantage of S corporation status is that (for federal tax purposes) net profits, losses, tax credits, and similar items are passed through to the shareholders without being taxed at the corporate level. Your state may or may not recognize S corporation status. Note that the detailed requirements for qualification for this status must be complied with fully. Consult an attorney for legal advice in this area.

## 1.2  Partnership Considerations

For entrepreneurs who are going to combine forces and go into business together, a partnership is the simplest and easiest way to set up a business. In fact, the formation of a partnership is often too easy, since no written agreement is required. Therefore, a group of two or more people may begin working together and enter into a partnership without pausing to work out the details that will control their relationship. This situation is more common than the one in which partners actually sit down and draft an agreement that meets their needs in advance.

## A. The Need for Written Agreements

The absence of a written agreement regulating the relations among partners is so common that nearly all of the states have enacted legislation that controls the relationship when there is no written agreement between the partners. Forty-nine out of fifty states have adopted some form of the UPA. (Louisiana, which bases its laws on the Napoleonic Code, is the only exception). The UPA is a piece of model legislation (originally drafted in 1916 and revised most recently in 1985) which covers the rights and obligations of all partners. Many of its provisions will not fit with the way you would prefer to define your relations among partners, and so it is best to formulate an agreement based upon your partnership needs.

Some of the key concerns that your agreement should cover include the following:

o   Initial contributions of capital

o   Sharing of management authority

o   Division of profits and losses

o   Withdrawal of a partner or adding new partners

o   Dissolution

These are covered in depth in chapter 4, "The Partnership Agreement."

Without exception, every partnership should have a written agreement. Besides the obvious benefits of having the agreement as you work together, it also forces all of you to discuss and think about the key elements of how your business will be run. A checklist for this discussion is included in chapter 4.

## B. Relations Among Partners

The partnership agreement should be used as a positive tool. In most businesses, once it is signed, it goes into a file, only to be forgotten until there is a serious question or dispute among partners. Do not let the relations among your partners ever reach the point where anyone is quoting terms of the agreement to try to settle a dispute.

Use preventative medicine! Everyone should agree that open communications are essential. Have regularly scheduled meetings where each partner can air ideas and grievances. If a grievance is raised, find a way to settle it to everyone's satisfaction. Your partnership will function best when there is a common understanding that an atmosphere of mutual respect must be maintained.

Chapter 7, "Partnership Problems" is designed to help you understand what can happen when things do not work out the way you have planned; Chapter 3, "Choosing Partners," discusses the careful selection of partners; and Chapter 8, "Partnership Lessons," provides additional insight into the relations among partners. Study these chapters carefully before you become a partner!

## C. Management and Control

In most small companies, day-to-day management responsibilities are shared by the owners. This is true whether the company is organized as a partnership or a corporation. Although a corporation is structured so that management can be easily separated from ownership, most small corporations are managed by their owners.

Unlike a partnership, however, a small corporation must have a formal structure, including shareholders, a board of directors, and managing officers. These groups are governed by the corporation's articles of incorporation and bylaws. Major decisions of the corporation are recorded formally at directors' meetings with minutes and resolutions. Except for the formalities, there are few differences.

The UPA requires that all partners share management responsibilities as co-equal managers. This can be modified by agreement to expand or limit the authority of any of the partners.

## D. Agency Law

In a partnership where management responsibility is shared, partners will take action on a daily basis on behalf of one another. In legal terms, the partners will act as *agents* for each other and the partnership as a whole. If you haven't been in this situation before, think about the consequences. How much authority do you want to give your partners to speak for you and take actions that will bind you?

As partners, you can agree to the exact amount of authority that each of you will have to represent the other partners in taking actions and making decisions. To make these grants of authority clear, you can also delineate those actions or decisions which can only be taken with the consent of a majority or all of the partners. The UPA supports your right to this by stating that an act of a partner which violates a restriction of authority is not binding on the partnership (UPA Section 9).

The UPA, in the absence of agreement, requires unanimous agreement of the partners to do any of the following (UPA Section 9):

o   Assign the partnership property in trust for creditors or on the assignee's promise to pay the debts of the partnership;

o   Dispose of the goodwill of the partnership;

o   Do any other act that would make it impossible to carry on the ordinary business of the partnership;

o   Confess (agree to) a judgment; and

o   Submit a partnership claim or liability to arbitration or reference.

Even if you set out clear limits on the authority held by each partner, there are two other areas of the law of agency with which you should be familiar.

First, no matter what the limits of authority are between partners, third parties that you deal with may not have knowledge of those limits. This leads to the concept of *apparent authority*. Each partner has apparent authority, as far as third parties are concerned, to bind your partnership to deals in the ordinary course of business. For example, you may have an agreement that limits each partner to $1,000 on the amount of goods or services that can be purchased on their own. One of your partners goes out and, on their own, contracts to buy a $6,000 copy machine. That contract will be valid between the seller of the copy machine and your partnership, although the other partners can hold the partner who exceeded his or her authority personally responsible for the purchase.

The second area of agency law is known as *ratification*. In the above example, the authority of one partner has clearly been exceeded. Let us assume, however, that the copy machine is delivered and everyone uses it for a month or two and says nothing about making the first two payments on it. At that point, the other partners complain about the unauthorized purchase. By then, it is probably too late. A court would hold that the other partners had *ratified* or implicitly agreed to the unauthorized action.

If one or more partners takes an unauthorized action and it is not acceptable to you (as a partner), you should give immediate written notice of your objection in order to best protect your rights.

There are a couple of related areas that can affect your partnership. A partner's admission or representation which is within the scope of his or her authority is usable as evidence against all of the partners. Similarly, if any partner receives notice of a matter relating to the partnership, the knowledge contained in that notice is imputed to the entire partnership.

For example, let us assume your partnership sells personal computers. If one partner is told by a customer that the personal computer she purchased was defective, then all of the partners are on notice that there is a potential problem, even if the partner she informed says nothing to the others. Let's further assume that this partner informs the customer that "she is right, the machine is defective," and then does nothing to remedy the problem. When the customer later take legal action, this admission is usable against all of the partners, even if another one of the partners could have solved the problem.

## E.  Liability

The insulation of corporate shareholders from liability seems to make a corporation a superior option. There is not much difference, however, between a corporation and a partnership when comparing small companies. It is a fact that corporate shareholders are not liable for the debts of the company. Creditors know this fact even better than those of us who own companies. When extending substantial amounts of credit to a small corporation, they will demand personal guarantees and/or other security from the owners if there are not sufficient assets in the corporation to secure the debts.

When considering partnerships' liability for claims filed against the business, general partners have unlimited liability; while shareholders of a corporation are insulated. However, there are some considerations that make this difference less clear. First, most successful small businesses purchase liability insurance. Even if the owners' assets are insulated from liability, those of the corporation are vulnerable. Second, for small corporations, courts traditionally do not like the way shareholders are insulated from liability. The courts have often allowed claimants who have sued successfully to *pierce the corporate veil.* This means that the claimants have been allowed to go after the personal assets of the shareholders. Thus, there is not absolute certainty that shareholders are totally insulated from liability.

In a partnership, the partners are *jointly and severally liable.* This means that each partner can be sued alone or together with all the other partners for the wrongs of the partnership. The choice belongs to the claimant. If one partner has the financial resources to satisfy a judgment and the others do not, that partner must pay the entire amount. For debts and obligations of the partnership, the partners are only jointly liable. That is, each is personally liable only for their proportionate share.

## F.  Taxes

At this point, let us look at the difference between corporations and partnerships from a practical point of view. Again the differences are not as great as they appear to be. While corporations theoretically have a problem of double taxation for their owners, this is usually avoidable. If the shareholders are also operating and managing the company, they can generally take out all of the money that would otherwise end up as net profit to the company as their salaries. This is permissible as long as the salaries taken are *reasonable* and as long as you are actively managing the business. Some fairly high salaries will qualify as reasonable.

Another difference is that corporations are allowed to retain some earnings without any personal income tax due on the earnings from the shareholders. Corporations pay federal income tax on earnings at the rate of 15% up to $50,000 in earnings; and earnings over $50,000 can result in taxes up to 39%.

Income taxes are covered at length in chapter 5.

G. **Continuity of Business and Transfer of Interest**

The UPA provides for the dissolution of a partnership upon the disability, death, or withdrawal of a partner for any reason. This automatic dis- solution can be modified by written agreement so that the partnership continues under a certain set of conditions. The key condition usually involves a buy-out of the withdrawing partner under a formula set out in the agreement.

Corporations have perpetual existence by law. They continue to exist regardless of whether the individual shareholders come or go.

Practically speaking, however, the differences between a partnership and a small corporation in this area are, again, not as great as they seem. In either case, if an owner who is absolutely essential to the success of the business withdraws, there is little chance that the business will continue. The only difference is that, in the case of a corporation, the remaining owners must take action to dissolve it, while in a partnership, it would dissolve by force of law.

In the absence of a partnership agreement, the UPA operates to dissolve a partnership upon any attempt to transfer ownership interest. At best, a partner may be able to assign his or her right to receive a share of the profit or loss distributions without any management authority. When writing an agreement, there is a careful balancing act that takes place. Each partner would like to be able to freely transfer his or her ownership interest and at the same time, would like to have complete control over those who will purchase other partners' interests.

Generally, the compromise that is agreed upon consists of a right to sell interests after offering the partnership itself or the other partners the right of first refusal. This means that any partner who receives a bona fide offer from a third party must first give the other partners an opportunity to buy their share at the same price and on the same terms and conditions. Some agreements let the other partners buy at a lower formula price that, in effect, penalizes the selling partner. In any event, you can see that some transferability, with or without restrictions, is possible in a partnership situation.

Corporations have the legal feature of free transferability of ownership shares. In practice, virtually every small corporation is set up with stock purchase agreements that restrict the free transferability of shares. This is done for the protection of the other shareholders. These agreements may or may not allow transfer after offering the right of first refusal to other shareholders.

## H. Fringe Benefits

The key consideration regarding fringe benefits is whether or not they are tax deductible to the company or the owners. Since 1982, many of the differences between corporations and partnerships have been eliminated as Congress has changed the tax laws several times. Before these changes, a corporation clearly offered more advantages to owners seeking fringe benefits.

The first area to consider in fringe benefits is pension plans. This is not a significant area of consideration until your business is providing a substantial income for the owners. When looking at the different types of pension plans available, you will find the same type of flexibility available to partners as are available to corporate share-holders/employees. Shareholders/employees are able to put more money into their pension plans when they reach substantial six-figure incomes. If you reach this point with your partnership, you will be able to afford sophisticated advice on tax planning, including help in determining whether it might be advisable to incorporate.

If a partnership's main consideration in adopting a pension plan is to reward and motivate employees, there are several options available, including Keogh, SEP, and 401(k) plans. These plans enable the employer or employee or both to save pre-tax dollars on a tax deferred basis until retirement.

A Keogh plan is a pension plan for self-employed persons, including partners. It can take several different forms depending on the retirement plans of the partners. The plan allows partners to deduct as much as 25% of compensation for the year, or $30,000, whichever is less. Note that the same percentage contribution must be made for employees. Contributions are kept in a tax-deferred trust where they are invested until retirement.

A Simplified Employee Pension (SEP) is a plan under which employees can make contributions to the IRAs of individual employees. Partners are considered employees of the partnership for purposes of these contributions. Annual contributions are excluded from each participants gross income to the extent that they do not exceed the lesser of 15% of compensation or $30,000.

A 401(k) plan is a qualified cash or deferred arrangement. Generally, this allows employees, including partners, to place up to $7,000 per

13

year of compensation into a tax-deferred account. The contributions can be invested with no taxes due until withdrawn at retirement. This is a plan that allows contributions at the option of each employee. Note that if the partners' compensation is relatively high compared with that of other employees, and if very few of them opt to contribute, the amounts that partners can contribute will be restricted to much less than $7,000 each.

Some of the fringe benefits that are still more beneficial for corporations include medical insurance plans, self-insured medical reimbursement plans, disability insurance, and group term life insurance. Under the current tax law, self-employed individuals, including partners, can deduct 25% of their medical insurance premiums. If Congress keeps up its current pace, partnerships can expect yearly changes in the tax laws affecting fringe benefits to continue.

## 1.3 Comparison of Partnerships, Limited Partnerships, and Corporations

|  | General Partnership | Limited Partnership | Corporation |
|---|---|---|---|
| **Start-up** | Relatively simple. No written agreement is required. No gov't approval required. Some filings and notices (e.g. fictitious business name statement) req. | Written agreement required. Certificate is filed with state + other formalities. Potential state and federal securities law compliance. | Articles of Inc. is filed with state + other formalities. Recordkeeping required (e.g. minutes). Additional accounting requirements. |
| **Management** | Control can be shared, or delegated to partners or managers. If not agreed to by partners, control is by a majority or by consensus. | General partners control management. In some cases, limited partners may have a vote in key decisions (e.g. major restructuring of the firm). | Centralized management, which can be separate from ownership. In small corporations, shareholders usually hold key management positions. |
| **Owner's Liability** | All partners have unlimited liability. Liabilities among partners are according to agreement. | General partners have unlimited liability. Limited partners have liability limited to their investment. | Shareholders are not liable for actions or obligations of the company. For small corporations, this insulation may not stand up in court. |
| **Taxes** | Business pays no taxes as an entity. Partners are taxed on profit. Losses also passed through to partners. | Same as general partnership except may be additional state taxes. | Pre-dividend profits and dividends paid to shareholders are taxed. Losses can't be passed through to shareholders. (Note exception of S corporations.) |
| **Transfer of Interest** | Restricted, generally only the right to receive distributions is transferable. Consent of remaining partners may be required or they may have right of first refusal to purchase under the agreement. | General partners--same as partnership. Limited partners have some rights to transfer interest with the consent of other limited partners. | Shares are freely transferable, but this is often restricted by agreement and the lack of a market for shares in smaller corporations. |
| **Continuity of Business** | Dissolved by death, disability, or withdrawal of a partner unless partners agree otherwise. | Has a finite life defined by agreement. Withdrawal of limited partner has no effect, but loss of a general partner may cause dissolution. | Perpetual existence. May be dissolved by agreement of shareholders. |
| **Fringe Benefits** | Limited benefits available to owners with favorable tax treatment. Partners can deduct 25% of health insurance premiums. Several pension plans now available: (Keogh, profit-sharing, 401(k), SEP). | Same as partnership for general partners. Not available for limited partners. | Full array of pension plans are available, as well as group insurance, accident, health, and sick pay plans. |

## 1.4 Summary

For new businesses and smaller existing businesses where two or more owners are joining forces, a general partnership is usually the simplest and best way to organize, since the formalities and expenses required to incorporate can be burdensome. This is not to say, however, that the legalities and rights and obligations among partners should be taken lightly. The purpose of this book is to give you a basic understanding of the relationships among partners and the means to put together a partnership agreement that makes sense for your situation.

# Chapter Two
# Choosing Partners

*"All tragedies are finished by a death. All comedies are ended by a marriage."*

Lord Byron (1788-1824)
Don Juan, Canto II

## 2.1 A Form of Marriage Vow

Let's take another look at a legal definition of *partnership:*

> "A voluntary contract between two or more competent persons to place their money, efforts, labor, and skills, or some or all of them, in lawful commerce or business, with the understanding that there shall be a proportioned sharing of the profit and losses between them." (Black's Law Dictionary, 4th ed., 1957, West Publishing Co.)

Although it sounds innocuous enough, entering into a partnership is serious business. When you do it, you have taken a form of marriage vow. It is more or less a permanent commitment that is binding and cannot be easily reversed. The effects on you and your family will be strong and lasting.

If we lived in a completely rational world, entering into a partnership would have two distinct phases. First, we would decide on a type of business, review the opportunity carefully, and then decide that it would work best as a partnership. Ideally, the "money, efforts, labor, and skill" required would be defined so well that the number and types of partners required could be listed in detail.

The second phase would then consist of finding the right people, structuring the organization so that these people complement one another, and then managing the business so that everyone works well together.

But we do not live in a completely rational world; and, in fact, partnerships rarely, if ever, occur in this way. If your experiences are like mine, you were not even thinking about a partnership when the opportunity presented itself. Nearly all of us skip the first phase of planning for a partnership and defining the types of partners who make the most sense.

Without making a value judgment as to whether this is good or bad, I want to help you recognize what is taking place. You will suddenly find yourself together with a friend or among a group of friends and friends of friends who are enthusiastically making plans for the future. At the very least, you should be aware that you did not plan for this situation. It just felt right, so you jumped into it.

## 2.2  Test Your Instincts

If possible, test your instincts. They may prove to be correct, but if they are not, your imagination is not the limit on how bad the down-side can be.

Testing your instincts about your future partners should not be difficult. First, ask yourself, "Why am I going into this partnership?" Complete the worksheet on page 21 and then ask, "Have I been completely honest with myself?"

Next, take a look at your new partners. How well do you know these people? Personalities are going to have a lot to do with your success or failure. What are their motivations for joining the partnership? Take a look at their reasons as stated on the worksheet on page 23, as well as your best guess. Compare these with your own.

Do you all have compatible long-term goals? This question cannot be over-emphasized. If there is one universal reason why partnerships do not make it, even when the underlying business is good, this is it.

Spouses play a dominant role in all of this. Think about your own spouse first. Does he or she support your plans to become a partner? What does he or she think about how you fit into the partnership? Does he or she agree with the reasons you have defined? What does he or she think about your partners? It is amazing how much insight your spouse can offer if you will just take the time to listen. In my case, I could have avoided many problems if I had given my wife more credit for her powers of observation on partnership issues when I was too emotionally involved to see them myself.

Have you met your partners' spouses? Are they supportive of the pro-posed venture? They can be incredibly powerful saboteurs if they are not.

By the same token, you should also listen carefully to friends' advice. On several occasions, I have had friends try to warn me about prospective partners. They were generally right; however, I was blinded by my enthusiasm and charged forward.

## 2.3  Skills and Money

Now you have stepped back and looked at whether your group includes the type of people you really want for partners. Next you should take a look at the skills that each of you is bringing to the party. Use the

"Partnership Skill Inventory" worksheet on page 25 to make an inventory of everyone's training and experience. This is an area where it should be possible to be fairly objective. How does your partnership's skill base stack up? Are you going to be able to hire any people for skills or experience that you lack?

You should be particularly careful to look for areas where skills overlap. Over the long haul, this has great potential for conflict. The most dangerous situation is where you have two people with nearly identical skills and you have decided that they are both such good people that they both belong on your team. How are you going to keep them from being at each other's throats? When the time comes to split up profits, are you going to be happy with a double-share going for the same skill contribution?

Now it is time to talk about capital contribution—the topic that everyone seems to want to avoid. The best possible situation is where each of you contributes your share of the capital, in cash, and takes your share of the obligations, including personal guarantees on debt. Any other arrangement is asking for trouble. For example, you may be tempted to include one person who has the skills you need, even though he or she is not able to come up with his or her share of the cash. Watch out! They may not have the same level of commitment as the other partners, and when that becomes clear, everyone else who picked up the tab for them will feel abused. So, if the person does not have the financial resources required, strongly consider hiring them as an employee. Perhaps they can buy in at a later date.

Also, think about the situation in which one partner provides the money (a *financial partner*), while the others provide the labor or expertise. This situation is difficult at best and there is an inevitable conflict. Those persons who become financial partners are taking a great deal of risk with their money. In order to minimize their risk, they will set up points of control over all the key aspects of the business. The partners who are doing the work soon realize that they are not only doing all the work, but their power to make key decisions is also very limited.

On the other side of the equation, the financial partners consider themselves sophisticated and unappreciated. They feel that the partners they are financing have no concept of how hard it is to accumulate the kind of money they are asking for. They also know that the other partners may be reckless and irresponsible, since it is not their money at risk.

Who's right? It doesn't matter. The point is that this situation has built-in feelings of animosity that you should understand. For more on this subject, see page 118.

The last thing to consider when you are stepping back and evaluating the team you are joining is this: Even if your partners have the skills, money, and enthusiasm, are they going to work? It almost boils down to this question: Is this project each partner's number one priority? If not, where does it rank for them? Would they rather be doing something else such as golfing, chasing women or men, or operating another business? If the partnership is a top priority for some of you, but not for the others, then you'll find some working hard and others coasting. This is not a blueprint for success.

## 2.4  Partner Scorecard

The "Partner Scorecard" at the end of this chapter (page 27) is a checklist summary of the concerns covered in this section. Fill one out for each of your new partners and one for yourself. This scorecard will help you quickly evaluate the strengths and weaknesses that will determine the success of your partnership.

The scoring points are fairly self-explanatory. For example, in number four, "Ability to be Honest with Self," symptoms of the problem are grabbing credit for the success of others, and an inability to admit mistakes. Number seven, "Extra-Curricular Activities," should include a look at the whole gamut of things that will divert a partner's attention—from sports and hobbies to drinking, gambling, extra-marital affairs, and drug abuse.

## Form 2-A

### My Reasons for Entering into This Partnership

1. _____
   _____
   _____

2. _____
   _____
   _____

3. _____
   _____
   _____

4. _____
   _____
   _____

5. _____
   _____
   _____

6. _____
   _____
   _____

7. _____
   _____
   _____

8. _____
   _____
   _____

9. _____
   _____
   _____

10. _____
    _____
    _____

**Form 2-B**

## My Prospective Partner's Reasons for
## Entering This Partnership

1. _____
_____
_____

2. _____
_____
_____

3. _____
_____
_____

4. _____
_____
_____

5. _____
_____
_____

6. _____
_____
_____

7. _____
_____
_____

8. _____
_____
_____

9. _____
_____
_____

10. _____
_____
_____

**Form 2-C**

## Partnership Skill Inventory

Name: _____

Training: _____

_____

_____

Experience:_____

_____

_____

How Experience and Training is Applicable to the New Business:

_____

_____

_____

_____

Name: _____

Training: _____

_____

_____

Experience:_____

_____

_____

How Experience and Training is Applicable to the New Business:

_____

_____

_____

_____

## Form 2-D

## Partner Scorecard

Score 1 to 10 (10 = highest)

1. Long-term goal match up? _____

2. Spouse's support for project? _____

3. Complementary skills? _____

4. Ability to be honest with self? _____

5. Team player? _____

6. Financially able to weather start-up period? _____

7. Extra-curricular activities (such as another business or other interests that would be damaging to the partnership)? _____

8. Past pattern of success? _____

9. Getting a free ride from others? _____

10. Gut feeling? _____

Total: _____/100

# Chapter Three
# Setting Up Your Partnership

*"A man of action, forced into a state of thought, is unhappy until he can get out of it."*

John Galsworthy (1867-1933)
*Maid In Waiting* - 1931

## 3.1  Name

Probably one of the first things that comes to mind in setting up a business is selecting a name.

First, consider the purpose that your name will serve and the message it will convey as it becomes the identification for your company. Here are some possibilities:

o The names of the owners;

o The type of product or service you provide;

o The geographic area you will serve;

o A clever, attention-grabbing name; or

o An abstract or fanciful name.

There is a legal dilemma in name selection. Most new companies prefer a name that is fairly descriptive of the product or service provided, so that customers will readily find the company and identify its product. However, the more descriptive the name, the more difficult it is to protect it from use by others.

Certain names are categorically prohibited for partnerships. These include the following:

o "Incorporated" or "Inc.," "Corporation" or "Corp."

o "Bank"

o "Insurance"

o "Trust" or "Trustee"

o "Limited" or "Ltd."

If you develop a name separate from the names of the partners, you may wish to obtain trademark or servicemark protection for it. The first step toward protecting your business name is conducting a search to determine its availability. The scope of this search will depend upon your plans for growth of the business. If you plan to form a partnership that will do business in a small geographical area, your search will be fairly simple and inexpensive. If, on the other hand, you plan to function over a large region or even nationally, then you should undertake an exhaustive search in preparation for federal registration of your name.

A good way to start a search is by contacting the state agency or agencies that reserve names for corporations and limited partnerships. (In most states, this is the secretary of state's office.) To conduct exhaustive searches, most business owners use a professional trademark search service. These firms conduct searches from computer data banks which not only look for your exact name, but also for those that are similar. The legal test that applies in trademark law is whether your name is "confusingly similar" to one already in use. It is interesting to note that there is no right to use one's own name in a business if it could cause confusion.

Once you find a name that is available, and if you plan to conduct business across state lines, you should register your name with the federal Patent and Trademark Office. The address is as follows:

U.S. Department of Commerce
Patent and Trademark Office
Washington, D.C. 20231

If you plan to conduct business in a large region within your state, there may be a state registration available. For example, in California, the Trademark Division of the Office of the Secretary of State handles trademark and servicemark registrations.

In many states, the name of a general partnership that does not include the surname of each partner or one that suggests additional owners, is a *fictitious business name* as defined by law; and usually this name must be registered with the state. In California, for example, partnerships engaging in business under a name that does not include the surname of each partner must file a *fictitious business name statement* in each county where it does business not later than 40 days from the time it begins to transact business for profit. This statement is good for five years and gives the partnership a presumption in favor of using the name in the county of its principal place of business. Most states have a similar registration requirement for fictitious names. You should check with your local county for its requirements. (The *fictitious business name statement* form on page 43 is the prescribed form for use in California.)

Note that the act of complying with the required filing of a fictitious name does not confer trademark or servicemark rights. A trademark or servicemark gives your business the legal right to use a name to the exclusion of all others, where the competitive use would be similar enough to confuse customers. A fictitious business name filing, on the other hand, is a requirement that is designed to protect those who do business with your firm. It enables them to discover the names of the principals or owners, so that they can discover their identities, if necessary.

## 3.2 Statement of Partnership

Under California law, a partnership or one or more of the partners may file a *statement of partnership*. This statement should be filed in any county where the partnership owns real estate and in the county of the partnership's principal place of business.

For real estate transactions, the statement provides a conclusive presumption that the partners listed are the correct owners of the property and have the authority to convey, encumber, or transfer interests in the property. This recorded statement is nearly always required by purchasers, lenders, and title insurance companies. In completing the form, you should note that if you include a provision restricting the authority of individual partners to sell, encumber, or transfer any kind of an interest in real estate, all partners must then participate.

The statement of partnership has an additional purpose. If a partnership is not dissolved by the death or withdrawal of a partner under the partnership agreement, the statement or amended statement may set forth the name and date of death or withdrawal of such deceased or withdrawing partner and whether the withdrawal was voluntary or involuntary. It can also point out that the partnership is still in existence through operation of its agreement.

Recording a statement which contains notice of a withdrawal of a partner is for the protection of this partner or his or her estate in the case of a death. It gives constructive notice to the rest of the world that this partner is no longer responsible for the debts or obligations of the partnership. *Constructive notice* means that everyone is charged with notice of withdrawal whether they actually see the publicly recorded notice or not.

See page 45 for an example of the prescribed form for the *statement of partnership.*

## 3.3 General Requirements

There are numerous laws and regulations that apply to setting up any business. The following is a brief summary of what you can expect to experience in the way of government regulation. For a more in-depth discussion of these requirements, see *Starting and Operating a Business In* (your state), available from Oasis Press.

31

## A. Licenses and Permits

Nearly all cities or counties require *business licenses* for every business operated within their jurisdiction. You should obtain this local license before you open for business in order to avoid problems with angry regulators who have to catch up with you later. The fee is usually fairly nominal; however, it does have the effect of registering you for any other local business taxes that are collected in your area. These can include gross receipts, income, payroll, and personal property taxes.

*Permits* may be required for special kinds of businesses. An obvious example is in the area of construction. If your business will build or remodel any buildings, you must first obtain permits. Permits are also required in other businesses where local authorities take a great interest in the public health, welfare, or morals. Other businesses that require permits are restaurants, hotels, and other public gathering places such as theatres. Zoning regulation is another form of local regulation which may have a great deal of impact on your business. Review the zoning regulations carefully before selecting locations.

On the state level, many businesses are again subject to license fees and various forms of taxes. State governments are also in charge of licensing and regulating the professions and other occupations where the public health, safety, welfare, or morals is deemed to require protection. Many regulated occupations have educational and testing requirements which must be fulfilled before the state will grant a license to practice them. These requirements should be researched carefully if your partnership will operate in any of these areas. In addition to professions like architecture, law, and medicine, states may require licenses from the following:

o   Automotive repair shops

o   Barbers

o   Cemeteries

o   Collection agencies

o   Building contractors

o   Employment agencies

o   Furniture manufacturers

o   Pest control services

o   Tax preparers

o   Insurance agents

o   Real estate agents

o   Horseracing tracks

32

Federal licensing requirements generally do not apply to small businesses. However, if your business falls in a category that requires federal licensing, such as drug or clinical manufacturing, you would be well-advised to use the services of an attorney who specializes in that area of regulation to deal with the complexities involved.

B. **Taxes**

1. **Sales and Use Tax Permits.** If you will sell tangible goods, your state will require some form of *seller's permit* so that it can collect sales tax from you. In recent years, most states have expanded this type of tax to include many services, such as the rental of goods. Some states collect a *gross receipt* or *gross income* tax rather than a sales tax.

   A *seller's permit* requires that you collect sales tax and hold it for the state when sales are made to retail customers. Depending on your state's requirements, you will have to file a sales tax return and pay the tax collected at monthly, quarterly, or annual intervals. If you make wholesale sales, it will be your duty to verify that your purchasers have resale permits.

2. **Real Estate Taxes.** If your partnership purchases real estate, you should receive tax notices from the county assessor's office on at least an annual basis.

3. **Employee Taxes.** If your partnership will have employees, you will have significant responsibilities to collect and pay various payroll taxes. As you might expect, the IRS and your state income tax agency are most anxious to accommodate these payments. The IRS makes available a helpful business tax kit, which includes *Circular E, Employers Tax Guide.* This contains the tables and instructions you will need for federal withholding and social security tax payments. The following are some of the employee taxes you may be liable for.

   o **Social Security (FICA).** For 1988, 7.51% of an employee's wages, up to $45,000 in wages per employee, must be withheld from the employee's paycheck. This is matched by another 7.51% paid by you as employer, for a total FICA tax of 15.02%.

   o **Federal Income Tax (FIT).** Each employee must complete a *Form W-4* when hired. This form states the employee's social security number and number of exemptions claimed. These forms are kept on file and are not forwarded to the IRS, unless an employee claims exemptions from withholding on more than 10 exemptions. Based on the exemptions claimed in the *W-4*, the tables contained in *Circular E* are used to calculate the amount of income tax to be withheld from each employee for each pay period. Read the rules carefully to learn how and when the withheld income tax is to be transmitted to the IRS.

Employees must be provided with a *Form W-2* by January 31 of each year showing wages paid and deductions for the preceding year. The IRS must be provided with the original *W-2s* and a summary *Form W-3* by the last day of February.

If your partnership uses *independent contractors* to perform services that would otherwise be performed by employees, you must file *Form 1099-MISC* for each contractor who receives over $600 from your business during the year. (An *independent contractor* is one who contracts to do certain work according to his or her own methods and who is not subject to any direction except as to the product or result of his or her work.) An *employer-employee* relationship is generally said to exist when the employer retains the right to direct the manner of performance as well as the result to be accomplished.

These *1099-MISCs* must include the social security number or taxpayer identification number of the contractor. Many states now have similar reporting requirements for independent contractors. Note that the IRS prefers that you treat persons who perform work for you as employees, since it benefits from withholding and higher taxes. If you plan to characterize people as independent contractors, make sure that you are on solid legal ground.

There is no hard and fast rule in this area and each case is a question of fact. The following are the primary factors considered by a court:

o The degree of supervision and control;

o Whether or not there is a requirement to devote full time to the work; and

o Whether the person views himself or herself as an employee or independent contractor.

o **Unemployment Taxes.** Your next area of responsibility for taxes as an employer is unemployment taxes. Here you will pay both the federal and state government. The federal unemployment tax is known as FUTA (Federal Unemployment Tax Act). In most cases, you will be required to pay 0.8% of the first $7,000 of annual wages for each employee. Again, the payment requirements are complex, so read your *Circular E* carefully. By January 31 of each year, you must file *Form 940*, which is the FUTA tax return for the preceding year.

For state unemployment tax requirements, you should check with your state taxing authority. In addition to learning the requirements for payment of tax, you should familiarize yourself with the operation of unemployment insurance in your state. Your business's hiring and firing practices may affect the unemployment tax you pay. This is due to the fact that unemployment benefits are an insurance system. If you as an employer cause the state to pay out a large number of claims, your premium is increased to compensate for this. This is true even if the benefits paid are due to layoffs caused by a lapse in your business.

o **Local Taxes.** The last area of employee taxes is local taxes. Your local city or county government may have imposed payroll or income taxes and may require withholding of the tax from the pay of employees. Information on this should be provided to you when you obtain a business license.

For a comprehensive discussion of income taxes, see chapter 5, "Partnership Income Taxes."

## 3.4 Insurance

In the past, insurance coverage for a business has not been a high priority consideration. But recently, the U.S. has been in the midst of an "insurance coverage crisis," and regardless of what the reasons are for this, it has caused tremendous difficulties for business owners. For many businesses, insurance carriers have refused to offer coverage at any price. For most of those "lucky" enough to be able to obtain coverage, the premiums are now two to ten times what they were a short time ago.

### A. Liability Insurance

Before you form your partnership, you should check to see if general liability insurance is available and, if it is, at what price. Even if they will offer your business coverage, nearly all insurance companies now write only *claims made* policies. This means that you are covered only while the policy is in force. For example, let's assume that someone is injured when one of your employees causes a car accident out of negligence. Depending on the statute of limitations in your state, the injured person may have several years to file a claim or sue you. If you have not kept your liability policy in force or, worse yet, if the insurance company has refused to renew your policy, you will be without coverage, although you had it when the accident occurred.

Besides the claims made limitation, watch out for other problems with the insurance offered to you. Many policies are now available only with a high deductible amount, or a low coverage limit, or both.

If your business will offer any type of professional advice or has the potential to generate claims for defamation of character or invasion

invasion of privacy, you should note that a general liability business policy will not provide coverage for these areas. You will need additional *errors and omissions* or *professional liability* coverage. This is now even harder to obtain and more expensive than general liability coverage.

If it hasn't already, this discussion should lead you to the conclusion that a competent insurance agent is a must. Unfortunately, many insurance agents are either unable or unwilling to go through the extra effort of finding coverage that makes sense for a new business. **Get competitive bids!** You will be shocked by what you will find. It is not uncommon to see variations of 300-400% in the premium for the same coverage. Insurance agents are paid a commission based on the premium, therefore they do not have much incentive to find you the lowest rate.

When you do find a rate and coverage that you can live with, ask the agent for the *A.M. Best* rating of the insurance company. *A.M. Best* is an independent service which rates the financial condition of insurance companies. Avoid companies that do not have at least an A or A+ rating or you may end up with an insurance company that cannot stand behind its coverage.

B.  **Health Insurance**

Health insurance is the next area of concern. Like liability insurance, it is becoming increasingly expensive and requires a great deal of study to find a plan that will fit your needs and budget. If you will have several employees, find an agent who can present you with a proposal for self-insuring up to a large deductible. Many employers now buy coverage with a deductible of about $2,000. Although employees are offered a $100 deductible, it turns out that it is a better value for the employer to have a third party administrator handle claims and to pay outright for claims between $100 and $2,000, rather than paying the actual premiums for $100 deductible coverage.

C.  **Life and Disability Insurance**

Life and disability insurance coverage are the other types of insurance you may consider. Life and disability coverage may be a required part of your partnership agreement or a consideration for fringe benefits.

First, a word on disability insurance. Good quality disability insurance is expensive and hard to obtain. This is coverage that pays if you are "unable to perform your own occupation for any reason," and it is "non-cancellable." Generally, the best coverage is not available during the first year or second of a new business, since insurance companies categorically refuse to underwrite it.

For those of us who are in good health (especially non-smokers), life insurance can be purchased at fairly reasonable rates. If the purpose is to fund your buy-sell section of your partnership agreement, calculate the amount you need and buy life protection only (*term*) insurance at the lowest rate available from an A.M. Best A or A+ rated company. **Do not** buy life insurance with a savings account or any other investment feature attached to it no matter what it is called. These policies are so lucrative for the agents and the life insurance companies that every new business is deluged with sales efforts for them. They are bad deals for you.

D.  **Workers' Compensation Insurance**

Nearly all states require that you obtain some form of workers' compensation insurance for employees. This is a cost of doing business that is becoming increasingly important as states have liberalized the claims allowed and payments made under those claims.

It is also important to coordinate this insurance coverage with your other general liability coverage, since there is an increasing trend to allow workers to sue employers for on-the-job injuries, in spite of the fact that workers' compensation is supposed to be the employees' exclusive remedy.

## 3.5 Real Estate

Entering into lease or purchase obligations for real estate are serious long-term. commitments for your partnership. They should not be under-taken until all partners have entered into a written partnership agreement covering the terms of the relationship. Nearly all lenders will require such an agreement, and it is not uncommon for landlords to want to assure themselves that your partnership is based on a written agreement. In addition to having an agreement, you should record a *statement of partnership* in the county where the real estate will be located. See the discussion on this in section 3.2.

Most new businesses lease the real estate they will occupy. This is often the largest commitment made early in the life of the business and it is one that should be made carefully. A commercial lease is a contract that is binding on the *lessees* (you and your partners) for its entire term. Courts have historically had a bias in favor of *lessors* (your landlord) and they will be given the benefit of the doubt in the event of a dispute. There is even a cliche to the effect that the only one who makes any money with respect to most new small businesses is the landlord.

The following is a discussion of a few points which may apply to your lease negotiations.

### A.  Real Estate Agents

Like insurance transactions, you may want to work with an agent to help you find space and negotiate the lease. But there is an inherent problem for you in this type of transaction—your agent receives his or her commission from the lessor. No matter how scrupulous your agent may be in representing your interests, it is hard for him or her to forget who is paying them. It is best for you to take the attitude that your real estate agent will be good at finding a location and facilitating compromises between you and the lessor. Do not count on your agent to be an advocate for your rights.

The real irony of this situation is that you do in fact pay the entire commission. It is built into the lease price, but the lessor gets to hand the money to the brokers and use this leverage to his or her advantage.

### B.  Location

Anyone with experience in real estate will tell you that the location of your business is the key to its success, particularly if you will conduct retail trade. Ask yourselves whether the location you have decided upon gives you the best chance for success. Optimum locations have a way of costing more than you would like to pay, so you should have a budget based on conservative cash flow projections for your business that lets you know just how much the budget can be stretched. Be sure to check the zoning laws carefully and research all permits you will need to operate at the location **before** signing a lease.

Once you find a location, it is not uncommon for the lessor to ask you to prove the credit worthiness of your partners and the viability of your business. It would be wise to prepare for this in advance by having a package of personal financial statements, bank and credit references, and a summary of your business plan which shows that your concept is exciting and well-conceived.

### C.  Term of Lease

When you have found a location that makes sense at a price you can live with, the next consideration is the term of the lease. Often the term will be controlled by the amount of investment required to prepare the property for your business. Regardless of whether the property improvements are paid for by you or the lessor, generally the more money spent, the longer the term of the lease will be.

When negotiating a term, remember that it works both ways. On one hand, you would like to tie up a location for as long as possible; but on the other hand, if you wish to change locations or should have to close your business, you would like the maximum amount of flexibility to do so. A way to compromise on this is to negotiate a relatively short term of a year or two, followed by an option or options to renew the lease for longer terms.

There is a quirk in California law regarding lease renewal options that you should keep in mind. To be enforceable, the renewal option must have a specific formula for the rent increase at that time. It cannot simply state "to be renewed at a market rate" or "at a rate to be determined". You should check to see if your state's law has followed California on this point.

A couple of provisions in the lease relate directly to the section on term. The first concerns your right to sub-lease the premises. If you wish to move, do you have the right to sub-lease to another tenant for the remainder of the term? If the lease is silent on this, your state's law will almost certainly say you do not. Thus it is helpful to include a sub-letting clause in your agreement, if you can negotiate it.

A directly related provision deals with mitigation of damages. You should always state in the lease that if you have to *vacate for any reason*, the lessor has a duty to mitigate your damages. This means that the lessor must actively seek another tenant to replace you and that the rent collected from the new tenant is subtracted from your obligation under the remaining lease term.

The clause should state *vacate for any reason*, since it is not always foreseeable what might cause you to vacate the premises. For example, what if the building you occupy is purchased by the state under its rights of eminent domain and is torn down for road construction? Although the lessor has been paid for the building that no longer exists, he or she may allege you still owe rent. You do not want to have to spend time and money to defend against this. This clause would also be important in the event of a fire. Do you owe rent while the building is being re-built? Does the lessor have a duty to expedite the re-construction?

D.  **Assignment**

Another section of the lease that may not seem like it is important when you first start your business deals with your right to assign the lease to a third party. This is known as *assignment*. What are your rights if you should decide to sell your business? Since the lessor nearly always presents you with a lease, it should come as no surprise that this provision usually gives the lessor complete discretion to say no to any request to assign the lease.

Think about how much your business would be worth if you could not transfer your premises lease with it. At the very least, this provision should be modified to state that the lessor's discretion is limited to

39

determining whether or not the *assignee* (new owner) is a similar credit risk to your partnership, and that the lessor's consent will not be unreasonably withheld.

You may hit a nerve in negotiating this point, because many lessors have obtained financing for their properties by assuring the bank that they have tied up credit-worthy tenants. They may have even asked for personal guarantees from all partners, as well as large rent and security deposits.

This point, however, should hit a similar nerve for you. No one wants to start a business with the possibility that it could be rendered worthless for resale on the whim of a landlord during a lease term. It is hard enough to make plans knowing that you can be tossed or priced out at the end of a lease term.

E. **Rent Increases**

Rent increases are another key section of the lease. Review carefully how often your rent can be raised and by how much. If your lease is *triple net*, this means that you pay your proportionate share of any increases in taxes, maintenance, and insurance for the property. Many leases also call for an automatic increase at a fixed percentage rate or at the rate of increase of the consumer price index. When negotiating on these, remember that the lessor's biggest cost is the mortgage payment and, if it is at a fixed rate of interest, the costs for the lessor are not affected substantially by inflation.

Rent increases mean a lot to the lessor. Commercial buildings generally sell for multiples of the net rental income. For each $1,000 your rent increases, the value of the building goes up about $10,000.

F. **Additions to the Property**

There is an old tradition in landlord-tenant law that anything you physically attach to the building or land becomes a fixture. This means that it becomes the property of the landlord. To avoid this problem, your lease should contain a written schedule of the items that will remain the property of your partnership even if they are physically attached to the lease premises. Store fixtures are an example of this.

Signs are another possible area of dispute between lessors and lessees. Make sure the section of the lease that covers this is to your liking. If it is not, change it. Do not accept the explanations that "This is just a boilerplate section of the lease" and "Don't worry, this has never been a problem!"

Finally, carefully note how your relations develop with the lessor as you negotiate the lease. If the person you are working with is inaccessible, unreasonable, or unfriendly, ask yourself whether you can live with this treatment over the course of several years. Many landlords have adopted the attitude that they are doing you a favor and tend to forget that you are a customer.

## Form 3-A

### FICTITIOUS BUSINESS NAME STATEMENT

#### THE FOLLOWING PERSON(S) IS (ARE) DOING BUSINESS AS:

Fictitious Business Name(s)

Street Address, City & State of Principal Place of Business in California      Zip Code

Full name of Registrant     –     (if corporation - show state of incorporation)

Residence Address     City     State     Zip Code

Full name of Registrant     (if corporation - show state of incorporation)

Residence Address     City     State     Zip Code

Full name of Registrant     (if corporation - show state of incorporation)

Residence Address     City     State     Zip Code

(If business is conducted by more than three registrants, attach separate page.)

**This business is conducted by**   ( ) an individual    ( ) a general partnership    ( ) a limited partnership
( ) an unincorporated association other than a partnership    ( ) a corporation    ( ) a business trust    ( ) copartners
   ( ) husband and wife    ( ) joint venture or    ( ) other-please specify _____ _(CHECK ONE ONLY)_

The registrant(s) commenced to transact business under the fictitious name or names listed

above on _____ 19_____

(If Registrant a corporation sign below.)

Signed _____     Corporate Name _____

Signed _____     Signature & Title _____

Type or
Print Name(s) _____     Print Name of Officer_____

This statement was filed with the County Clerk of _____ County on date indicated by file stamp above.

#### FOR OFFICIAL USE ONLY

I HEREBY CERTIFY THAT THIS COPY IS A CORRECT COPY OF THE
ORIGINAL STATEMENT ON FILE IN MY OFFICE.

_____ COUNTY CLERK

BY _____ DEPUTY

File No _____

**Form 3-B**

## Statement of Partnership

Recording requested by:

_____

When recorded return to:

_____

_____

The undersigned partnership declares and states that:

1) The name of the partnership is:_____

_____

_____

2) The names of each of its partners are:_____

_____

_____

3) The partners named are all the partners of the partners of the partnership.

4) Any conveyance, encumbrance, or transfer of an interest in the partnership's real property must be filed on behalf of the partnership by:

_____

_____

This statement was executed on_____,

at_____

_____

The undersigned, each for himself or herself, declares that the foregoing is true and correct.

SURVIVING AND PROSPERING IN A BUSINESS PARTNERSHIP

This declaration was executed on_____

at_____

_____

by_____

(name)_____

by_____

(name)_____




(NOTARY'S NOTICE AND SIGNATURE)

# Chapter Four
# The Partnership Agreement

*"To be prepared for war is one of the most effectual means of preserving peace."*

George Washington (1732-1799)
First Annual Address to Both
Houses of Congress

There is no standard agreement that covers all partnerships. In fact, partnerships are as diverse as the ventures they are formed to operate.

There is also no requirement that your partnership have a written agreement. A typical state law simply defines a *partnership* as an "association of two or more persons to carry on as co-owners a business for profit." In the absence of a written agreement, the relationship between you and your partners will be governed by the UPA and a long history of case law developed by the courts.

In spite of the fact that it is not required, it is always advisable to have a written agreement which sets out the rights and obligations of each partner. You will find that the exercise of writing the agreement will force everyone to discuss most of the key issues concerning how your business will be organized, funded, operated, and eventually sold.

Normally, by the time you are ready to work out the details of a partnership agreement, you already have your team in place and you have been working together for some time to start your business. Whether you realize it or not, you have already been operating as a partnership. The written agreement will now serve to formalize and define your future relations.

Although you are busy with the essentials of starting your new venture, do not overlook the importance of the agreement that controls the relations among partners. It covers issues that may seem distant and unimportant at this moment. These same issues may later be the key to the success or failure of your business, or even your own financial future.

Each partner should be involved in structuring your agreement. The purpose of this chapter is to give you sample terms along with some explanations that you can use as the basis for your discussion about the rights and obligations you will share. The more specifically you can define your partnership relationship, the stronger your partnership will be. Due to the large scope of this book, the sample terms here are fairly general and broad in scope. In your agreement, however, you should feel free to define the parameters that best fit your partnership's situation.

The "Partnership Agreement Checklist" (pages 49-54) contains items that you should be prepared to discuss and cover when writing your partnership agreement. Preparing answers for the questions on the checklist will prepare you and your partners for most of the decisions you will need to make in drafting your partnership agreement.

Following the checklist is a sample format of a partnership agreement with comments on each provision. The entire agreement is set forth without comments in Appendix A. Remember that this is just one suggested way of formalizing your agreement. Each partnership situation is different and you will need to write an agreement that fits your specific needs. The important thing is that you have a written agreement that defines the rights and obligations of each partner to your satisfaction.

If you make any changes to this agreement by crossing out portions of text or adding language in the margins, or both, this should be accompanied by the initials of each partner in the adjacent margin in order to make the changes effective.

## Form 4-A

### Partnership Agreement Checklist

1. **The Partners**

    Name _____

    Address _____

    Current occupation _____

    Age _____ Marital status _____

    Business relationships outside of partnership._____

    _____

    _____

    If partner is a business, all pertinent facts about form of organization and owners._____

    _____

    _____

2. **Business Activity**

    General activities of the business._____

    _____

    _____

    Where will it be conducted?_____

    _____

    _____

    Future activities._____

    _____

    _____

3. **Employees and Consultants**

    List those who will be employed._____

    _____

    _____

## 4. Capital Contributions

Amounts to be contributed, by whom? when?_____

_____

_____

Any services or property in lieu of capital?_____

_____

_____

Contribution of all or part of an existing business?_____

_____

_____

Will the partnership borrow money at the outset?_____

_____

_____

Will there be future contributions of capital?_____

_____

_____

## 5. Management

Who will manage the business?_____

_____

_____

Will management and administration be separated?_____

_____

_____

One vote per partner or voting weighted by capital contribution?_____

_____

_____

If there are two partners or an even number, how will tie votes be resolved?

_____

_____

_____

6. **Agency**

Limits of authority of each partner to bind the partnership._____

_____

_____

_____

_____

7. **Distributions and Allocations**

How will profits and losses be divided?_____

_____

_____

Salaries?_____

_____

_____

Draws?_____

_____

_____

Fringe benefits?_____

_____

_____

Any guaranteed payments to partners?_____

_____

_____

8. **Time devoted to the business**

How much time will each partner devote to the business?_____

_____

_____

_____


9. **Outside activities**

Are outside activities permitted? If so, can they be in areas related to the business?_____

_____

_____

_____


10. **Transferability of Ownership**

Is free transferability acceptable to all partners? If not, what are the limitations?_____

_____

_____

Right of first refusal for partnership? Other partners?_____

_____

_____

Should there be a non-competition agreement for departing partners?_____

_____

_____


11. **Dissolution or Continuation**

Is there an option for buyout upon death, disability, or withdrawal? Is this voluntary or mandatory? What is the formula? _____

_____

_____

If there is not a buyout option, what are the terms of dissolution? _____

_____

_____

_____

_____


## 12. Regulation

Will the business be subject to regulation?_____

_____

Is ownership restricted?_____

_____

Permits and licenses required?_____

_____


## 13. Risks

What are the risks of liability to customers and others?_____

_____

_____

Are risks insurable? At what cost?_____

_____

_____

Will there be initial operating losses? When is the business projected to have a profit?_____

_____

_____

If additional capital is required, how will it be raised?_____

_____

_____

## 14. Term of Partnership

What is the term of the partnership? _____

_____

_____

What events will cause termination of the partnership?_____

_____

_____

_____

_____

## Form 4-B

## General Partnership Agreement

This Agreement is made on _____,
19_____, by and among _____
_____,
referred to as "Partners" under the following provisions.

**Note:** *The effective date of your agreement may be set to coincide with your contributions of capital, beginning of operations for tax purposes, liability for partnership debts, or other significant date. None of these dates is required as the effective date.*

*Include the full names of all partners. Partners can be individuals, partnerships, corporations, and other associations. If any of the partners are corporations, make sure that their articles of incorporation permit them to become a partner.*

### 1. Name

The name of the Partnership is_____

_____

_____

It will be referred to in this Agreement as the "Partnership."

**Note:** *See the discussion concerning selection of a name in chapter 2.*

### 2. Type of Business

The Partnership is formed for the purpose of engaging in the business of_____

_____

_____

This purpose may be modified or expanded by the written agreement of all Partners.

**Note:** *Here you should define the activities that your partnership will pursue. If you are continuing an existing business, then state this clearly. The* *real importance of this section of your agreement is to define the nature of the partnership so that the partners' individual pursuits can be distinguished from those reasonably related to the partnership.*

## 3. Term

The Partnership will begin on the date of this Agreement and will continue until _____.

**Note:** *Use either a specific date or state that it will continue until dissolved by mutual agreement of the partners. You can also provide that it will continue indefinitely until one partner gives 60 days prior written notice; or that it will continue year to year unless one or more partners give prior written notice before an anniversary date.*

*This section is particularly important if your partnership is formed for a specific purpose. If you wish to continue the partnership for other purposes, the entire agreement should be reviewed.*

## 4. Place of Business

The Partnership's principal place of business shall be _____

_____.

The principal place of business may be changed and other places of business may be established by agreement of the partners.

**Note:** *The principal place of business is the address used for notices to the partnership in your fictitious business statement and other official filings.*

## 5. Capital Contributions

The Partnership's initial capital shall consist of cash to be contributed by the Partners in the following amounts:

| Name | Amount |
|------|--------|
| _____ | $ _____ |
| _____ | $ _____ |
| _____ | $ _____ |

56

Each Partner's contribution shall be paid in full within _____ days after the date of this Agreement.

If any Partner fails to make their capital contribution by this date, the Partnership shall immediately dissolve. Partners who have made their contribution shall be entitled to an immediate return of it, unless all Partners agree in writing to modify this section.

**Note:** *If initial contributions include property or services, this section should be modified to specifically identify the property or services and the exact value attributed to them. The tax consequences of contributing property or services are covered in chapter 5.*

*Contributions may also consist of existing businesses, including partnerships. If this is the case, you will need to provide for the assumption of assets and liabilities by this partnership. Again, carefully define the exact capital contribution each partner is credited with from the transfer. The transfer of an ongoing business into your partnership is generally a complex transaction that should be reviewed by an accountant.*

*Another way of dealing with contributions is to develop a formula for those partners who will buy in over time. There are many possibilities for formulas. For example, a partner can be required to make a monthly contribution or contribute a percentage of his or her share of distributed profits.*

*You may also want to consider a provision making each partner assessable for additional capital contributions upon a vote of the partners. This would be useful if your plans show that the business will most likely require additional capital investment from the partners.*

### 6. Voluntary Contributions and Withdrawals of Capital

No Partner may make any voluntary contribution or withdrawal of capital without the written consent of all partners.

**Note:** *This section is to assure that you remain partners in the same percentages, unless all Partners consent to a change. If any of you plan to loan money or property to the partnership, your agreement should cover this contingency. Loans should require approval of at least a majority of the Partners. There should be a written promissory note covering the terms of the loan, including interest, payments, and due date.*

## 7. Division of Profits and Losses

Profits and losses shall be shared among the Partners in the same share as their capital contribution.

**Note:** *If you wish to share profits and losses according to percentages other than capital contributions, state the percentages clearly in this section. Each partner's share of profits does not necessarily have to be the same as their percentage of losses.*

## 8. Distributions to Partners

Within _____ days after the end of each fiscal year of the Partnership, there shall be distributed in cash, to the Partners, in proportion to their respective shares in the Partnership's profits, an amount equal to the Partnership's profit for that fiscal year as computed under this Agreement.

**Note:** *The number of days should allow enough time for the year's accounting to be completed.*

*You should consider several alternatives for this section. Net profits may not be the correct definition for money to divide. If you will have non-cash expenses that result in the accumulation of cash, you may wish to base distributions on net cash flow.*

*Similarly, if your partnership will sell capital assets from time to time, you should provide for whether the money generated will be distributed to partners or remain in the partnership. Generally, this would apply for a real estate partnership. This section should be reviewed carefully for tax consequences, especially if one or more of the partners contributed the capital assets being sold.*

*Distributions may be made at any interval you choose. However, it is advisable that they be made only after your accounting is complete for that period. A better alternative may be to use "partner draws," which are covered in the next section.*

*Finally, you may want to consider placing a general or specific limitation on the amount of distributions. This provision would make the final determination of the amount of distribution subject to a majority vote or consensus of all the partners. In spite of your formula for distributions, your business may need cash for continuing operations or expansion. This provision would protect against one or more partners making a demand that they receive a distribution when the business needs the money.*

### 9. Partners' Drawing Accounts

Each Partner shall be entitled to draw against profits such amounts as from time to time are agreed on by a majority of the Partners. These amounts shall be charged to the Partner's drawing accounts as they are drawn.

**Note:** *This is such an important consideration that you may wish to require that all· partners agree on draws unanimously. If you can forecast your cash flow well enough, exact monthly sums can be substituted for discretionary draws.*

*Review this section carefully in light of each partner's personal financial situation.*

*If there is any chance that partner draws may exceed net profits for the year, you should consider adding a provision that makes it clear that such excessive withdrawals are clearly loans from the partnership. The loans must be unconditional, legally enforceable, and due at a determinable date. Otherwise, they are considered to be taxable distributions by the IRS.*

*As an alternative to draws, you can define salaries that each partner will be paid. This, however, is usually not done for new businesses.*

### 10. Fiscal Year and Accounting Method

The Partnership's fiscal year shall end on_____each year. The Partnership's books shall be kept on the _____ basis.

**Note:** *For most partnerships, a calendar year will be used. For a calendar year, enter December 31 above. The IRS requires that the partnership's taxable year be the same as that shared by partners who own greater than a 50% share, unless there is a business purpose supporting a different fiscal year.*

*Either cash or accrual should be selected as the accounting method. If you are not sure of the difference, consult an accountant.*

### 11. Accountings

Within _____ days after the end of each fiscal year, the Partnership shall furnish to each Partner a copy of the Partnership's income tax returns for that fiscal year, a profit and loss statement, and balance sheet showing the Partnership's financial position at the end of that fiscal year.

**Note:** *Generally, individual partners will want this information as soon as possible, so that they can meet individual federal and state tax filing deadlines. Thirty days should give your accountant time to complete this reporting if the partnership books have been kept up to date.*

*Depending on the nature of the business, you may wish to require financial statements for partners on a monthly or quarterly basis.*

*Note also that partnership books must be kept at the principal place of business, unless the partners agree otherwise. All partners have the right to access, inspect, and copy of the books at all times under the UPA.*

## 12. Management and Authority

Each Partner shall have an equal right in the management of the Partnership. Each Partner shall have authority to bind the Partnership in making contracts and incurring obligations in the Partnership name or on its credit. This authority is subject to a limit of $_____. No Partner shall incur obligations in excess of this limit without the prior written consent of a majority of Partners.

**Note:** *Control of the business operations should be discussed carefully. See the discussion on the Law of Agency in chapter 1 (page 9). You may wish to require the written consent of all partners for obligations above the limitation amount. You may also wish to designate a "managing partner." His or her authority should be clearly defined in this section. The ability to remove the managing partner should also be clearly stated.*

## 13. Partnership Funds

All Partnership funds shall be deposited in the Partnership's name. Accounts will require the signature of at least _____ Partners for withdrawals or checks written above $_____.

**Note:** *You should decide on the check writing authority available to each of you in the normal course of business. Include this limit in the signature authority established with your bank.*

*In the absence of this provision, each of you will have co-equal rights in the management of all the partnership's monies.*

60

## 14. Employment and Dismissal

No Partner shall hire any employee or fire any employee, except in the case of gross misconduct, without the consent of a majority of the Partners.

**Note:** *For smaller partnerships, you may wish to require consent of all partners. Again, you may wish to designate a "managing partner" who will handle employee matters.*

## 15. Time Devoted to Partnership

Each Partner shall devote full time and attention to the conduct of Partnership business.

**Note:** *This can be modified to allow competing or non-competing outside activities. In the absence of any provision on this, each partner has a duty not to compete with the partnership.*

*If one or more partners will actively continue outside business activities, the permissible activity should be defined and the amount of time they will devote to the partnership should also be carefully defined.*

*If you choose to allow one or more partners to conduct outside activity that will compete with the partnership, you may still wish to disallow more direct forms of competition. Exercise care in this area to avoid disputes later.*

## 16. Vacations and Leaves of Absence

Each Partner shall be entitled to _____ days of vacation and _____ days of absence for illness or disability each fiscal year. Days of vacation or absence for illness that exceed these amounts shall result in a proportionate reduction of that Partner's share of the profits for the fiscal year.

**Note:** *Experience shows that this provision serves to protect all partners. If any of the partners express concern about the loss of income should their days of absence for illness or disability exceed the allotted amount, then disability insurance should be considered.*

## 17. Admission of New Partners

A new Partner may be admitted to the Partnership, but only with the written approval of _____ of the Partners. Each new Partner shall be admitted only if he or she shall have executed this Agreement or a supplement to it in which the new Partner agrees to be bound by the terms of this Agreement. Admission of a new Partner shall not cause dissolution of the Partnership.

**Note:** *The consent of all partners is required to admit a new partner unless you modify this requirement in your agreement. Similarly, you must have a written agreement allowing the admission of a new partner or it will trigger the dissolution of your partnership. An amended statement of partnership should be recorded and an amended fictitious business name statement should be filed and published.*

## 18. Interest of New Partner

A newly admitted Partner's capital contribution and share of profits and losses shall be set forth in the written consent of the Partners consenting to the admission of the new Partner.

**Note:** *This section can go on to state "but admission of a new partner shall not reduce the participation in the Partnership's profits or losses of any partner who has not consented to that admission." This highlights the problem of allowing a majority or less than unanimous approval of new partners. Should those who don't consent be rewarded by having their share remain intact or should they be subject to the decision of the majority?*

## 19. Dissolution

The Partnership shall dissolve and terminate on any Partner's death, permanent physical or mental disability, becoming a party to a divorce action or voluntary withdrawal, unless within _____ days after the Partnership has received notice of the Partner's death, disability, becoming a party to a divorce action or desire to withdraw, it elects in writing to purchase that Partner's interest. This election shall require the consent of _____ of the remaining Partners. The price to be paid for the interest of the deceased, disabled, party to a divorce action, or withdrawing Partner shall be computed according to the terms of this Agreement.

**Note:** *In the absence of agreement to the contrary, the death or withdrawal of a partner, dissolves the partnership. Permanent disability will generally cause a court to order dissolution. The language which states "becomes a party to a divorce action" has been added to cover the concerns discussed in chapter 7.*

*With slight modification, this same provision can be used for a two-person partnership to allow one remaining partner to purchase the interest of the other and continue the business as a sole proprietorship.*

*For professional partnerships, there are special needs which should be addressed in this section. It would be best to consult an attorney with experience in this area.*

*You should also note that a partner's bankruptcy causes the dissolution of the partnership by law. If you wish to have the option to continue the business without this partner, a specific provision should be added to allow a buyout following this contingency.*

## 20. Non-Competition Covenant

Following withdrawal from the Partnership, the withdrawing Partner shall not carry on a business similar to the business of the Partnership within the

_____ of _____ for a period of

_____ years.

**Note:** *The first spaces are to define a geographical area, such as City of Oakland, or County of Alameda. Both the geographical area and the number of years must be reasonable, in order to make this provision enforceable. "Reasonable" generally means a year or two at most and a geographical area where you actively do business.*

## 21. Transfers of Partnership Interests

**Note:** *There are at least three options that apply to this contingency: 1) free transferability, 2) no allowed transfers, and 3) limited transferability. This is a difficult issue, since for themselves most partners would like a great deal of freedom and at the same time, the assurance that other partners cannot readily transfer their interest.*

### Option 1: Free Transferability

Each Partner may transfer his or her interest in the Partnership without dissolving the Partnership by the transfer.

**Note:** *By law, the new partner will not have management rights or the right of access to the books. Their rights are restricted to the receipt of the transferring partner's share of distributions.*

### Option 2: Non-Transferability

A Partner's interest may not be transferred, in whole or in part.

**Note:** *This provision fits with the structuring of your agreement so that the withdrawal of a partner for any reason will trigger a dissolution as contemplated by the UPA.*

### Options 3: Limited Transferability

A Partner may transfer his or her interest in the Partnership only as follows:

1. To the Partnership or to any other Partner only after the Partnership declines;

2. By intestate succession or by will on the Partner's death;

3. By a gift to the Partner's spouse or children, or to a trustee for the Partner's spouse or children or both;

4. To any other person after the Partner making the transfer has first offered the Partnership and other Partners their rights of first refusal in accordance with the provisions of this Agreement.

**Note:** *"Intestate succession" is the distribution of property upon the death of a person who dies without a will. If this option is chosen, your agreement should include sections on valuation of a Partner's interest and right of first refusal.*

*Again, it should be noted that by law, the substituted partner will have the right to distributions only, unless you have modified this by your agreement.*

## 22. Right of First Refusal

If a Partner desires to transfer his or her Partnership interest, that Partner shall give written notice to the Partnership. The notice shall set forth the name of the party, the terms on which the interest is to be transferred, and the price. For _____ days after the notice is received, the Partnership shall have the right to purchase the Partner's entire interest at the same price and on the same terms.

**Note:** *This provision can be extended by first giving the partnership a right of first refusal and then the individual partners. It 'can also define the price as the lesser of the offer from a third party or the value of the partner's interest as determined under your agreement's valuation clause. This is to protect against unwanted partners who will pay a premium for the selling partner's interest. Remember, however, that you may be the partner who wants to sell!*

## 23. Valuation of Interest

**Note:** *If your partnership develops a successful business, this section is potentially the most important part of your agreement. Each partner will want to know what his or her share is worth, especially for tax and estate planning purposes. If you should ever experience a dispute or breakdown in relations among partners, this provision will be a key element in the resolution of the dispute.*

*There are many variations of the valuation clause. The best way to understand them is to assume that your business is operating success-fully after some period of time, perhaps 5 to 10 years, and then apply the formula to your respective interests. Is the outcome some-thing that you can all live with?*

*In a dispute situation, this provision will be scrutinized so closely that you may wish to set out a specific example of the application of the formula in your agreement or a supplement to it. If you use a supplement, it should become an exhibit to the agreement and should be incorporated by reference in this section.*

The following are a few of the more common options used to cover valuation. Some are fairly lengthy due to the fact that they are so crucial in dispute situations.

### Option 1: Value Based on Capital Account

The value of a Partner's interest in the Partnership, for purposes of this Agreement, shall be the sum of the following items as of the date the value is to be determined, as these items are reflected on the Partnership's regularly maintained accounting books and records:

1) The balance in the Partner's capital account;

2) The balance in the Partner's drawing account;

3) The Partner's proportionate share of the Partnership's net profit for the current fiscal year to the date as of which the computation is made and not yet reflected in the Partner's capital or drawing account; or, if the Partnership operations for that period show a loss, the Partner's proportional share of any such loss shall be deducted; and

4) Any debt or other amount due to the Partner from the Partnership; but

5) Less any debt owed by the Partner to the Partnership.

**Note:** *This method of valuation is most accurate while your business is new. Once you have achieved some lasting success, it will tend to undervalue each partner's interest when compared with the fair market value. You may decide that this is a desirable effect of your valuation clause. In other words, any partner who wishes to withdraw can be bought out by the remaining partners at a low price. Remember that this same valuation will apply to a buyout triggered by a partner's death or disability.*

**Option 2: Value Based on Equity and Earnings**

The value of a Partner's interest in the Partnership for purposes of this Agreement, shall be calculated by taking an average of the net profits of the business as shown on the Partnership's federal tax return for the past _____ years. This average of the net profits shall then be multiplied by a multiple of _____ to determine the value of the business. This value shall then be multiplied by that Partner's ownership percentage on the date of valuation to determine the value of that Partner's interest.

**Note:** *The key to this method is agreeing on a multiplier that will make sense for your business. This is known as the "capitalization of earnings" method. It is common in the real estate industry where buyers use a multiplier of net rents to approximate the purchase price which will give them the return on investment they require.*

66

*In some industries, multipliers are fairly well-established for going concerns. They may be based on sales, gross profits, or other measures of a company's performance as well as net profits. If there is any possibility of confusion, net profits or the other figure used, should be defined specifically.*

### Option 3: Valuation by Agreement

The value of a Partner's interest in the Partnership for purposes of this Agreement shall be calculated by applying that Partner's ownership interest percentage to the value of the Partnership, which shall be determined as follows:

1. Within _____ days after the end of each fiscal year of the Partnership, the Partners shall, after due consideration of all factors they consider relevant, determine the Partnership's value by unanimous written agreement, and that value shall remain in effect for the purposes of this Agreement from the date of that written determination until the next such written determination, except as otherwise provided below. The valuation shall be entered on Exhibit _____ and all Partners shall initial the entry.

2. Should the Partners be unable to agree on a value or otherwise fail to make any such determination, the Partnership's value shall be the greater of (a) the value last established under this section, or (b) the Partnership's net worth, determined in accordance with generally accepted accounting principles, consistently applied, as of the end of the Partnership's next preceding fiscal year.

3. Until it is otherwise determined under this section, the Partnership's value shall be the aggregate initial capital contributions required under this Agreement and actually paid or conveyed to the Partnership.

**Note:** *Like other methods, there are pros and cons to this one. It has the beneficial effect of requiring the partners to discuss and apply their personal knowledge of the business on an annual basis. An* *exhibit to the agreement should be attached where the annual figure can be recorded.*

*On the negative side, many partnerships forget or fail to make the annual valuation. Even if it is made, there may be substantial changes in value between valuations. There has also been litigation when all remaining partners have tried to set a low valuation after one of the partners has died. In this situation, the court has stepped in and found that a duty of "good faith and fair dealing" towards the deceased partner's estate was violated.*

### Option 4: Valuation by Appraisal

The value of a Partner's interest in the Partnership for purposes of this Agreement shall be determined by appraisal as follows:

Within _____ days after the event requiring appraisal or, in the case of a Partner's death or legal disability, within _____ days after appointment of that Partner's personal representative, the Partnership and the Partner whose interest is to be appraised, or that Partner's personal representative, either 1) shall jointly appoint an appraiser for this purpose, or 2) failing this joint action, shall each separately designate an appraiser and, within _____ days after their appointment, the two designated appraisers shall jointly designate a third appraiser. The failure of either the Partnership or the Partner whose interest is being appraised (or that Partner's personal representative) to appoint an appraiser within the time allowed shall be deemed equivalent to appointment of the appraiser appointed by the other party.

If, within _____ days after the appointment of all appraisers, a majority of the appraisers concur on the value of the interest being appraised, that appraisal shall be binding and conclusive. If a majority of the appraisers do not concur within that period, the determination of the appraiser whose appraisal is neither highest nor lowest shall be binding and conclusive. The Partnership and the Partner whose interest is to be appraised, or that Partner's estate or successors, shall share the appraisal expenses equally.

A Partner's interest in the Partnership so appraised shall be based on that Partner's ownership interest.

**Note:** *Appraiser or appraisers may be limited to those with a certain certification or professional designation which applies to the field of your business.*

*This method may prove to be very costly, especially if three appraisers are employed. You can provide for use of an average of the three, rather than the value of the middle appraiser. If necessary, you can state in your agreement the standards of appraisal that will be used by the appraiser. If you reach a point where you wish to make the agreement this technical, it would be best to confer with a CPA or other financial expert.*

### 24. Payment of Purchase Price

#### Option 1: Cash

Except as otherwise provided, whenever the Partnership is obligated or, having the right to do so, chooses to purchase a Partner's interest, it shall pay for the interest in cash within _____ days after the date on which the Partnership's obligation to pay has become fixed.

#### Options 2: Cash or Note

Except as otherwise provided, whenever the Partnership is obligated or, having the right to do so, chooses to purchase a Partner's interest, it shall pay for that interest, at its option, in cash or by promissory note of the Partnership, or partly in cash and partly by note. Any promissory note shall be dated as of the effective date of the purchase, shall mature in not more than _____ years, shall be payable in installments of principal and interest that come due not less frequently than annually, shall bear interest at the rate of _____ percent per annum, and may, at the Partnership's option, be subordinated to existing and future banks and other institutional lenders for money borrowed.

**Note:** *It is generally advisable to give the partnership the alternative of paying by note, since it may be impossible for the remaining part-*

69

*ners to raise the cash required. A middle position would be to require a cash payment of some percentage, such as 10% or 20% and the balance paid in installments.*

*The provision that allows the partnership to subordinate the note is to help it retain flexibility for credit arrangements. If you feel that a withdrawing partner should have better protection, you can delete this and, if you wish, require that the note be secured by partnership assets or personal collateral of the remaining partners.*

*This section should also be viewed in light of whether or not you choose to carry life or disability insurance for the partners. If you carry life insurance in sufficient amounts to fund the buyout of each partner's interest upon death, the all-cash option should be required for purchase upon death.*

## 25. Arbitration

It is agreed that all disputes arising out of this Agreement shall be submitted to binding arbitration in accordance with the rules of the American Arbitration Association.

**Note:** *This provision requires that all disputes be arbitrated rather than litigated. For a discussion of the wisdom of this requirement, see chapter 7, "Partnership Problems."*

*You may also want to consider a mediation provision. It is a voluntary process that is less formal than arbitration. If your dispute is friendly enough to warrant mediation, you most likely will be able to agree to settle it without having your agreement require it.*

## 26. Amendments

This Agreement may be amended by the written agreement of all Partners.

## 27. Notices

All notices between the Partners shall be in writing and shall be deemed served when personally delivered to a Partner, or on the second day after being deposited in the mail, certified, first-class postage prepaid, addressed to the Partner's address shown after his or her signature to this Agreement or a more recent address given to the Partnership in writing.

## 28. Entire Agreement

This instrument contains the entire Agreement of the parties. It correctly sets out the Partners' rights and obligations. Any prior agreements, oral representations, or modifications shall be of no force or effect unless contained in a subsequent written modification signed by all parties to this Agreement.

## 29. Severability

If any term, provision, covenant, or condition of this Agreement is held by a court of competent jurisdiction or arbitrator to be invalid, void, or unenforceable, the rest of this Agreement shall in no way be affected, impaired, or invalidated.

**In witness whereof,** the Partners have executed this Agreement as of the date first shown above.

**Signature**                          **Residence Address**

_____         _____

_____         _____

_____         _____

_____         _____

_____         _____

_____         _____

**Note:** *Type or print the name of each partner below the signature lines.*

## Form 4-C

## Consent of Spouses

We certify that:

1. We are the spouses of the persons who signed the foregoing Partnership Agreement and who constitute the members of the Partnership described in that Agreement.

2. We have read and approve the provisions of that Partnership Agreement, including but not limited to those relating to the purchase, sale, or other disposition of the interest of a deceased, retiring, withdrawing, divorcing or terminating Partner.

3. We agree to be bound by and accept those provisions of that Partnership Agreement in lieu of all other interests we, or any of us, may have in that Partnership, whether the interest may be community property or otherwise.

4. Our spouses shall have full power of management of their interests in the Partnership, including any portion of those interests that are our community property; and they have the full right, without our further approval, to exercise their voting rights as Partners in the Partnership, to execute any amendments to the Partnership Agreement, and to sell, transfer, encumber, and deal in any manner with those Partnership interests.

Executed on _____, at _____

_____.

**Signature of Spouses**

_____

_____


_____

_____


_____

_____

**Note:** *Again, type or print the name of each spouse below the signature lines. This section is absolutely essential for the protection of all partners and generally will be required by lenders.*

73

# Chapter Five
# Partnership Income Taxes

*". . . but in this world nothing is certain but death and taxes."*

Benjamin Franklin (1706-1790)
Letter to M. Leroy - 1789

This chapter will introduce you to how the tax laws treat partnerships. In spite of the fact that we all received "tax simplification and fairness" from Congress in 1986, the rules and regulations for partnerships are still complex. You should find an accountant with experience in this area (especially if your partnership is new) who can advise you on the best way to organize, conduct, and report the activities of your partnership for tax purposes.

If this is your first venture into the world of business ownership, you will find that there are still several tax advantages available for small businesses. The price of these advantages is complying with fairly complex recordkeeping and reporting requirements. To make the best of the tax situation, advance planning should be used for your major business decisions, including the organization of and the eventual sale or dissolution of the partnership.

The following discussion covers the basics of how the tax laws treat a partnership. A sample of the annual partnership tax return form is included for your review. If any of this discussion sounds like Swahili or Sanskrit to you, don't be alarmed. On many occasions, our courts have held that the tax code is incomprehensible to even the experts. What you should recognize is that you may need the services of a competent accountant to help you with setting up tax recordkeeping and reporting systems for your business and to help with advice on the tax ramifications of major decisions.

## 5.1  A Word on Accountants

In my experience and in the experience of my clients, accountants have not only been one of the best sources of advice for new businesses, but also the primary source of fee disputes and misunderstandings. For some reason, the bills issued by accountants to new businesses are often far out of line of the expectations of the owners. Many times the fees are not billed until the relationship has continued for several months and the clients are shocked to find that they total two, three, or four times their expectations.

To avoid this problem, you should reach an understanding with the accountant you retain. Get a clear estimate of what the fees will be for the services you require. If the estimate fits within your budget and is acceptable, then write a letter to the accountant confirming the estimate. In this letter, you should state that since you are a new business and on a tight budget, there are two main requirements for the relationship. First, you will receive monthly bills for all work performed for your business during the month. These bills will be fully itemized, showing the amount of time spent on each task and who performed it. This will allow you to see if you are being billed for a CPA's time when a secretary or bookkeeper could perform the task. Second, no work above the estimated amount you are confirming is to be performed without your prior written authorization.

If this seems a little strong, ask yourself how you would feel if you budgeted $2,000 for accounting during your first year and received a bill for $8,000. This same type of letter will also serve you well in avoiding costly misunderstandings with other professionals such as attorneys and consultants. They are also business owners; and they should understand when someone forming a new business asks for their cooperation in order to stay within their budget.

## 5.2 Contributions to Partnership

If all partners put in cash for their contribution when forming a partnership, there are no tax consequences from these transactions. The value for tax purposes (or *basis*) of each partner's ownership share is clear. If any partner withdraws all or part of this original cash contribution, there are also no tax consequences.

Things become more complicated when partners contribute property to the partnership. The property contributed does not result in any gain or loss to the partnership or any of its partners, including the contributing partner. However, the value that the partnership places on this property for purposes of the contribution will most likely not be the value of that property for tax purposes. The *adjusted basis* of the property before it was contributed to the partnership becomes the new *carryover basis* for the partnership. *Adjusted basis* means the original cost of the property, plus or minus any improvements to, or depreciation from, the property. *Carryover basis* means that the same basis is used for the property for the partners, even after the property is re-titled and placed into the partnership.

What is the importance of your *basis* in the partnership? First, it is the maximum amount of partnership losses that can be deducted by a partner. Second, it is used in determining gain or loss on the sale or liquidation of your partnership interest. It is also used in determining the tax consequences of certain distributions to the partner.

Let us assume, for example, that partners X and Y form a partnership. Partner X contributes $100,000 cash and partner Y contributes a small building with a $100,000 *fair market value* (what it could be sold for to a disinterested third party in the open market). Partner Y has owned the building for several years and his adjusted basis in the building, after depreciating it over the years, is $40,000. Partner X will have basis of $100,000 in the partnership and Partner Y's basis will be $40,000. If the partnership continues to depreciate the building, it will start with a carryover basis (for tax purposes) of $40,000. Each partner will have a capital account (for partnership accounting purposes) of $100,000.

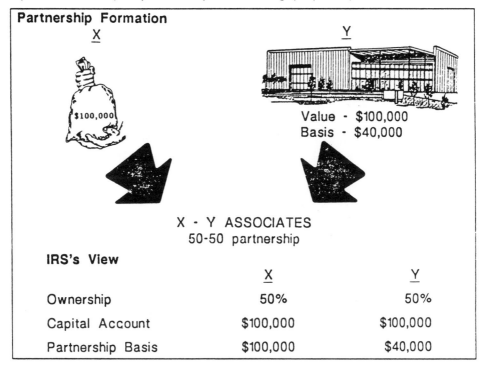

This situation becomes more complicated if the property contributed is subject to a mortgage. In that case, the mortgage is now assumed by the partnership, so that if there are two partners, the partner contributing property is regarded as having received a distribution equal to the amount assumed by other partners (or 50% in this example). This distribution can be taxable income to the contributing partner, so caution should be used for this type of contribution (for example, consult an accountant).

Another situation which may arise is where one or more partners contribute services rather than cash or property. In this case, the contributing partner must include the fair market value of the interest received as taxable income on their personal income tax return.

## 5.3 Operating the Partnership

The tax laws treat your partnership as an entity. However, it is an entity that reports the results of operations rather than paying tax. As an entity, the partnership must make several elections. First, it must elect to be either a *cash basis* or *accrual basis* taxpayer. The *cash basis* is a method of accounting under which you book receipts and expenditures of money when they actually occur. The *accrual method* makes certain adjusting entries for implicit transactions. Under this method, income items are reported for the year in which all events fixing the right to receive income occur and for expense items when all events occur fixing the liability to pay. For example, if you have the contractual right to receive a payment or contractually must make a payment in the current year, but it is not received or paid until next year, under the accrual method, you will show the income or expense this year.

These methods are an attempt by the accounting profession to present a more meaningful measure of the firm's financial position. The importance of this election for tax purposes is to determine which method will be the most beneficial to the partners.

Second, the partnership must elect a taxable year. Since December 1986, the partnership is required to have the same taxable year as one or more of its partners who have an aggregate interest in partnership profits and capital greater than 50%. If the partners do not have the same taxable year, then a calendar year must be used; unless you can convince the IRS there is a legitimate business purpose for a different taxable year.

The partnership must also elect the method of 1) computing depreciation or cost recovery deductions for partnership property, 2) treatment of bad debt, and 3) reporting the sale of specified assets.

If these elections introduce concepts that are not familiar to you, get expert advice. These are items that can make a significant difference in the amount of tax that comes out of each partner's pocket.

The Internal Revenue Code, Rules and Regulations of the IRS, and rulings by the courts have developed an extensive body of tax law covering the operations of partnerships. The following is a list of some of the general areas of concern:

(1) Special dealings between the partnership and partners.

    a. Ordinary income from the sale of non-capital assets.

    b. Guaranteed payments from the partnership to partners.

    c. In the case of a limited partnership, payment of syndication and organization expenses.

    d. Loans by a partner to the partnership.

    e. Allocation of partnership income and expense items.

(2) Computing the tax basis of the partners' interest in the partnership.

(3) Distribution to partners—current versus liquidation distributions.

(4) Sale or exchange of partnership interests.

(5) Partnership termination.

(6) Partner's death or retirement.

(7) Family partnerships.

A discussion of these areas of tax law is beyond the scope of this book. Moreover, most normal, well-educated, and intelligent people find there is no logic to the rules and requirements. But try to remember that these areas all have potentially important tax consequences and, ideally, any decisions in these areas should be made after advance tax-planning.

(**Note:** A *family partnership* is a partnership among family members that is often used as a very sophisticated tax and estate planning device. For that reason, it is highly suspect by the IRS and has its own set of special rules. If your new small business happens to be a partnership among family members, you may inadvertently be in a category which the IRS treats as having great potential for abuse.)

## 5.4 The Partnership Tax Return

Although partnerships do not pay federal income taxes, they must file annual information returns on *Form 1065.* Regardless of the amount of income or loss, every partnership doing business in the U.S., or having U.S. source income during its tax year, must file one copy of *Form 1065* for that year. Generally, the partnership uses the official tax return form for the year in which its calendar or fiscal year begins.

*Form 1065* is a two-page report, designed as an information return for the reporting of partnership transactions and the partners' shares of partnership items. It does not provide for the computation of gross or taxable income or any tax, since no tax is paid by the partnership.

A copy of the official *Form 1065,* including schedules A and K and the instructions, can be found in Appendix B. The following is a brief review of *Form 1065* to help you understand how to complete the form.

(**Note:** A new partnership must create and file a form in addition to the federal income tax return indicating that it has adopted a taxable year which is the same as the taxable year of a majority of partners, all partners, or that it has adopted a calendar year.)

### A. Preliminary Information

The top of page one first asks for the partners' names, addresses, and the business activity, as well as the taxable period covered.

Box A on the top left of page one covers the general area of activity. (For example, retail, distribution, or manufacturing.) Box B covers the principal product or services. If there are multiple products or services and activities, boxes A and B should contain responses for those which the largest percentage of total assets are used.

The code number requested in box C can be found on page 20 of the instructions.

All partnerships must obtain a federal Taxpayer Identification Number (TIN). This is used in box D and on all other statements, schedules, or tax documents. To apply for this number, obtain *Form SS-4* from the IRS or the Social Security Administration.

Question M is to determine whether you are a *small partnership*. If you are, you can avoid Schedules L and M, Question F on page one of *Form 1065*, and Question I on Schedule K-1.

## B. Income

Items 1-7 on page one cover ordinary income.

*Gross receipts* are reported on the basis of the partnership's accounting method. Generally, the accrual method is used to clearly reflect income where inventories are needed. Credit allowances or other allowances made to customers are placed in 1b and subtracted to reach a net sales figure in 1c.

*Cost of Goods Sold* is computed on Schedule A if inventories are involved in the business. If inventories are not a factor, such as in service businesses, then the *cost of operations* is used. When cost of operations is used, a schedule must be attached to the return showing salaries and other costs in detail.

Inventories must be taken on a basis which conforms as closely as possible to the best accounting practice in the particular trade or business, and they should be based on consistent accounting practices. Physical inventories should be taken at reasonable intervals of at least once per year.

## C. Schedule A

The beginning inventory will normally agree with the year-end inventory reported for the preceding year. If there is a different number used, there must be a statement attached explaining the change in inventory method.

*Purchases*, line 2, includes merchandise bought for sale, and raw materials and parts for manufacture. Purchases are accounted for when title passes to your business, less trade discounts. Inventory losses due to theft or casualty can be used to reduce beginning inventory or purchases.

*Cost of labor*, line 3, includes salaries and wages, except those of partners, chargeable to the cost of manufacturing. This item will apply only to manufacturing concerns.

*Section 263A* and *other costs*, lines 4a and 4b, now include more indirect expenses. These include the following:

o   Utilities

o   Rental of equipment and facilities

o   Indirect labor and materials

o   Scrap and spoilage

o   Insurance

o   Administrative or support expenses

o   Current service costs of pensions

o   Profit-sharing

o   Storage costs

o   A portion of all tax depreciation

Other costs relate to manufacturing businesses and, if they apply, should be detailed on a separate schedule.

Line 6 calls for the *closing* or *year-end inventory*. The *cost of goods sold* can then be calculated by subtracting line 6 from line 5.

*Net gain or loss* from **Form 4797**, line 6, covers sales, exchanges, or other dispositions of non-inventory property. Note that capital asset transactions are reported on Schedule D. *Form 4797* is for those types of transactions when the result is ordinary income or loss due to a special provision.

D.  **Deductions**

Lines 9-19 are partnership deductions.

*Salaries and wages*, line 9, should not include any salaries or wages already included in calculating the cost of goods sold.

*Guaranteed payments to partners*, line 10, must be made under an arrangement where the payments are determined without regard to the partnership income and are ordinary and necessary expenses of the business. These do not include guaranteed payments while organizing your partnership.

*Business bad debts*, line 14, must arise from a bona fide debtor-creditor relationship based on a valid and enforceable obligation to pay a fixed or determinable sum of money. There must be a reasonable expectation and intent that repayment will be made; thus, loans made by partners and their relatives will be subject to scrutiny.

*Depreciation*, line 16, is detailed on *Form 4562.* This form also develops the amount of depreciation that will be allocated to each partner on Schedule K-1.

*Other deductions*, line 19, may include several items, which are detailed on an attached schedule. Here are some examples:

o   Advertising expenses

o   Travel and entertainment (note the 80% limitation)

o   Accounting and tax return preparation fees

o   Legal expenses

o   Inexpensive equipment and supplies

o   Utilities

o   Insurance premiums

o   Contributions or donations made with an intent to obtain a business benefit

E.   **Schedule K and K-1**

Schedule K is required only when more than ten K-1s are attached to your *Form 1065.*

Schedule K-1 is similar to Schedule K. One copy of each K-1 is attached to *Form 1065* and filed with the IRS. Each partner retains his or her copy of the K-1 for his or her tax records and uses it to report the appropriate amounts on his or her personal tax return. The allocations in the K-1s must correspond with the allocations in your partnership agreement.

Note that if any partner treats partnership items differently from the partnership, *Form 8082, Notice of Inconsistent Treatment or Amended Return,* must be filed.

## 5.5  Partners' Personal Returns

First, each partner should remember some of the general considerations that derive from entering into the partnership.

If the partnership has a different tax year from a partner's tax year, the income or loss from the partnership must be reported personally by that person in the tax year when the partnership's tax year ends.

There are limitations on the amount of loss each partner can deduct. A partner's share of losses cannot be deducted if it exceeds his or her adjusted basis in the partnership. In addition to this restriction, there is a separate limitation for losses that relate to the amount the partner is *at risk* with respect to partnership activities. This *at risk* limitation deals with personal liability for the partnership's loans and can become very technical. If you are an investor-partner, you may or may not be personally responsible should the partnership fail to repay loans. If you are not, it may have an effect on the amount of deductions you can take from the partnership. Consulut an expert if there is any question.

As pointed out above, the partnership must deliver a Schedule K-1 to each partner. The following is a brief description of how the items reported on Schedule K-1 are reported by an individual partner.

| Item | K-1 | Personal 1040 |
|------|-----|---------------|
| Guaranteed payments to a partner | Line 5 | Schedule E, Part II |
| Ordinary income or net loss | Line 1 | Schedule E, Part II |
| Dividends | Line 4b | 1040, line 10 |
| Salaries | Form W-2 | 1040, line 7 |
| Interest paid by partnership | Line 4a | 1040, line 8 |
| Gains or losses from sale of capital assets | Line 4d or 4e | Schedule D |
| Charitable contributions | Line 8 | Schedule A, line 14a or 14b |
| Net earnings from self-employment | | Schedule SE |

Note that this discussion on taxes has assumed that you are a partner who is active in the management of the business. If you are an investor-partner and do not "materially participate" in the business, your ownership may be defined as a "passive activity" under the Internal Revenue Code which will have a significant effect on the way you can use losses or credits generated by the partnership on your personal return.

## 5.6  Sale or Exchange of Partnership Interest

A partner who sells his or her partnership interest is selling something similar to a share of stock, and at the same time is selling a percentage interest in every partnership asset. Under the tax code, you may have a capital account that differs from your basis. Recall the example of partners X and Y who formed X-Y Associates. Assume that after one year of operations they sell the business for $300,000; and that during that year they took no depreciation deductions for the building that Y had contributed. The sale would then have the following effects:

|  | X | Y |
|---|---|---|
| Sale Proceeds | $150,000 | $150,000 |
| Basis | $100,000 | $40,000 |
| Gain on Sale | $50,000 | $110,000 |

Generally, the gain or loss from the sale of a partnership interest is treated as gain or loss from the sale of a capital asset, that is, an asset that is generally held for investment purposes, rather than property held in inventory for sale to customers.

The sale or exchange of a partner's entire interest closes the partnership's taxable year for that partner at that point.

If the partner's interest is purchased by the partnership or another partner, the corresponding re-adjustments of basis become fairly complicated. See your accountant for this. The same advice applies to the tax effects of terminating your partnership or the death or retirement of a partner.

The partnership must now file *Form 8308, Report of a Sale or Exchange of Certain Partnership Interests*, with the IRS when this occurs. *Form 8308* should be attached to *Form 1065* for the year in which the sale or exchange occurred.

## 5.7 State Taxes

Filing requirements for partnerships vary from state to state. They are usually similar to the federal requirements. However, you will need to research your state's laws to make sure that you comply with the proper reporting and payment requirements for your state.

# Chapter Six
# Limited Partnerships

*"We will now discuss in a little more detail the struggle for existence."*

Charles Robert Darwin (1809-1882)
*The Origin of Species* - 1859

This chapter will introduce you to limited partnerships and how they operate. The limited partnership is used as an investment vehicle; it features *general partners* and *limited partners*. *General partners*, which may be one or more individuals or a corporation, control and operate the business; while *limited partners* have liability limited to the amount of their investment, and have no control over the day-to-day operations of the business. LImited partners are investors and are similar to shareholders/investors in a corporation.

The main advantage of limited partnerships is that tax profits and losses can be passed directly through to limited partners, while their liability remains limited. In smaller limited partnerships in particular, the limited partners need to be careful not to exercise control over the business that is reserved for the general partner. For example, in a real estate partnership, it would be inappropriate for limited partners to make decisions regarding the day-to-day operations, such as tenant relations and maintenance. If the limited partners do exercise such control, the IRS will seek to characterize the limited partnership as a corporation so that it can tax profits at two levels.

This same dilemma applies to transfer of ownership units of the limited partners. Some transferability is permitted, particularly in death or emergency situations; however, free transferability is not permitted since it will jeopardize the tax status of the partnership.

The following is a list of advantages and disadvantages of joining a partnership as a limited partner:

**Advantages for the Limited Partner:**

o   Limited liability

o   Pass-through of tax advantages

o   Shared ownership of large assets through pooling of capital

o   Professional management provided by general partner

### Disadvantages for the Limited Partner

o   Illiquidity; units of ownership are not freely transferable

o   Lack of control over management decisions

The general partner has a fiduciary duty towards the limited partners; and, like any other fiduciary/investor relationship, there is a great potential for conflict. In most cases, the general partner has made little or no capital contribution and is (at least partly) compensated regardless of partnership profits. The general partner owes a duty of good faith and fair dealing toward the limited partners. The specifics of the relationship are covered in more detail in the following section on the limited partnership agreement.

A limited partnership generally raises many more legal questions than a general partnership, since there is a higher standard of protection for the limited partners. Most states have very detailed registration requirements to establish a limited partnership. In addition to this, the units of ownership in a limited partnership may be *securities*, and as such are subject to regulation under both state and federal law. The securities laws and regulations are a treacherous area even for lawyers. They set many requirements on the structuring of limited partnership offerings, such as who may invest and what must be disclosed to potential investors.

The general partners may be a partnership. In this case, they should have a partnership agreement between themselves in addition to the limited partnership agreement.

Most states (37 at last count) have adopted some form of the Uniform Limited Partnership Act (ULPA), which is similar to the Uniform Partnership Act (UPA). You should note that there are many requirements for a limited partnership which cannot be waived or modified by agreement. This is different from the situation for general partnerships, where there is a great deal of flexibility in putting together an agreement.

## 6.1   Limited Partnership Agreement

The following is a sample *limited partnership agreement* with comments on its provisions. **The basic purpose of setting out this agreement is to familiarize you with most of the issues involved in setting up a limited partnership. It is not designed to be a comprehensive agreement, and it is not designed for any specific situations.** Remember that this partnership relationship requires an extra level of caution because of the built-in protections for investors. Following the limited partnership agreement is a discussion of the registration certificate that must be filed for each limited partnership. (See final section of this chapter.)

## Form 6-A

## Limited Partnership Agreement

This Limited Partnership Agreement ("Agreement") is made on _____
between _____
the General Partner and the Limited Partners listed on the signature page. By
this Agreement, the Partners join together to form a limited partnership and
agree to all terms of this Agreement.

**Note:** *There must be at least one general partner and one limited partner.
They can be individuals, general or limited partnerships, or corporations.
If there are a significant number of limited partners, they can be listed
on the signature page or presented as an exhibit. This eliminates the
need to revise the entire agreement when limited partners are added
or deleted.*

1. **Purpose**

The purpose of the partnership is to engage in the business of _____
_____

a. In addition to this purpose, the partnership may purchase any real or
personal property, make any investment, and engage in any other business
activity proposed by the general partner and approved by a majority of the
limited partners.

**Note:** *You may wish to require approval of two-thirds or all of the limited
partners for additional purposes.*

2. **Name**

The name of the Partnership shall be _____,
a limited partnership.

**Note:** *Do not use the name of a limited partner. For more information on
choosing a name, see chapter 2. Most states require that the name
indicate that it is a limited partnership. For example, "ABC Partners, A
Limited Partnership."*

3.  **Place of Business**

    The principal place of business for the partnership shall be _____

    _____.

    **Note:** *This same address must be stated in the certificate. This address must refer to the place where partnership records must be kept as required by the ULPA.*

4.  **Term**

    The partnership term begins on the date of this Agreement and shall continue until _____, when it shall dissolve under the terms of this Agreement.

    **Note:** *A definite term should be stated to avoid IRS arguments that the partnership has continuity of life, similar to a corporation. The partnership should also dissolve upon retirement, removal, bankruptcy, or dissolution of a sole remaining general partner.*

5.  **Capital Contributions**

    Each partner has contributed, or will contribute by _____ the amount shown next to their signature to this Agreement.

    **Note:** *Future services cannot be exchanged for a limited partnership interest. Property, services, or a promissory note can be used for a contribution. Under this section, one of two options should be included to define future contributions:*

    a. Limited partners shall not be required to contribute additional capital; or

    b. Limited partners may be required to contribute additional capital to the partnership.

    **Note:** *This defines whether a limited partner's interest is assessable or non-assessable. If you choose to give the general partner the power to assess, you may wish to limit assessments to a percentage of original contribution, or make the power to assess subject to approval of a majority of the limited partners. This section can also contain elaborate provisions for the contingency that a limited partner fails to pay an assessment, including penalties.*

*A similar provision can be included for partnerships that allow contributions in installments. This provision would define the reduction in ownership and penalty for failure to make, or delinquency in making, an installment contribution.*

*This provision may also allow the general partner to admit additional limited partners in order to raise the capital required.*

## 6. Capital Account

Each partner shall have a capital account that includes invested capital plus that partner's allocations of net income, minus that partner's allocations of net loss and share of distributions.

**Note:** *There are specific IRS regulations on how to calculate a partner's capital account. If a partner contributes property, the fair market value is used in calculating the capital account.*

## 7. Distributions and Allocations

Net income and net loss shall be allocated as follows:

a. _____ percent to the General Partner.

b. _____ percent to the Limited Partners, according to their respective percentage ownership interests.

**Note:** *This is a key area of the agreement that is subject to negotiation between the general and limited partners. Basically, there are three possible types of fees or distributions to the general partner: Front end or organizational, during operations, and upon sale or dissolution. Distributions to the general partner during operations or upon sale or distribution may be made subordinate to a priority return to the limited partners. There is also discretion in how net income and net loss are allocated. For example, the limited partners can be given a disproportionate share of the net losses.*

## 8. Partnership Expenses

a. The Partnership shall reimburse the General Partner for the following expenses:_____

_____

_____

b. The General Partner shall pay and shall not be reimbursed by the Partnership for the following expenses: _____

_____

_____

**Note:** *This section should be thought out carefully in order to avoid arguments later.*

*Reimbursable expenses might include actual cost of goods or materials used for the partnership; organization costs incurred to form the partnership, including legal and accounting fees; salaries, compensation and fringe benefits of personnel involved in the partnership business (excluding officers and directors of the general partner); legal, audit, accounting, consulting; travel and entertainment; brokerage fees; etc.*

*Non-reimbursable expenses might include salaries, compensation and fringe benefits of officers and directors of the general partner; overhead expenses of the general partner; fees already paid to the general partner under another section of the agreement.*

*If the general partner is engaging in other business activities besides this limited partnership, extra care should be taken in defining the expenses which will apply.*

9. **Management**

Except as otherwise expressly stated in this Agreement, the General Partner shall manage the partnership business and have exclusive control over the partnership business, including the power to sign deeds, notes, mortgages, deeds of trust, contracts, leases, and direction of business operations.

**Note:** *The authority of the general partner can be set forth in much more detail, if necessary. The power to execute documents pertaining to real estate should be stated explicitly in order to satisfy title insurance companies, which will review the partnership agreement before issuing insurance.*

*Limited partners may retain the right to vote on matters allowed by each state's version of the ULPA. They must exercise care, however, not to jeopardize their limited liability and tax status by overly restricting the management authority of the general partner.*

## 10. Books and Records

The General Partner shall keep all required books and records at the principal place of business. Each limited partner shall have the right to inspect and copy all books and records during normal business hours.

**Note:** *The ULPA requires that annual financial reports be issued to each partner. You may wish to supplement this section with another section requiring more frequent and specific reporting to the limited partners.*

## 11. Accounting

The partnership's tax or fiscal year shall be _____. The General Partner shall make any tax election necessary for completion of the partnership tax return.

**Note:** *You may also want to require an annual audit of the books and records by an independent accounting firm. This is an expensive require- ment and may not be appropriate for small partnerships. The tax or fiscal year can be a calendar year or any appropriate fiscal year.*

## 12. Assignment

**Note:** *Two options are presented here. The first option allows free transferability of partnership units, while the second option restricts assignment rights.*

### Option 1

A limited partner may assign his or her rights to receive distributions, net income and net loss to any person. On receipt by the General Partner of a notice of assignment signed by both the assignor and assignee, in a form approved by the General Partner, and payment of a fee not to exceed $_____ to cover partnership costs, the assignment shall be completed. Any assignment under this section shall not cause dissolution of the partnership.

91

**Option 2**

No limited partner shall assign, transfer, or sell any interest in the partnership or any interest in partnership assets without the prior written approval of a majority of the limited partners. Any assignment under this section shall not cause dissolution of the partnership.

**Note:** *Unanimous, two-thirds approval, or another requirement can be substituted for "majority." It is usually best to allow some right to assign. Another option is to allow assignment only after granting a right of first refusal to the other limited partners.*

*It should also be noted that there are several types of involuntary assignments which can occur. These include: death, legal incapacity, foreclosure against a partner, court order, divorce decree or settlement or transfer from a fiduciary on termination of the relationship. For larger partnerships, a provision can be included which defines these assignments and the process which applies to them.*

## 13. Arbitration

Any controversy between the partners involving the construction or application of any of the terms, covenants, or conditions of the agreement shall be submitted to arbitration in the city of the principal place of business of the partnership, on the request of any partner. The arbitration shall be conducted under the rules of the American Arbitration Association.

## 14. Amendments

This Agreement may be amended by the written agreement of all Partners.

## 15. Notices

All notices between the Partners shall be in writing and shall be deemed served when personally delivered to a Partner, or on the second day after being deposited in the mail, certified, first-class postage prepaid, addressed to the Partner's address shown after his or her signature to this Agreement or a more recent address given to the Partnership in writing.

## 16. Entire Agreement

This instrument contains the entire Agreement of the parties. It correctly sets out the Partners' rights and obligations. Any prior agreements, oral representations, or modifications shall be of no force or effect unless contained in a subsequent written modification signed by all parties to this Agreement.

## 17. Severability

If any term, provision, covenant, or condition of this Agreement is held by a court of competent jurisdiction or arbitrator to be invalid, void, or unenforceable, the rest of this Agreement shall in no way be affected, impaired, or invalidated.

**In witness whereof,** the partners have signed this Agreement as of the date first shown above.

| Name & Address | Capital Contribution | Percentage Interest |
|---|---|---|
| General Partner(s): | | |
| _____ | $_____ | _____% |
| _____ | | |
| _____ | | |
| _____ | $_____ | _____% |
| _____ | | |
| _____ | $_____ | _____% |
| _____ | | |
| _____ | | |

|                | Capital<br>Contribution | Percentage<br>Interest |
|----------------|-------------------------|------------------------|
| **Name & Address** |                     |                        |

**Limited Partner(s):**

_____        $_____        _____%

_____

_____

_____        $_____        _____%

_____

_____

_____        $_____        _____%

_____

_____

**Note:** *As pointed out at the beginning of the agreement, if there are a large number of limited partners, their signatures can be attached as Exhibit A to the Agreement.*

## 6.2 Additional Terms

The limited partnership agreement set forth in the previous section is in a very simple format. It is designed to give you a basic overview of the key provisions. As you can probably guess, a limited partnership agreement can become extremely complex, depending on the situation. The following is a summary of some of the provisions and considerations that go into a more complex limited partnership agreement.

1. A section setting forth **definitions** of terms that are used within the agreement.

2. **Admission of Limited Partners** — A detailed section covering the procedures for admitting partners, including those admitted after initial organization.

3. **Escrow** — Covers use of an escrow agent for acceptance of subscriptions to the partnership.

4. **Captial Contributions** — Additional provisions can be included to cover contributions in installments or assessments requiring further contributions in the future.

5. **Delinquent Contributions** — Penalties, interests, legal costs, etc.

6. **Capital Account** — This section can be expanded to give your accountants explicit requirements, including compliance with applicable Treasury Department regulations.

7. **Reserves** — Instructs the general partner as to reserves that must be kept out of initial capital and during operations.

8. **Distributions and Allocations** — As mentioned in the note to this section of the agreement, there are many variations that can be used to cover the apportionments between limited partners and between the limited partners and the general partner. Included in these are alternatives which give limited partners the right to priority in distributions or a fixed rate of return. These rights can be covered in detail for distributions during operations, from re-finance proceeds and upon sale or dissolution.

9. **Payments to General Partner** — Especially in large partnerships, it is common for the agreement to define several types of fees and payments in detail. These fees and payments can include management fees, leasing commissions, loan broker's commission, insurance commission, and payment on removal of the general partner.

10. **Tax Matters Partner (TMP)** — The IRS now requires the appointment of a TMP for partnerships of ten or more partners. The TMP is usually the general partner, who then has the authority to negotiate with IRS on behalf of the partnership.

11. **Devotion of Time** — This section defines whether the general partner will be full-time or part-time. In any event, it should require the general partner to devote an amount of time reasonably necessary to manage partnership business.

12. **Indemnification** — This section requires the partnership to indemnify, hold harmless, and defend the general partner from liability claims. You should decide whether to indemnify for all claims or to limit this to those arising out of actions taken in good faith on behalf of the partnership. Gross negligence, intentional misconduct, or criminal actions should be excluded.

13. **Investment Opportunities** — Where the general partner is in a business or is in an investor in opportunities that are similar to the partnership's pursuits, this section allows the general partner to pursue them without first presenting them to the partnership. Without this section, such action is potentially a breach of fiduciary duty.

14. **Conflicts of Interest** — Here the general partner should disclose all potential conflicts of interest to the limited partners. Particularly important are disclosures of any transactions between the partnership and the general partner or its affiliates.

15. **Limited Partners' Voting Rights and Meetings** — This section can range from granting minimum voting rights to the limited partners to requiring approval of a long list of specific actions that might be proposed by the general partner. This should be compared with your state's version of the ULPA to see which actions require a vote of the partners by law.

    Regularly scheduled meetings, as well as the right to call special meetings can also be covered here. Again, this should be written in light of your state's version of the ULPA.

    Where there is great concern on the part of the limited partners, some states allow the appointment of an audit committee. This allows limited partners to review and approve or disapprove of major partnership actions without becoming liable for partnership debts. The agreement can also require the submission of an annual budget to the audit committee.

16. **General Partner's Withdrawal, Removal, Bankruptcy, or Dissolution** — These events should all result in the dissolution of the partnership, even if it is immediately reconstituted with a new general partner. This is to remove any argument on the part of the IRS that the partnership is in fact a corporation because it has continuity of life.

    Among the provisions that can be included are majority vote for removal, notice of removal, purchase of a general partner's interest, partnership liability on general partner's removal or withdrawal, successor and predecessor general partners, and contribution of partnership in the event of a change of general partner.

17. **Special Power of Attorney** — Your state may require that the general partner be appointed attorney-in-fact for purposes of filing partnership documents.

## 6.3 Certificate of Limited Partnership

The ULPA requires each limited partnership to file a registration certificate, which contains basic information about the partnership. The state government agency which accepts this filing varies from state to state. In many states, filing is done with the secretary of state. There may also be a requirement that you publish a copy of the certificate in a local newspaper. Check with your state's secretary of state or Corporations Commission for filing requirements.

Requirements for the certificate have been simplified since 1985. It must now contain at least the following information:

o The name of the Limited Partnership;

o The address of the partnership's office and the name and address of its agent for service of process;

o The name and business address of each general partner;

o The latest date upon which the limited partnership is to dissolve;

o Any other matters the general partners determine to include therein.

These significantly reduced requirements grew out of a recognition of the fact that the limited partnership agreement, not the certificate, has become the authoritative and comprehensive document for most limited partnerships, and that creditors should refer to it for facts concerning capital and finances.

If during the course of your limited partnership there are any significant changes such as the name, general partner, or address, the certificate should be amended.

# Chapter Seven
# Partnership Problems

*"A man never lost any money on a fast horse; it's the slow ones that cause all the damn trouble."*

Editor
Calgary, Alberta newspaper

## 7.1  Subjects Most of Us Would Rather Avoid

While you are making plans for success and working together with your new partners, it is natural that you are not considering the down-side of things. In fact, you don't even want to think about this. But your attorney should be planning for any negative possibilities (this is what he or she is paid for); and attorneys know it is more likely that you will experience difficulties in your partnership. Ironically, even if your business is successful, you may have a partnership that is not. In fact, if you pause to consider this for a moment, all partnership problems worth fighting over involve commercially successful partnerships. If the businss is a failure, everyone will simply walk away from it.

Following are some of the problems attorneys usually associate with partnerships:

o Divorce

o Dispute/Dissolution

o Disability/Death

These are subjects that most of us would rather avoid. In fact, most business people want to avoid them so much that they turn to attorney-bashing when forced with dealing with them. In fact, one popular piece of advice is "Attorneys are deal-killers."

Regardless of what you think of attorneys, be practical. You should plan for success and understand the potential pitfalls in an area that is particularly treacherous. This is especially true for the first-time partner.

Even if you are never going to die or become disabled, or if you would never have a marital or debt problem, or if it is unthinkable that you would enter into a dispute or dissolution, then accept this fact—your partners would!

Since it is no coincidence that written partnership agreements concentrate on these same areas, it goes without saying that you should invest the time and money to have a well-conceived and well-written partnership agreement.

Most partnerships do not have written partnership agreements. This fact is so well-established that 49 out of 50 states (Louisiana is the exception) have adopted the Uniform Partnership Act (UPA) which codifies the legal rights and obligations among partners. "Why," you might ask, "would our state legislatures spend so much time on this subject?" The answer lies in the fact that we in business have historically spent a lot of time in court arguing with our partners. As a matter of public policy, state governments would rather have us spend less time in court, so they have tried to make the law clear on where we stand when we get into a partnership dispute.

Even if you have a written agreement, it will remain in the file drawer as long as the partnership is making money and everyone is happy with one another. I hope you never have to refer back to it. But if you do, what can you expect?

## 7.2 Divorce

To illustrate this potential problem, let's look at the partnership of Smith and Jones. They were 50/50 partners in an extremely successful dry-cleaning business with two retail locations. Before entering into the business, they both had several years of experience in the business and had been personal friends for ten years.

By joining forces, Smith and Jones were able to buy a large dry-cleaning operation with two locations. They recognized that the purchase of these businesses was a turn-around opportunity with high profit potential. Before entering into the partnership, they had lengthy discussions about their plans for the business and their personal objectives. Following these discussions, they entered into a written partnership agreement and completed the purchase of the two locations.

The agreement split everything down the middle, including initial investment, debt, profits, losses, and management responsibility.

When they commenced operation of the business, it quickly became apparent that the two partners brought a different level of commitment and skills to the partnership. Jones, it turned out, was a much better manager and knew more about what it took to make the business successful. He dedicated himself to the new venture and worked long hours to assure its success. Smith, on the other hand, was more interested in playing than working. He had constant excuses for his failure to show the same commitment to the business as Jones.

In spite of the differences in work ethic and commitment, Jones worked diligently for several years to bring the business to a high level of profitability. He was disappointed with Smith, but accepted his fate of not having the best possible partner. Smith had at least made some contributions in the area of planning for business expansion.

This mode of operation was to end abruptly. At one point, Smith announced he was taking a trip to visit his ailing mother. He returned after four weeks and looked happier than Jones had ever seen him. While visiting his mother, he had met a younger woman who understood him. He had fallen in love and had decided to divorce his wife of forty years. As he explained to Jones, they hated each other anyway and as far as he could see, his wife would be happy to be rid of him.

Smith asked Jones for his support through the divorce. Jones could see that he was upset and agreed to give his partner the emotional support he requested. Smith also assured Jones, "Don't worry, I'll protect you no matter what happens in the divorce."

After that, Smith's performance as a partner dropped to new lows. When he did show up at work, all he could talk about was the divorce. It distracted him so badly that he became error-prone. Jones had to review everything he did so that he made no major mistakes which would have hurt the business.

Once the divorce was filed by Smith, his wife went on the offensive. She was going to teach him a lesson that he would not forget. The lesson was that if he was going to leave her for a younger woman, he would do it with little or no money.

Mrs. Smith had her attorney file *lis pendens notices* on both the real estate and business assets of the partnership. *Lis pendens* is a recording of public notice that all of the business property was subject to a legal action. The notice had a chilling effect on vendors, creditors, and several parties considering entering into contracts with the partnership. Mrs. Smith also alleged that Jones had encouraged her husband to leave her and that he was responsible for the divorce.

Smith informed Jones that he could not do anything about this. He told his partner that Mrs. Smith had gotten this "crooked" lawyer and that the two of them were plotting against him. He assured Jones that the situation was temporary and that soon he would be vindicated in court and everything would be back to normal. He would have a new wife and be motivated to work harder than ever.

As the divorce proceedings progressed over the months, Jones found himself being dragged into it. He had to help answer a set of interrogatories from Mrs. Smith's attorney. This consisted of about two hundred questions and a request for supporting business documents. The questions were designed to support the allegation that Mrs. Smith was being cheated out of her share of the business profits. Jones also found himself the subject of a deposition. He spent eight hours in her attorney's office answering questions which implied that he and his partner had conspired to cheat her and deprive the Smith children of their inheritance.

Mrs. Smith's attorney also threatened to seek restraining orders, injunctions, accountings and to ultimately have a receiver appointed to take over management of the business. (Receivers are discussed at more length in section 7.3 "Disputes/Dissolution," page 103).

The more these tactics upset her husband and Jones, the more Mrs. Smith seemed to derive satisfaction from them.

Jones was most shocked when he learned about a property settlement offer that Smith had submitted to his wife. In this offer, Smith proposed that when the assets were divided up, Mrs. Smith would take title to his one-half interest in the partnership with Jones. This possibility was inconceivable to Jones. His partner, who had assured him that he would be protected, was now trying to make him partners with an ex-wife who had accused Jones of causing the divorce and conspiring to cheat him. Jones consulted with his attorney to see if this was possible and was shocked to learn that it was.

Ultimately, Mr. and Mrs. Smith reconciled and the divorce action was withdrawn. Jones breathed a sigh of relief at having escaped a situation which could have ruined the business he had worked so hard to make a success.

## A. Lessons

If you are in a similar situation and you check your partnership agreement for remedies, you will find that it is silent on this point. You will have no right to take corrective action for your business, and conversely your partner has no obligation to compensate you for the loss. The standard forms used in drafting partnership agreements are silent on the subject of divorce, as is the UPA.

What you have on your hands is a partner who is basically "emotionally disabled." You will not be able to prove that they fit the definition of "disability" in your agreement and you will find it nearly impossible as a matter of practicality to prove that he or she isn't meeting their obligation to "use best efforts and devote himself or herself full time to the business."

At the same time, you are dealing with a friend, who also happens to be a business partner. Not very many of us are dispassionate enough to invoke legal arguments against our friends at a time like this. Your partner will tell you that it is only temporary and that they need support. In this type of crisis, people tend to use a simple sorting process where everyone they are associated with is either "one of us" or "part of the opposition." Thus, even if you try to sit down and talk this over with your partner, you will probably be characterized as a cruel and uncaring enemy of your emotionally volatile partner.

Divorces nearly always start out as "friendly." Both parties are going to behave in an adult manner. They will divide up property and kids and then go their separate ways with no hard feelings. I'm sure I do not need to tell you that this is a fairy tale. Even in "no fault divorce" states like California, if there is any property involved, chances are that there will be a battle royale.

Now at this point, your partner will say, "I can't prevent my 'no good' spouse from doing this. She/he has got this crooked attorney and you wouldn't believe all the crazy things they're pulling." You'll also be reminded that this is only temporary. Soon your partner will win the day in court and all will be normal again—don't worry!

But this is all a rationalization. First of all, "temporary" is a relative term. Where assets are involved, it is not uncommon for the divorce action to drag on for two, three, or four years. How well will you and your business be able to weather a storm of this duration? What if you couldn't obtain bank credit for a period of three years due to your assets being subject to lis pendens notices? Can you survive this sort of period with a preoccupied and emotionally bothered partner?

What can you do to protect yourself from this kind of situation?

I would suggest that you and your prospective partners discuss the subject and agree that all of you have the right to be free of the possibility of being dragged into it. You can do this by including a clause in your partnership agreement that gives all partners the right to buy out any partner who becomes part of a divorce action. The buyout can be tied to the price stated in the buy/sell formula in the agreement. If, however, you think this is cold-hearted, I suggest you re-read the preceding section or discuss the subject with anyone who has ever been in the situation.

I would also suggest that if you include this clause in the partnership agreement, you should have the spouse of each partner indicate their acceptance and understanding of it in the spousal consent form. These changes have been added to the sample agreement discussed in chapter 4.


## 7.3  Dispute/Dissolution

To illustrate this potential problem, let us continue with the example of partners Smith and Jones. Remember that the importance of these examples is to help you avoid a similar problem. By reviewing various probable situations, you will be able to prevent your partnership from coming anywhere near experiencing similar problems. These situations are avoidable as long as everyone is committed to making your business and your partnership a success.

In this example, Smith never went through with his divorce action. He and Mrs. Smith reconciled. At that point, however, he decided that he wanted out of the partnership with Jones.

The partnership, as you will recall, involved the very successful operation of a dry cleaning business with two retail locations. Jones was responsible for this success. He had the expertise required for the management of the business and he had spent long hours, seven days a week, in making the business profitable. Smith, on the other hand, had shirked his responsibilities and had even avoided being present at the business wherever possible. Discussions about this had done no good. They simply had a different work ethic and a different set of personal objectives.

In spite of Smith's poor work habits and attitude, it should be noted that he was always there when it was time to divide the profits. He was very diligent in his efforts to be sure that he received his half. He regularly let Jones know that he was watching closely and that nobody could get away with taking advantage of him.

When Smith indicated his desire to get out of the partnership, Jones was the logical buyer of his one-half interest. They discussed this possibility, but were not able to arrive at a purchase price that was acceptable to both of them. Smith wanted a price for his half that Jones considered astronomical.

Since they could not agree on a price between themselves, they agreed that the entire business would be offered for sale to third parties at the price that Smith thought it was worth.

At this point, relations between the two partners became very bad. Smith refused to do any further work on the business and left all the responsibility to Jones. Open hostility developed between them.

The business was offered for sale to third parties. Since it was so successful, several potential buyers were interested in it. Their review of the business was conducted carefully and slowly. Several months passed from the time Smith had first stated his desire to get out.

During this time, many unpleasant incidents took place. Smith decided to take the position that Jones was a "crook" and accused Jones of stealing from him. Smith showed up at the business on several occasions and shouted physical threats at Jones in front of the employees and customers, and, at a later point, had the locks changed and locked Jones out of the business. Smith also set up a bank account in his name only and put all the business's cash into it. His explanation for this was that it was necessary to prevent Jones from stealing from him.

When Jones was locked out of the business and separated from his share of the cash, he felt he had no alternative but to visit his attorney, who was experienced in handling this type of dispute. When Jones finished explaining the facts of the situation, the attorney told him that unfortunately, this type of dispute was very common. In his experience, fistfights, lockouts, and similar behavior were regular occurrences in partnership disputes.

Jones then asked the attorney what his rights were. The attorney first explained that this partnership dispute was in the realm of what attorneys call *partnership dissolution.* Whenever a partner wants out, or the other partners want to throw one partner out of the business, and it cannot be resolved in a friendly manner, a dissolution proceeding usually follows.

The attorney's first question for Jones was whether he and Smith had a partnership agreement. Jones had brought the agreement with him. This was the first time anyone had looked at it since their business was started. The attorney immediately turned to the section covering buyout rights of the partners. This provision in the agreement between Smith and Jones allowed the remaining partner to buy the interest of the other partner upon his death, disability, or voluntary withdrawal. It also contained a formula for calculating the price at which this buyout option could be exercised.

Jones explained to the attorney that when he had entered into the partnership with Smith, this was the one section of the agreement that had captured Smith's interest. Smith had, in fact, written the formula it contained and Jones had agreed to it. When Smith had first told Jones that he wanted to sell out, he had also informed him that he shouldn't bother to try to use this buyout formula, since it resulted in a price that was too low.

Jones then asked his attorney if it was possible to enforce this provision, especially since Smith had written it. The price that it generated was about the price that Jones felt was fair for the business. The formula was based on well-accepted principles of valuation in the industry.

The attorney informed Jones that it was possible to enforce the buyout formula; however, Jones should understand the practicalities of what he was facing in trying to enforce this provision.

He explained that a partnership dissolution proceeding is similar to arms negotiations between the superpowers. Any of the partners has the right to file an action for dissolution in court. Filing is similar to "pushing the button" and launching the missiles.

He continued his explanation to Jones by pointing out that most partners assume that even if they file an action in court, they will be able to continue to operate the business until a judge can hear the evidence in the matter and issue a decision. In almost every case, he explained, the scenario will go like this:

First, a hearing will be held shortly after you file. At this hearing, it will become clear that you and your partner have an irreconcilable breakdown in your relations, and putting you together in the same courtroom will prove conclusively to any third party observer that you cannot get along. No matter how eloquently or logically any of you present a plan to continue operation of the business until your dispute is resolved, the judge has one primary way of dealing with this sort of problem. He or she will throw both of you out of the management of the business and appoint a receiver to take over its operations. This is for your collective protection—at least in theory.

The receiver will most likely be a person who knows nothing about your business or your industry, and their fees will probably run about $500 per day. They are usually a friend of the judge, such as a retired banker. The receiver will then hire a lawyer to represent the business. Billing will range from $100-$200 per hour with you having no control over the amount billed. If there is any day-to-day management required, the receiver will also hire a manager at another $200-$300 per day.

The receiver will also hire an accountant to come in and do a complete audit of the business. Once again, cost is no object. Knowing that the court is scrutinizing their work, the accountant will no doubt be exceptionally thorough at an hourly fee between $50 and $150 per hour. It may even take a team of accountants to do the audit justice.

If you do not believe this assures destruction of your business, then ponder your business credit situation once the button has been pushed. All the loans you have with banks will have a provision that allows the bank to call the loan upon appointment of a receiver for the business. *Calling* the loan means that it is due, in cash, immediately. This is generally true for real estate loans as well.

It is also likely that your contracts with major suppliers have a provision that they can be canceled upon appointment of a receiver. Appointment of a receiver is likewise defined as a default under equipment and real property leases. You will be faced with being thrown out of your locations and any leased equipment can be repossessed.

The attorney then said, "Perhaps you can see why I have labeled this situation 'mutually assured destruction' and made an analogy to nuclear war. Filing in court will not protect your interests; it will destroy them. Your only satisfaction will be that you dragged your partner down with you, so that no one survived financially."

The attorney then informed Jones that during this action, his fees would be $150 per hour and that it was not uncommon for this type of lawsuit to take 200-300 hours of his time. In addition, at least one expert witness would be necessary to address the question of valuation of the business. This person's fees would be an additional several thousand dollars.

## A. Lessons

Partnership disputes are obviously lucrative business for the lawyers, accountants, and other advisers who work on them. There is already a new specialty developing in psychology, where principles from marriage counseling and relationship therapy are being applied in a business partnership context.

The partnership agreement between Smith and Jones did not call for binding arbitration to settle disputes. This is a provision that you may want to consider for your agreement. Under this procedure, the partners agree to submit the dispute to an independent arbitrator. The procedures are more informal than a trial in a court of law and everyone is bound by the decision without the right of appeal. This is not cheap, however, since all parties are still represented by lawyers and it often takes as much time as going to court.

In some cases, however, entering into an arbitration proceeding may bring warring parties to their senses while avoiding a receivership. But this is not a foolproof solution. What if one partner refuses to arbitrate? The only recourse again is to file in court and you are back into the mutually assured destruction scenario.

You should also note that arbitrators are not bound by law or by what your agreement contains; and there is no appeal from their ruling, no matter how inept it might be. Most arbitrators are competent, but it is possible to get one who is not the greatest.

Dissolution disputes inevitably center around the buy/sell formula in your agreement. This clause should be drafted as clearly as possible. As you have seen, a partner may try to pull shenanigans with the clause. If possible, include a clear example or exhibit which applies the formula in the agreement. Leave no room for disagreement or interpretation. You may want to avoid a formula and leave the valuation to an appraiser. The clause then states that if you cannot agree on an appraiser, each of you selects one and they, in turn, select a third. The appraised values are then averaged.

There is no way to guarantee that you will not end up in a serious dispute or dissolution situation. But at least you now have an idea how serious the problem can become. Keep this in mind when you select partners and negotiate a partnership agreement.

## B. Causes of Dissolution

If you have a partnership agreement, the most common causes of dissolution are by operation of the agreement or from a violation of the agreement. Where there is not a violation of the partnership agreement, dissolution may be caused by operation of law for the following reasons:

1.  The termination of the definite term or particular undertaking specified in the partnership agreement;

2.  The express will of any partner when no definite term or particular undertaking is specified;

3.  The express will of all of the partners;

4.  The expulsion of any partner.

Generally, for any partner to sue another partner or the partnership, there must be a request for dissolution. Courts must usually issue a decree of dissolution whenever any of the following occur:

1.  A partner has been declared a lunatic in any judicial proceeding or is shown to be of unsound mind;

2.  A partner becomes in any other way incapable of performing his or her part of the partnership contract;

3.  A partner has been guilty of such conduct as tends to prejudicially affect the carrying on of the business;

4.  A partner willfully or persistently commits a breach of the partnership agreement, or otherwise so conducts himself or herself in matters relating to the partnership business that it is not reasonably practical to carry on the business and partnership with him or her;

5.  The business of the partnership can only be carried on at a loss;

6.  Other circumstances render a dissolution equitable.

Numbers 2, 3, and 4 are very difficult to prove, and, even if you can, the most likely result is that a receiver will be appointed to take over the business.

Note that whenever a partnership is dissolved, a notice of dissolution should be published in order to provide public notice, especially to creditors. The notice of dissolution on page 111 is an example of the form used by one state.

## 7.5 Disability/Death

These pleasant topics round out this discussion. Once again, the question is, "What would be the effect on your partnership if you or one of your partners could no longer participate in management due to death or a long-term disability?" Like the other topics covered in this chapter, these need to be considered from the point of view of protecting yourself and your family in the event that you or one of your partners has the problem.

These happen to be the two contingencies that are insurable. In the case of long-term disability, an individual partner can buy an insurance policy that will replace earnings. This is a good idea to the extent that your family is dependent on these earnings and does not have investment income or spouse's income sufficient to replace them. Similarly, life insurance can be purchased to protect a partner's family. In a partnership situation, life insurance is generally used to fund a buy/sell agreement between the partners.

Let us assume, for example, that there are two equal partners and that their partnership agreement states that upon the death of either partner, the surviving partner will have 90 days to buy the interest of the deceased partner. Let us further assume that the business is worth about $1 million—that is, each partner's share of the assets after subtracting debts is approximately $500,000. If neither partner has the means to finance this amount, they can agree to purchase life insurance policies on one another's lives. Each partner will then be the beneficiary of the other partner's policy and the proceeds upon death are required to be used to fund the buyout of the deceased partner's interest.

This type of arrangement is generally advisable. For most people, the value of their share of a successful business is one of the largest portions of their estate. If your surviving spouse did not receive cash for your interest, would you feel comfortable with him or her taking your place in the business? Would your spouse or another member of your family be capable of assuming your role in the business? Even if one of them could, how would your partner react to this? Your family may end up in a dispute/dissolution mode, where the loss of everything due to the appointment of a receiver is threatened after your death.

On the other hand, how would you feel about suddenly having your partner's spouse or child as your partner? If this prospect frightens you, it is best to have a buyout provision upon your partner's death and a means to fund it.

A disability in the partnership should be dealt with similarly. Assume your partner suffers a stroke or disabling heart attack. How long would you feel charitable enough to pay them their portion of the profits while you did all the work? How do you think your partner would treat you if you were the unfortunate one with the disability?

Another interesting question in this area is "What constitutes a *disability*?" Does alcoholism or drug addiction qualify? Consider this case. Two partners operated a business with eight retail locations open seven days a week. One partner had a drinking problem. This problem escalated to the point where he became institutionalized for his drinking and his wife filed for divorce. He was hospitalized and his wife was appointed his *conservator* (the legal equivalent of a guardian for adult) and took over his interest in the business partnership. Although the other partner was able to avoid losing everything, it took several years of agony and thousands of dollars in attorney's fees to dissolve the partnership.

When drafting a clause that deals with disability, remember that there will not be a lump sum of cash available from insurance proceeds to fund a buyout. You and your partners will most likely need the right to make installment payments to satisfy the buyout obligation.

One of the solutions that has been proposed for all of the problems discussed in this chapter is an *expulsion clause*. This allows partners to hold a vote and expel a partner by a relatively large percentage vote, which is set out in your agreement. This may sound like a democratic solution, but in practice it nearly always leads to a dissolution proceeding in court. The expelled partner will fight like a cornered tiger when he or she feels attacked unfairly by everyone else.

The best solution is preventative medicine. Select partners who have objectives similar to yours. Get to know them as well as possible in advance so that you can form a judgment as to whether they share your enthusiasm and work ethic. Make sure that all of you bring appropriate and complementary skills to the partnership and that each of you has the time, inclination, and incentive to use them. Meet the spouses; find out if they are supportive of the partnership, and if you all get along. They may even have more influence on your business than the partners themselves.

Ben Franklin was absolutely correct about an "ounce of prevention." Use the attorney's perspective as preventative medicine, so that you avoid these problem areas. You will have enough challenges in making the business itself a success.

## Form 7-A

# NOTICE OF DISSOLUTION OF PARTNERSHIP

Public notice is hereby given that_____

_____ , and _____

_____ , heretofore doing

business under the fictitious name and style of_____

(Please Print)

_____ at_____ , City of

(Street Address)

_____ , County of _____ State of California, did on the _____ day of_____

(Multiple Choice)
by withdrawal,
19_____ by Mutual consent, dissolve the said partnership and terminate their relations as partners therein.
by _____
(Strike off the two above choices that do not apply)

(NOTE: The following two paragraphs are optional features of this form and either, or both, may be amended if they are not adequate or stricken off if they do not apply.)

Said business in the future will be conducted by_____

_____ , and _____ , who will

pay and discharge all liabilities and debts of the firm and receive all monies payable to the firm.

Further notice is hereby given that the undersigned will not be responsible, from this time on, for any

obligation incurred by the other(s) in (his) (her) (their) own name(s) or in the name of the firm.

Dated at _____ , California, this _____ day of _____ 19_____.

_____
Mail to:

_____                    (Signature) _____
Address

_____                    _____
City                                        Zip                         (Please type or print signature)

_____
Phone

Section 15035.5 of the Corporations Code requires that whenever a partnership is dissolved notice of the dissolution shall be published at least once in a newspaper of general circulation in the place, or in each place if more than one, at which partnership business was regularly carried on, and a printer's affidavit showing such publication shall be filed with the City Clerk within 30 days after such publication.

111

# Chapter Eight
# Practical Suggestions for Your Partnership

*"Few things are harder to put up with than the annoyance of a good example."*

Mark Twain (1835 -1910)
*Puddin' Head Wilson's Calendar*

This chapter covers some of the many situations that can arise in forming and operating your partnership. It is designed to help you think about each situation from the perspective of someone who has had years of experience with partnerships. Again, the key to these situations and suggestions is to use them as preventative medicine. By reviewing situations that can lead to potential problems, you will be able to stress the strengths in the relationship between your partners. You can then build on these strengths and at the same time recognize any potential weaknesses. At the end of this chapter, a checklist has been included to help you quickly review your partnership. If you discover any areas of potential weakness, discuss these with all of your partners and work out a plan to deal with them before they actually turn into problems. In this way, you will be able to spend more time working together to make your business a success.

## 8.1 Potential Situations

**SITUATION: You've been approached to be a partner.** This may actually be the opportunity of a lifetime; however, it is best to pause for a moment and think about this.

**SUGGESTION:** First, ask yourself why you have been so honored. Nearly all of us are subject to flattery, and nothing strokes the ego like being asked to join a partnership. If you were not part of the original planning for and conceptualization of the business, then probably you have been asked to become a partner because the existing partners have a plan for you. Does their plan fit with your plans?

Generally, avoid partnerships with anyone who says they are going to make you rich. Everyone wants the business to be a financial success, but this is a goal you develop together. It is not something that someone else is going to accomplish for you.

Note carefully the original reasons for entering into the relationship by using the questionnaire in chapter 2. If you notice that the very things that enticed you to join are rapidly disappearing or gradually withering away, then ask yourself, "Is this still what I want to do?"

Finally, consider whether you would be better off as a consultant (independent contractor) rather than a partner. Maintaining your independence may make the most sense. After working as a consultant for a while, you can still join the partnership and you'll have a better feel for the business and your partners.

**SITUATION: You're not quite sure partnership is right.** For whatever reason it just doesn't feel quite right.

**SUGGESTION:** Entering into a partnership is a very serious commitment that is not easy to walk away from. Try a *joint venture*. This is a partnership formed for one project. As an experiment, plan a joint venture with your partners for a limited test period such as 60 or 90 days. Evaluate your progress at the end of the test period and decide if you are ready for a long-term commitment. You will know a lot more about each other after working together for a while.

**SITUATION: Large age difference between partners.** This is an especially difficult problem in a two-person partnership.

**SUGGESTION:** There are a lot of positives to matching maturity and experience with youthful vigor and optimism. There is, however, a potential mismatch of goals inherent in this arrangement.

If you are the younger part of the equation, test to see if the older partner will agree to a buyout arrangement at a defined retirement point in the future. You should also test to see what sort of reception your aggressive plans for expansion will get.

If you are the older part of the equation, check to see if your younger partner has the maturity to respect your experience and judgment. When you offer reason and caution, will your partner recognize that his or her youthful enthusiasm needs to be tempered at times?

**SITUATION: Spouses.** In many cases, your partners come with partners. Their spouse will have a great impact on your partnership. This impact is usually supportive and helpful; it can, however, have the opposite effect.

**SUGGESTION:** Meet and get to know the spouses. Determine whether they are supportive of your business venture, and get a feel for the marital relationship. A divorce can be devastating to your business. You should also get a feel for whether the spouse may try to dominate your partner and consequently affect the running of your business. Also, watch carefully for any feelings of animosity. You may have a partner with whom you are on friendly terms, but is constantly hearing negatives about you at home. Finally, ask your own spouse directly whether he or she likes all of your partners and is enthusiastic about the business venture.

**SITUATION: Partners who are dishonest with themselves.** Most people are sincere and straightforward, however, once in a while you will find a potential partner who is not, because he is not being honest with himself.

**SUGGESTION:** The first symptom of this trait is taking credit for others' ideas and actions. In the most advanced state, these people actually believe their exaggerations. The inability to accept any criticism, even the smallest and most positive criticism, is another indicator. When these potential partners relate their past experiences, they claim they "never made a mistake in their life." It was always someone else's fault.

People who are dishonest with themselves are likely to be dishonest with others. Such people may frequently volunteer the statement that "I am honest" or make repeated statements like "We have a good partnership, don't we?" It is as if they are going through a process of convincing themselves.

The problem with partners who are dishonest with themselves is that you can never really get their agreement on anything. For example, when you discuss personal and business goals, it is essential that all of you have compatible goals. With this type of partner, you may have a partner who is saying all the right things, but who, in fact, has no intention of committing to the hard work and sacrifice that is necessary, and who does not have similar long-term goals.

**SITUATION: Grabbing.** This is shorthand for greed in relations with other partners.

**SUGGESTION:** This is a common problem since nearly all entrepreneurs are by definition assertive people. After all, they take the risks in order to reap the rewards.

Entrepreneurs who become partners have to understand and agree that, while it may be "open season" on the rest of the world, it is unacceptable to grab from their partners. This is such a common problem that I suggest the "Diamond Merchant" method. This is an honor system where all of you agree that a healthy distrust for the rest of the world is probably wise, but among your group there has to be absolute trust and openness. To enforce this, you should all agree that any act of dishonesty or grabbing towards another partner can result in permanent expulsion from the partnership.

You should note that, in practice, it is much easier to enforce this while you are planning for your partnership than after you have formed it.

Testing for grabbing can be done by initiating a discussion about ownership shares. You should listen to and observe carefully how everyone behaves during this discussion. Generally, there will be a preliminary division of ownership percentages, which is continued at a later meeting. If you have grabbers for prospective partners, you will find them coming back with propositions that boil down to your share going down and their shares going up. They always have great rationalizations for the changes; but no matter what the reasoning, you will find that you are always getting the shorter end of the stick.

The same pattern applies to salaries or draws. These people always have a reason why they deserve more and you should be satisfied with the same or less.

In the case of a 50/50 partnership, you will know you have a potential grabber on your hands if they can't stand to split things evenly. They go out of their minds unless they take at least a little extra for themselves. This type of person is also generally paranoid that others are similarly greedy and are grabbing from them. You may find yourself being tested or accused of taking something from them when you didn't.

Taking credit for the ideas of others is another symptom that you have a grabber on your hands. If you find your partners either taking credit for your ideas or trying to shift the blame for mistakes, correct them immediately. Watch how they react to see how serious the problem is. If they will not admit their "mistakes" and agree to stop the behavior, it's serious.

**Corollary Situation: Cheapness.** Strict cost control is a very positive strength in business. Some people confuse this strength with the weakness of always being cheap.

**Suggestions:** I'm sure you know a person like this. They just always seem to disappear or have an excuse when it is time to pay a check in a restaurant. Anytime they have to pay their share of something, they make excuses and delay. At the same time, these people are the first ones to be extra-generous with themselves when there is money or when there are goodies to be divided. You should review this type of behavior to see if you will have a partner who has a potential problem that will affect your relations later.

**SITUATION: Politics.** We all enjoy some degree of office politics. Some people carry these to an extreme, so that they operate in a manner that becomes sneaky or manipulative.

**SUGGESTION:** This kind of behavior may be found among partners who come out of large organizations. They may have learned over the years that playing politics is the way to get ahead in the organization.

You may be able to jolt them out of this behavior pattern by confronting them several times. Again, if they have been rewarded for acting this way for several years, they probably have a chronic case. Unfortunately, this behavior can cause very serious problems for your partnership in the long run.

**Corollary Situation: Bureaucratic behavior.** All organizations need some rules, policies, and procedures. However, in a small business, these need to be kept to a minimum.

**Suggestion:** This is another potential problem endemic among people who come out of large organizations. In the unfamiliar terrain of small business, they may return to this type of behavior. Many rules, procedures and policies just do not fit in a small organization. In the worst case, they start taking action or avoiding participation in decisions solely for the purpose of covering their tail.

**SITUATION: Coattail latching.** You want to be part of a team where everyone is success-driven and eagerly takes his or her share of the responsibility and workload. Unfortunately, people who are along for a "free ride" sometimes make their way into a partnership.

**SUGGESTION:** Take a close look at yourself to make sure that you are not a talented and generous giver and producer, while any of your partners are users and takers. If you are unselfishly creative, you might attract users and takers. For a partnership to work over the long run, everyone must contribute his or her share.

**Corollary Situation: Victimization.** There is just no positive way to view this situation. It happens in partnerships and you should seek to avoid it.

**Suggestion:** If you find yourself doing the work of, or taking responsibility for, the actions of a partner, you are being victimized. These people have an uncanny ability to become your good friend and then slowly but surely, load their work and responsibilities onto you. They are skilled in finding the people who are nice enough to go along with this. If you are sought out to join an existing team as a partner, there is a chance that you have been hand-picked as a potential "nice-person" victim. Although this may be only a slight possibility, spend a moment reviewing it for your own peace of mind.

**SITUATION: Extracurricular Activities.** The saying, "Everything in moderation" might apply to this particular situation. All of you need to agree that if this business is not your number one priority, it is close to it. Everything else must be "in moderation."

**SUGGESTION:** Alcoholics, drug users, gamblers and those enjoying extra-marital affairs make good characters in movies, but you don't want to be partners with one. Their problems become yours—whether you like it or not. It is no coincidence that all of these things have a high probability of ending up in court. If you are involved with these people as a partner, you and your business usually get invited to court with them. This is time-consuming and costly, as they drag you down with them.

**SITUATION: Holding meetings and making decisions to the exclusion of other partners.** This is similar to the grabbing situation. With a group of strong and assertive partners, you may find someone who needs to be reminded of the boundaries of their shared authority as a partner.

**SUGGESTION:** It should go without saying that holding key meetings and making key decisions without the consent of other partners are not acceptable practices. The person who is guilty of this may think that this is a natural assertion of leadership ability. However, it is not natural in a partnership situation. If a leader is called for, then make a conscious choice. Do not let someone grab this position through aggressive behavior.

In legal terms, this is an *agency* question. When, if ever, does one partner have the actual authority to act on behalf of the others? You should agree specifically on actual authority, since each of you will have the apparent authority to bind your partnership as far as third parties are concerned.

**SITUATION: Inadequate leader.** This is a situation that develops after you have operated together for a while. It may be very awkward if your leader does not recognize his or her shortcomings.

**SUGGESTION:** If your partnership is a full team, you have probably chosen a leader, or perhaps the partnership was started by a leader. Is this person a strong leader who provides the right representation and has a vision for your company? Once again, this requires a fine balance. You want someone who is strong, but not authoritarian and autocratic. A partnership is by definition a democratic or participative undertaking.

If you are part of a team where talented people are being taken in the wrong direction by an inadequate leader, whether weak or strong, you will need to take corrective action for the sake of the survival of the business. Remember, one of the primary reasons for joining a partnership is to have some influence over and a vote on your own destiny.

Corollary Situation: 50/50 partnership decisions.

**Suggestion:** A two-person partnership has a potential inherent problem. Whenever you disagree (and you will), there is a potential tie vote. Will you be able to work out these disagreements in an adult manner? It is possible, but it takes planning and a lot of give and take in an atmosphere of mutual respect. Some advisers recommend setting up a dispute-settling mechanism such as mediation. If you reach the point where it is necessary to invoke a clause like this, it may be too late- you've probably lost all respect for each other, so recognize this in advance and plan for it!

**SITUATION: Financial partners.** This is the label that financiers of assorted types give to themselves.

**SUGGESTION:** There are thousands of success stories where businesses have been financed by financial partners. If you need outside capital investment, you want to become another one of these success stories. Without a doubt, your financial partners will also want you to become a success.

Financial partners, you will quickly learn, are extremely careful about where they invest their money. You should be equally careful about who you accept it from.

The first thing to remember is that financial partners are knowledgeable and experienced. Most of them did not get their money by chance and they don't throw it away by chance. If you find a reputable financial partner, he or she may be your best friend in the way they critique your business and make suggestions. Make sure that this behavior is reinforced by structuring your agreement with them so that you will benefit as much as they do.

One thing you will notice is that financial partners always have a lawyer. Never try to deal with them without one of your own. And do not fall for the trap of using their lawyer, who, they will assure you, can represent all of you, since you are "partners."

In negotiating for money, you should always pursue multiple sources. Do this no matter how good your deal sounds with any one source or how offended they might act that you don't trust them to close the deal. Financial partners are notorious for taking you right up to the altar and then jilting you when it is time to hand over the check. Legally, you have almost no recourse should this happen to you.

When you are starting a business, time is nearly always of the essence. Financial partners, on the other hand, are always trying to delay the date of investment. This is the safe and conservative thing for them to do. They can learn more about you and the business; and do all the other things they do to avoid mistakes. Since you have opposite motivations (that is, you want the money as soon as possible), work out a compromise. Set a deadline for funding that gives your financial partner sufficient time for "due diligence" and gives you a date certain, so you can make plans and know whether or not you are going to get the promised money.

If you take a financial partner, they will dictate much of the way you structure and operate your business. Your partnership should decide in advance how much restructuring you will allow and which demands are acceptable. In other words, where do you draw the line? If you do not make these advance decisions, you will soon find that you are in fact employees of the financial partner, rather than business partners running your own business.

**One final note:** Financial partners often require that you and your partners earn your full share of ownership over time. That is, each partner is subject to a *vesting schedule.* Imagine, for example, that each partner is entitled to a 12% share of the business, and a 24-month vesting schedule is used. Each partner will therefore earn 1/2% per month. After 6 months, a partner would be vested in 3% of the company, and after a year 6%.

This is for the protection of all the partners, so that no one can leave after a short time with a full ownership share. Financial partners require this so that the key people they have financed have a great incentive to stay. If one of the partners should leave, their forfeited share of ownership can be used to entice another key person to replace them.

If your financial partner has contracted to raise money for you, tie their ownership share to performance of what they have promised. For example, let's assume your financial partner promises to raise $1 million for your business, but only comes up with $600,000. They should then only vest in 60% of the ownership share they were to ordinarily receive. Don't forget to tie their vesting to raising the money by the time you have agreed upon.

**Corollary Situation: Negotiating the partnership agreement.**

**Suggestion:** While financial partners always retain lawyers to represent them in negotiating, this is not typical in negotiations among partners. Each of you has a perfect right to individual representation by a lawyer. The actual negotiating, however, should be done among partners themselves. Once you have worked out the details of your arrangement, a lawyer or lawyers should then be instructed to put together an agreement that reflects what you have agreed upon. Use the checklist and agreement in chapter 4 as a guide to go over the relevant issues concerning your relationship.

If one of your partners insists on having their lawyer negotiate for them, you should explain to them that this forces you to have your lawyer talk with their lawyer. This can get very expensive and awkward.

**SITUATION: Quitters.** Unfortunately, becoming an entrepreneur is not right for everyone.

**SUGGESTION:** This type of partner is scared and nervous right from the start. At the slightest problem, he or she is ready to throw in the towel. A little skepticism and fear is normal, but not when it gets out of hand.

A partner with this problem lacks the self-confidence required to make it as a business owner. You generally find them looking for a sure thing and trying to minimize risk in every way they possibly can. Again, it is normal and healthy to try to minimize risk to some extent, but this should not be your primary focus. If this person has the skills you need, suggest that they become an employee. They will most likely be happy with the security that provides.

**SITUATION: Employees.**

**SUGGESTION:** Employees should have one boss. To have more than one is known as *duplicity*. All supervision should come only through one person and other partners should resist exercising their authority by circumventing this structure.

## 8.2 Partner Checklist

For your convenience, I have prepared a checklist for some of these major areas of potential problems in a partnership. This is a way to help you quickly review a partner for potential problems. You will be pleasantly surprised to see that few, if any, of these apply to your situation. Most likely this checklist will confirm that you have chosen wisely and that there is no need for concern. If you should turn up potential problems, take them seriously, for even the small ones can eventually turn your attention from business to arguing and worse.

## 8.3 Planning for Success

Have you taken a close look at your own style? The bottom line is whether you are comfortable with sharing decision-making and responsibility. If you prefer running things yourself, the odds are that you are not going to like the idea of not having the last word on important business decisions.

Some people enter into a partnership with the illusion that it will lessen the risk of a new business. If you have read this far, it shouldn't be necessary to correct this myth. Adding the dimension of partners obviously adds to both the potential rewards and risks. The question is, "Do the benefits of the rewards clearly outweigh the risks?"

I hope that I have at least given you some food for thought as you consider entering into a business partnership. My purpose has been to enable you to take this step from a more knowledgeable position. The path is fraught with danger, but you can put yourself in a position to avoid the traps and pitfalls with some good planning and prevention. My sincere hope is that yours becomes one of the all-time great partnership successes.

## Form 8-A

### Partner Checklist

Have you investigated your future partner(s) thoroughly?          Yes/No

1. Past business or job performance?. . . . . . . . . . . . . . . . . . . . . . \_\_\_\_\_

2. Compatible long-term goals?. . . . . . . . . . . . . . . . . . . . . . . . \_\_\_\_\_

3. Compatible management styles?. . . . . . . . . . . . . . . . . . . . . \_\_\_\_\_

4. Similar work ethic?. . . . . . . . . . . . . . . . . . . . . . . . . . . . \_\_\_\_\_

5. Extracurricular activities?. . . . . . . . . . . . . . . . . . . . . . . \_\_\_\_\_

6. Grabbing, greed?. . . . . . . . . . . . . . . . . . . . . . . . . . . . \_\_\_\_\_

7. Honest with self and others?. . . . . . . . . . . . . . . . . . . . . \_\_\_\_\_

8. Excludes partners from key meetings and/or decisions?. . . . . . . . \_\_\_\_\_

9. Partnership is first business priority?. . . . . . . . . . . . . . . . . \_\_\_\_\_

10. Mutual respect?. . . . . . . . . . . . . . . . . . . . . . . . . . . . \_\_\_\_\_

11. Sneaky or devious?. . . . . . . . . . . . . . . . . . . . . . . . . . \_\_\_\_\_

12. Coattail latcher?. . . . . . . . . . . . . . . . . . . . . . . . . . . \_\_\_\_\_

13. Quitter?. . . . . . . . . . . . . . . . . . . . . . . . . . . . . . . \_\_\_\_\_

14. Self-confident?. . . . . . . . . . . . . . . . . . . . . . . . . . . . \_\_\_\_\_

15. If a financial partner, do you have a written commitment
    with a deadline for money?. . . . . . . . . . . . . . . . . . . . . . \_\_\_\_\_

    o  Are you using an attorney to negotiate with their attorney? . . . \_\_\_\_\_

16. If a partner is the team leader, does he or she have:

    o  A vision for the partnership?. . . . . . . . . . . . . . . . . . . \_\_\_\_\_

    o  Solid leadership abilities? . . . . . . . . . . . . . . . . . . . . \_\_\_\_\_

    o  Respect of and for all team members?. . . . . . . . . . . . . . \_\_\_\_\_

17. Bureaucratic behavior?. . . . . . . . . . . . . . . . . . . . . . . . \_\_\_\_\_

18. Large age spread between partners?. . . . . . . . . . . . . . . . . \_\_\_\_\_

19. Terminally cheap?. . . . . . . . . . . . . . . . . . . . . . . . . . . . . . . \_\_\_\_\_

20. Spouse supports project?. . . . . . . . . . . . . . . . . . . . . . . . . . \_\_\_\_\_

    o  All spouses like all partners and each other?. . . . . . . . . . . \_\_\_\_\_

21. If it is a 50/50 partnership, do you have a:

    o  Pre-determined decision-making process?. . . . . . . . . . . . . \_\_\_\_\_

    o  Dispute resolution process?. . . . . . . . . . . . . . . . . . . . . \_\_\_\_\_

22. Have friends warned you about a partner?. . . . . . . . . . . . . . \_\_\_\_\_

23. Any other psychological games?. . . . . . . . . . . . . . . . . . . . \_\_\_\_\_

24. Have you considered a test period pre-partnership joint venture
    relationship?. . . . . . . . . . . . . . . . . . . . . . . . . . . . . . . \_\_\_\_\_

Do you have a written agreement?. . . . . . . . . . . . . . . . . . . . \_\_\_\_\_

Does it include:

o  Explicit duties and rights of each partner?. . . . . . . . . . . . . \_\_\_\_\_

o  Buyout formula with example?. . . . . . . . . . . . . . . . . . . . . \_\_\_\_\_

o  Instructions in case of a partner's divorce?. . . . . . . . . . . . . \_\_\_\_\_

o  Binding method of settling disputes?. . . . . . . . . . . . . . . . . \_\_\_\_\_

o  Rights on dissolution?. . . . . . . . . . . . . . . . . . . . . . . . . \_\_\_\_\_

Are all partners contributing their share of capital?. . . . . . . . . . . \_\_\_\_\_

Are all partners taking their share of liabilities?. . . . . . . . . . . . . \_\_\_\_\_

o  Continued responsibility for liabilities after dissolution?. . . . . . . . \_\_\_\_\_

o  Sharing of overhead equally?. . . . . . . . . . . . . . . . . . . . . \_\_\_\_\_

Does your partnership have frequent and regularly scheduled
meetings with all partners where problems with each other as
well as business issues are discussed openly?. . . . . . . . . . . . . . \_\_\_\_\_

## Appendix A

## General Partnership Agreement

This Agreement is made on _____,
19_____, by and among _____
_____,
referred to as "Partners" under the following provisions.

### 1. Name

The name of the Partnership is_____

_____

_____

It will be referred to in this Agreement as the "Partnership".

### 2. Type of Business

The Partnership is formed for the purpose of engaging in the business
of_____

_____

_____

This purpose may be modified or expanded by the written agreement of all
Partners.

### 3. Term

The Partnership will begin on the date of this Agreement and will
continue until_____.

### 4. Place of Business

The Partnership's principal place of business shall be_____

_____.

The principal place of business may be changed and other places of
business may be established by agreement of the partners.

### 5. Capital Contributions

The Partnership's initial capital shall consist of cash to be contributed by the Partners in the following amounts:

| Name | Amount |
|------|--------|
| _____ | $ _____ |
| _____ | $ _____ |
| _____ | $ _____ |

Each Partner's contribution shall be paid in full within _____ days after the date of this Agreement.

If any Partner fails to make their capital contribution by this date, the Partnership shall immediately dissolve. Partners who have made their contribution shall be entitled to an immediate return of it, unless all Partners agree in writing to modify this section.

### 6. Voluntary Contributions and Withdrawals of Capital

No Partner may make any voluntary contribution or withdrawal of capital without the written consent of all partners.

### 7. Division of Profits and Losses

Profits and losses shall be shared among the Partners in the same share as their capital contribution.

### 8. Distributions to Partners

Within _____ days after the end of each fiscal year of the Partnership, there shall be distributed in cash, to the Partners, in proportion to their respective shares in the Partnership's profits, an amount equal to the Partnership's profit for that fiscal year as computed under this Agreement.

## 9. Partners' Drawing Accounts

Each Partner shall be entitled to draw against profits such amounts as from time to time are agreed on by a majority of the Partners. These amounts shall be charged to the Partner's drawing accounts as they are drawn.

## 10. Fiscal Year and Accounting Method

The Partnership's fiscal year shall end on_____each year. The Partnership's books shall be kept on the _____ basis.

## 11. Accountings

Within _____ days after the end of each fiscal year, the Partnership shall furnish to each Partner a copy of the Partnership's income tax returns for that fiscal year, a profit and loss statement, and balance sheet showing the Partnership's financial position at the end of that fiscal year.

## 12. Management and Authority

Each Partner shall have an equal right in the management of the Partnership. Each Partner shall have authority to bind the Partnership in making contracts and incurring obligations in the Partnership name or on its credit. This authority is subject to a limit of $_____. No Partner shall incur obligations in excess of this limit without the prior written consent of a majority of Partners.

## 13. Partnership Funds

All Partnership funds shall be deposited in the Partnership's name. Accounts will require the signature of at least _____ Partners for withdrawals or checks written above $_____.

## 14. Employment and Dismissal

No Partner shall hire any employee or fire any employee, except in the case of gross misconduct, without the consent of a majority of the Partners.

### 15. Time Devoted to Partnership

Each Partner shall devote full time and attention to the conduct of Partnership business.

### 16. Vacations and Leaves of Absence

Each Partner shall be entitled to _____ days of vacation and _____ days of absence for illness or disability each fiscal year. Days of vacation or absence for illness that exceed these amounts shall result in a proportionate reduction of that Partner's share of the profits for the fiscal year.

### 17. Admission of New Partners

A new Partner may be admitted to the Partnership, but only with the written approval of _____ of the Partners. Each new Partner shall be admitted only if he or she shall have executed this Agreement or a supplement to it in which the new Partner agrees to be bound by the terms of this Agreement. Admission of a new Partner shall not cause dissolution of the Partnership.

### 18. Interest of New Partner

A newly admitted Partner's capital contribution and share of profits and losses shall be set forth in the written consent of the Partners consenting to the admission of the new Partner.

### 19. Dissolution

The Partnership shall dissolve and terminate on any Partner's death, permanent physical or mental disability, becoming a party to a divorce action or voluntary withdrawal, unless within _____ days after the Partnership has received notice of the Partner's death, disability, becoming a party to a divorce action or desire to withdraw, it elects in writing to purchase that Partner's interest. This election shall require the consent of _____ of the remaining Partners. The price to be paid for the interest of the deceased, disabled, party to a divorce action, or withdrawing Partner shall be computed according to the terms of this Agreement.

20. **Non-Competition Covenant**

Following withdrawal from the Partnership, the withdrawing Partner shall not carry on a business similar to the business of the Partnership within the _____ of _____ for a period of _____ years.

21. **Transfers of Partnership Interests**

**Option 1: Free Transferability**

Each Partner may transfer his or her interest in the Partnership without dissolving the Partnership by the transfer.

**Option 2: Non-Transferability**

A Partner's interest may not be transferred, in whole or in part.

**Options 3: Limited Transferability**

A Partner may transfer his or her interest in the Partnership only as follows:

1. To the Partnership or to any other Partner only after the Partnership declines;

2. By intestate succession or by will on the Partner's death;

3. By a gift to the Partner's spouse or children, or to a trustee for the Partner's spouse or children or both;

4. To any other person after the Partner making the transfer has first offered the Partnership and other Partners their rights of first refusal in accordance with the provisions of this Agreement.

## 22. Right of First Refusal

If a Partner desires to transfer his or her Partnership interest, that Partner shall give written notice to the Partnership. The notice shall set forth the name of the party, the terms on which the interest is to be transferred, and the price. For _____ days after the notice is received, the Partnership shall have the right to purchase the Partner's entire interest at the same price and on the same terms.

## 23. Valuation of Interest

The following are a few of the more common options used to cover valuation. Some are fairly lengthy due to the fact that they are so crucial in dispute situations.

### Option 1: Value Based on Capital Account

The value of a Partner's interest in the Partnership for purposes of this Agreement shall be the sum of the following items as of the date the value is to be determined, as these items are reflected on the Partnership's regularly maintained accounting books and records:

1) The balance in the Partner's capital account;

2) The balance in the Partner's drawing account;

3) The Partner's proportionate share of the Partnership's net profit for the current fiscal year to the date as of which the computation is made and not yet reflected in the Partner's capital or drawing account; or, if the Partnership operations for that period show a loss, the Partner's proportional share of any such loss shall be deducted; and

4) Any debt or other amount due to the Partner from the Partnership; but

5) Less any debt owed by the Partner to the Partnership.

## Option 2: Value Based on Equity and Earnings

The value of a Partner's interest in the Partnership for purposes of this Agreement, shall be calculated by taking an average of the net profits of the business as shown on the Partnership's federal tax return for the past _____ years. This average of the net profits shall then be multiplied by a multiple of _____ to determine the value of the business. This value shall then be multiplied by that Partner's ownership percentage on the date of valuation to determine the value of that Partner's interest.

## Option 3: Valuation by Agreement

The value of a Partner's interest in the Partnership for purposes of this Agreement shall be calculated by applying that Partner's ownership interest percentage to the value of the Partnership, which shall be determined as follows:

1. Within _____ days after the end of each fiscal year of the Partnership, the Partners shall, after due consideration of all factors they consider relevant, determine the Partnership's value by unanimous written agreement, and that value shall remain in effect for the purposes of this Agreement from the date of that written determination until the next such written determination, except as otherwise provided below. The valuation shall be entered on Exhibit _____ and all Partners shall initial the entry.

2. Should the Partners be unable to agree on a value or otherwise fail to make any such determination, the Partnership's value shall be the greater of (a) the value last established under this section, or (b) the Partnership's net worth, determined in accordance with generally accepted accounting principles, consistently applied, as of the end of the Partnership's next preceding fiscal year.

3. Until it is otherwise determined under this section, the Partnership's value shall be the aggregate initial capital contributions required under this Agreement and actually paid or conveyed to the Partnership.

**Option 4: Valuation by Appraisal**

The value of a Partner's interest in the Partnership for purposes of this Agreement shall be determined by appraisal as follows:

Within _____ days after the event requiring appraisal or, in the case of a Partner's death or legal disability, within _____ days after appointment of that Partner's personal representative, the Partnership and the Partner whose interest is to be appraised, or that Partner's personal representative, either 1) shall jointly appoint an appraiser for this purpose, or 2) failing this joint action, shall each separately designate an appraiser and, within _____ days after their appointment, the two designated appraisers shall jointly designate a third appraiser. The failure of either the Partnership or the Partner whose interest is being appraised (or that Partner's personal representative) to appoint an appraiser within the time allowed shall be deemed equivalent to appointment of the appraiser appointed by the other party.

If, within _____ days after the appointment of all appraisers, a majority of the appraisers concur on the value of the interest being appraised, that appraisal shall be binding and conclusive. If a majority of the appraisers do not concur within that period, the determination of the appraiser whose appraisal is neither highest nor lowest shall be binding and conclusive. The Partnership and the Partner whose interest is to be appraised, or that Partner's estate or successors, shall share the appraisal expenses equally.

A Partner's interest in the Partnership so appraised shall be based on that Partner's ownership interest.

### 24. Payment of Purchase Price

#### Option 1: Cash

Except as otherwise provided, whenever the Partnership is obligated or, having the right to do so, chooses to purchase a Partner's interest, it shall pay for the interest in cash within _____ days after the date on which the Partnership's obligation to pay has become fixed.

#### Options 2: Cash or Note

Except as otherwise provided, whenever the Partnership is obligated or, having the right to do so, chooses to purchase a Partner's interest, it shall pay for that interest, at its option, in cash or by promissory note of the Partnership, or partly in cash and partly by note. Any promissory note shall be dated as of the effective date of the purchase, shall mature in not more than _____ years, shall be payable in installments of principal and interest that come due not less frequently than annually, shall bear interest at the rate of _____ percent per annum, and may, at the Partnership's option, be subordinated to existing and future banks and other institutional lenders for money borrowed.

### 25. Arbitration

It is agreed that all disputes arising out of this Agreement shall be submitted to binding arbitration in accordance with the rules of the American Arbitration Association.

### 26. Amendments

This Agreement may be amended by the written agreement of all Partners.

### 27. Notices

All notices between the Partners shall be in writing and shall be deemed served when personally delivered to a Partner, or on the second day after being deposited in the mail, certified, first-class postage prepaid, addressed  to the Partner's address shown after his or her signature to this Agreement or a more recent address given to the Partnership in writing.

## 28. Entire Agreement

This instrument contains the entire Agreement of the parties. It correctly sets out the Partners' rights and obligations. Any prior agreements, oral representations, or modifications shall be of no force or effect unless contained in a subsequent written modification signed by all parties to this Agreement.

## 29. Severability

If any term, provision, covenant, or condition of this Agreement is held by a court of competent jurisdiction or arbitrator to be invalid, void, or unenforceable, the rest of this Agreement shall in no way be affected, impaired, or invalidated.

**In witness whereof,** the Partners have executed this Agreement as of the date first shown above.

**Signature**                                   **Residence Address**

_____          _____

_____          _____


_____          _____

_____          _____


_____          _____

_____          _____

| Form **1065** | **U.S. Partnership Return of Income** | OMB No. 1545-0099 |
|---|---|---|
| | ▶ For Paperwork Reduction Act Notice, see Form 1065 Instructions. | **1987** |
| Department of the Treasury Internal Revenue Service | For calendar year 1987, or fiscal year beginning _____ 1987, and ending _____ 19 __ | |

| A Principal business activity | Use IRS label. Otherwise, please print or type. | Name | D Employer identification number |
|---|---|---|---|
| B Principal product or service | | Number and street (or P.O. Box number if mail is not delivered to street address) | E Date business started |
| C Business code number | | City or town, state, and ZIP code | F Enter total assets at end of tax year $ |

G Check accounting method: (1) ☐ Cash  (2) ☐ Accrual (3) ☐ Other

H Check applicable boxes: (1) ☐ Final return  (2) ☐ Change in address  (3) ☐ Amended return

|  | Yes | No |
|---|---|---|
| I Number of partners in this partnership ▶ _____ | | |
| J Is this partnership a limited partnership (see the Instructions)? | | |
| K Is this partnership a partner in another partnership? | | |
| L Are any partners in this partnership also partnerships? | | |
| M Does the partnership meet all the requirements shown in the Instructions for **Question M**? | | |
| N Was there a distribution of property or a transfer (for example, by sale or death) of a partnership interest during the tax year? If "Yes," see the Instructions concerning an election to adjust the basis of the partnership's assets under section 754 | | |

|  | Yes | No |
|---|---|---|
| O At any time during the tax year, did the partnership have an interest in or a signature or other authority over a financial account in a foreign country (such as a bank account, securities account, or other financial account)? (See the Instructions for exceptions and filing requirements for Form TD F 90-22.1.) If "Yes," write the name of the foreign country. ▶ _____ | | |
| P Was the partnership the grantor of, or transferor to, a foreign trust which existed during the current tax year, whether or not the partnership or any partner has any beneficial interest in it? If "Yes," you may have to file Forms 3520, 3520-A, or 926 | | |
| Q Was this partnership in operation at the end of 1987? | | |

R Number of months in 1987 that this partnership was in operation ▶ _____

S Check this box if the partnership has filed or is required to file Form 8264, Application for Registration of a Tax Shelter ☐

T Check this box if this is a partnership subject to the consolidated partnership audit procedures of TEFRA. (See page 7 of the Instructions.) ☐

**Caution:** *Include **only** trade or business income and expenses on lines 1a–21 below. See the instructions for more information.*

**Income**

| | | | |
|---|---|---|---|
| 1a | Gross receipts or sales $ _____  1b Minus returns and allowances $ _____ Balance ▶ | 1c | |
| 2 | Cost of goods sold and/or operations (Schedule A, line 7) | 2 | |
| 3 | Gross profit (subtract line 2 from line 1c) | 3 | |
| 4 | Ordinary income (loss) from other partnerships and fiduciaries (attach schedule) | 4 | |
| 5 | Net farm profit (loss) (attach Schedule F (Form 1040)) | 5 | |
| 6 | Net gain (loss) (Form 4797, line 18) | 6 | |
| 7 | Other income (loss) | 7 | |
| 8 | **TOTAL** income (loss) (combine lines 3 through 7) | 8 | |

**Deductions** (see instructions for limitations)

| | | | |
|---|---|---|---|
| 9a | Salaries and wages (other than to partners) $ _____  9b Minus jobs credit $ _____ Balance ▶ | 9c | |
| 10 | Guaranteed payments to partners | 10 | |
| 11 | Rent | 11 | |
| 12 | Deductible interest expense not claimed elsewhere on return (see Instructions) | 12 | |
| 13 | Taxes | 13 | |
| 14 | Bad debts | 14 | |
| 15 | Repairs | 15 | |
| 16a | Depreciation from Form 4562 (attach Form 4562) $ _____  16b Minus depreciation claimed on Schedule A and elsewhere on return $ _____ Balance ▶ | 16c | |
| 17 | Depletion (**Do not deduct oil and gas depletion.**) | 17 | |
| 18a | Retirement plans, etc. | 18a | |
| b | Employee benefit programs | 18b | |
| 19 | Other deductions (attach schedule) | 19 | |
| 20 | **TOTAL** deductions (add amounts in column for lines 9c through 19) | 20 | |
| 21 | Ordinary income (loss) from trade or business activity(ies) (subtract line 20 from line 8) | 21 | |

**Please Sign Here**

Under penalties of perjury, I declare that I have examined this return, including accompanying schedules and statements, and to the best of my knowledge and belief, it is true, correct, and complete. Declaration of preparer (other than taxpayer) is based on all information of which preparer has any knowledge.

▶ _____
Signature of general partner

▶ _____
Date

**Paid Preparer's Use Only**

| Preparer's signature ▶ | | Date | Check if self-employed ▶ ☐ | Preparer's social security no. |
|---|---|---|---|---|
| Firm's name (or yours if self-employed) and address ▶ | | | E.I. No. ▶ | |
| | | | ZIP code ▶ | |

## Schedule A    Cost of Goods Sold and/or Operations

| | | |
|---|---|---|
| 1 | Inventory at beginning of year. | 1 |
| 2 | Purchases minus cost of items withdrawn for personal use | 2 |
| 3 | Cost of labor. | 3 |
| 4a | Additional section 263A costs (see instructions) | 4a |
| b | Other costs (attach schedule) | 4b |
| 5 | Total (add lines 1 through 4b). | 5 |
| 6 | Inventory at end of year . | 6 |
| 7 | Cost of goods sold (subtract line 6 from line 5). Enter here and on page 1, line 2 | 7 |

8a Check all methods used for valuing closing inventory:

    **(i)** ☐ Cost

    **(ii)** ☐ Lower of cost or market as described in regulations section 1.471-4

    **(iii)** ☐ Writedown of "subnormal" goods as described in regulations section 1.471-2(c)

    **(iv)** ☐ Other (specify method used and attach explanation) ▶ ...........................................

    **b** Check if the LIFO inventory method was adopted this tax year for any goods (if checked, attach Form 970) . . . . . ☐

    **c** Do the rules of section 263A (with respect to property produced or acquired for resale) apply to the partnership? . . ☐ Yes ☐ No

    **d** Was there any change (other than for section 263A purposes) in determining quantities, cost, or valuations between opening and closing inventory? If "Yes," attach explanation . . . . . . . . . . . . . . . . . . ☐ Yes ☐ No

## Schedule H    Income (Loss) From Rental Real Estate Activity(ies)

1 In the space provided below, show the kind and location of each rental property. Attach a schedule if more space is needed.

Property A ...........................................................................................

Property B ...........................................................................................

Property C ...........................................................................................

| Rental Real Estate Income | | Properties | | | Totals (Add columns A, B, C, and amounts from any attached schedule) |
|---|---|---|---|---|---|
| | | **A** | **B** | **C** | |
| 2 Gross Income | 2 | | | | 2 |
| Rental Real Estate Expenses | | | | | |
| 3 Advertising | 3 | | | | |
| 4 Auto and travel | 4 | | | | |
| 5 Cleaning and maintenance | 5 | | | | |
| 6 Commissions | 6 | | | | |
| 7 Insurance | 7 | | | | |
| 8 Legal and other professional fees | 8 | | | | |
| 9 Interest expense | 9 | | | | |
| 10 Repairs | 10 | | | | |
| 11 Taxes | 11 | | | | |
| 12 Utilities | 12 | | | | |
| 13 Wages and salaries | 13 | | | | |
| 14 Depreciation from Form 4562 | 14 | | | | |
| 15 Other (list) ................. | | | | | |
| ................................ | | | | | |
| ................................ | | | | | |
| 16 Total expenses. Add lines 3 through 15 | 16 | | | | 16 |
| 17 Net income (loss) from rental real estate activity(ies). Subtract line 16 from line 2. Enter total net income (loss) from all properties on Schedule K, line 2. | 17 | | | | 17 |

## Schedule K — Partners' Shares of Income, Credits, Deductions, etc.

| | (a) Distributive share items | | | (b) Total amount |
|---|---|---|---|---|
| **Income (Loss)** | **1** Ordinary income (loss) from trade or business activity(ies) (page 1, line 21) . . . . | | 1 | |
| | **2** Net income (loss) from rental real estate activity(ies) (Schedule H, line 17) . . . | | 2 | |
| | **3a** Gross income from other rental activity(ies) . . . . . | 3a | $ | | |
| | **b** Minus expenses (attach schedule) . . . . . | 3b | $ | | |
| | **c** Balance net income (loss) from other rental activity(ies) . . . . . . . ▶ | | 3c | |
| | **4** Portfolio income (loss): | | | |
| | **a** Interest income . . . . . . . . . . | | 4a | |
| | **b** Dividend income . . . . . . . . . | | 4b | |
| | **c** Royalty income . . . . . . . . . | | 4c | |
| | **d** Net short-term capital gain (loss) (Schedule D, line 4) | | 4d | |
| | **e** Net long-term capital gain (loss) (Schedule D, line 9) | | 4e | |
| | **f** Other portfolio income (loss) (attach schedule) | | 4f | |
| | **5** Guaranteed payments . . . . . . . . | | 5 | |
| | **6** Net gain (loss) under section 1231 (other than due to casualty or theft) | | 6 | |
| | **7** Other (attach schedule) . . . . . . . | | 7 | |
| **Deductions** | **8** Charitable contributions (attach list) . . . . . . . | | 8 | |
| | **9** Expense deduction for recovery property (section 179) . . . . | | 9 | |
| | **10** Deductions related to portfolio income (do not include investment interest expense) | | 10 | |
| | **11** Other (attach schedule) . . . . . . . . . | | 11 | |
| **Credits** | **12a** Credit for income tax withheld . . . . . . . . | | 12a | |
| | **b** Low-income housing credit (attach Form 8586) . . . . | | 12b | |
| | **c** Qualified rehabilitation expenditures related to rental real estate activity(ies) (attach schedule) . . . | | 12c | |
| | **d** Credit(s) related to rental real estate activity(ies) other than 12b and 12c (attach schedule) . . . | | 12d | |
| | **e** Credit(s) related to rental activity(ies) other than 12b, 12c, and 12d (attach schedule) | | 12e | |
| | **13** Other (attach schedule) . . . . . . . . | | 13 | |
| **Self-Employment** | **14a** Net earnings (loss) from self-employment . . . . . | | 14a | |
| | **b** Gross farming or fishing income . . . . . . | | 14b | |
| | **c** Gross nonfarm income . . . . . . . . | | 14c | |
| **Tax Preference Items** | **15a** Accelerated depreciation of real property placed in service before 1/1/87 | | 15a | |
| | **b** Accelerated depreciation of leased personal property placed in service before 1/1/87 | | 15b | |
| | **c** Depreciation adjustment on property placed in service after 12/31/86 | | 15c | |
| | **d** Depletion (other than oil and gas) . . . . . . | | 15d | |
| | **e** (1) Gross income from oil, gas, and geothermal properties . | | 15e(1) | |
| | (2) Deductions allocable to oil, gas, and geothermal properties | | 15e(2) | |
| | **f** Other (attach schedule) . . . . . . . | | 15f | |
| **Investment Interest** | **16a** Interest expense on investment debts . . . . . | | 16a | |
| | **b** (1) Investment income included on lines 4a through 4f, Schedule K | | 16b(1) | |
| | (2) Investment expenses included on line 10, Schedule K . . . | | 16b(2) | |
| **Foreign Taxes** | **17a** Type of income _ _ _ _ _ _ _ _ _ _ _ _ _ _ _ _ _ _ _ _ _ _ _ | | | |
| | **b** Foreign country or U.S. possession _ _ _ _ _ _ _ _ _ _ _ _ _ _ _ | | | |
| | **c** Total gross income from sources outside the U.S. (attach schedule) . . | | 17c | |
| | **d** Total applicable deductions and losses (attach schedule) . . . | | 17d | |
| | **e** Total foreign taxes (check one): ▶ ☐ Paid ☐ Accrued . . . . | | 17e | |
| | **f** Reduction in taxes available for credit (attach schedule) . . . . | | 17f | |
| | **g** Other (attach schedule) . . . . . . . | | 17g | |
| **Other** | **18** Attach schedule for other items and amounts not reported above. See Instructions | | | |

## Schedule L Balance Sheets

(See the Instructions for Question M Before Completing Schedules L and M.)

| Assets | Beginning of tax year (a) | (b) | End of tax year (c) | (d) |
|---|---|---|---|---|
| 1 Cash . . . . . . . . . . . . | | | | |
| 2 Trade notes and accounts receivable . . . . . | | | | |
| a Minus allowance for bad debts . . . . . . | | | | |
| 3 Inventories . . . . . . . . . | | | | |
| 4 Federal and state government obligations . . | | | | |
| 5 Other current assets (attach schedule) . . . . | | | | |
| 6 Mortgage and real estate loans . . . . . . | | | | |
| 7 Other investments (attach schedule) . . . . . | | | | |
| 8 Buildings and other depreciable assets . . . . | | | | |
| a Minus accumulated depreciation . . . . . | | | | |
| 9 Depletable assets . . . . . . . | | | | |
| a Minus accumulated depletion . . . . . | | | | |
| 10 Land (net of any amortization) . . . . . . | | | | |
| 11 Intangible assets (amortizable only). . . . . | | | | |
| a Minus accumulated amortization . . . . | | | | |
| 12 Other assets (attach schedule) . . . . . | | | | |
| 13 TOTAL assets. . . . . . . . | | | | |
| **Liabilities and Capital** | | | | |
| 14 Accounts payable . . . . . . | | | | |
| 15 Mortgages, notes, bonds payable in less than 1 year | | | | |
| 16 Other current liabilities (attach schedule) . . . . | | | | |
| 17 All nonrecourse loans . . . . . . | | | | |
| 18 Mortgages, notes, bonds payable in 1 year or more | | | | |
| 19 Other liabilities (attach schedule) . . . . | | | | |
| 20 Partners' capital accounts. . . . . | | | | |
| 21 TOTAL liabilities and capital . . . . | | | | |

## Schedule M Reconciliation of Partners' Capital Accounts

(Show reconciliation of each partner's capital account on Schedule K-1 (Form 1065), Question I.)

| (a) Capital account at beginning of year | (b) Capital contributed during year | (c) Income (loss) from lines 1,2, 3c, and 4 of Sch. K | (d) Income not included in column (c), plus nontaxable income | (e) Losses not included in column (c), plus unallowable deductions | (f) Withdrawals and distributions | (g) Capital account at end of year |
|---|---|---|---|---|---|---|
| | | | | | | |
| | | | | | | |

## Designation of Tax Matters Partner

The following general partner is hereby designated as the tax matters partner (TMP) for the tax year for which this partnership return is filed:

Name of designated TMP ▶ _____    Identifying number of TMP ▶ _____

Address of designated TMP ▶ _____

✿ U.S. GOVERNMENT PRINTING OFFICE: 1987-183-165 E.I. 43-0787287

# 1987
# Instructions for Form 1065
## U.S. Partnership Return of Income
*(Section references are to the Internal Revenue Code unless otherwise noted.)*

**Department of the Treasury**
**Internal Revenue Service**

## Paperwork Reduction Act Notice

We ask for this information to carry out the Internal Revenue laws of the United States. We need it to ensure that taxpayers are complying with these laws and to allow us to figure and collect the right amount of tax. You are required to give us this information.

## Changes You Should Note
### Changes to Form 1065

The 1987 Form 1065 is a four page form. Page 3 of Form 1065 provides a **Schedule K**, Partners' Shares of Income, Credits, Deductions, etc. **Schedule L**, Balance Sheets; and **Schedule M**, Reconciliation of Partners' Capital Accounts, are on page 4. A new schedule, **Schedule H**, Income (Loss) From Rental Real Estate Activities, has been added to page 2. **Schedule B**, Distributive Share Items, has been eliminated.

Please note these other major changes to Form 1065:

• Page 1 is used only to report income and expenses related to a trade or business activity of the partnership. Rental activities and portfolio income such as interest and dividends are not reported on page 1 of Form 1065 but are instead reported on Schedule K. This change was made to enable partners to comply with the new passive activity limitations of section 469. See page 5 for more information on section 469.

• Partnerships subject to the consolidated audit procedures of TEFRA (see sections 6221 through 6231) may designate a Tax Matters Partner (TMP) on page 4 of Form 1065.

• All partnerships, including those with 10 or fewer partners, are required to complete Schedule K, which is on page 3 of Form 1065. Schedule K provides totals of amounts separately reported to partners on Schedule K-1.

### Tax Reform Act of 1986

The Tax Reform Act of 1986 (hereafter referred to as "the Act") made many changes that affect partnerships and partners. Included below are some of the changes.

**Tax Year Changes.**—For partnership tax years beginning in 1987, all partnerships generally will be required to adopt the same taxable year as the partners who own a majority (more than 50%) interest in the partnership profits and capital. An exception applies if the partnership establishes to the satisfaction of IRS that there is a business purpose for having a different taxable year. Partnerships required to change tax years because of section 706(b) must file short-year returns. Question H has been added to Schedule K-1 to help partners in these partnerships

consider the relief provision that generally allows partners to take into account the short period income in excess of expenses ratably over 4 years. See **Tax Years** on page 3 for more information.

**Depreciation.**—The rules for figuring depreciation have been substantially changed. The Accelerated Cost Recovery System (ACRS) has been modified. The new system is effective for property placed in service after 1986. The new system provides specific depreciation methods for each class of assets. See **Form 4562**, Depreciation and Amortization.

**Long-Term Contracts.**—Section 460 provides new rules for accounting for long-term contracts entered into after February 28, 1986. See that section for more information.

**Passive Activities.**—Section 469 limits the amount of losses and credits that partners may claim from "passive activities." Generally, a passive activity is any activity that involves the conduct of any trade or business in which the partner does not materially participate. Except as may be provided in the regulations, limited partners are treated as not materially participating in the trade or business activities of the partnership. A rental activity is also considered a passive activity. See **Passive Activity Limitations** on page 5 for more information.

**Tax Preference Items.**—The Act made many changes to the alternative minimum tax provisions. New or revised tax preference items include the following: depreciation on real or personal property placed in service after 1986: use of the completed contract method; installment sales of certain property; passive farm losses; and passive activity losses. See **Publication 909**, Alternative Minimum Tax, and the instructions for **Form 6251**, Alternative Minimum Tax—Individuals, for more information.

**Section 179 Deduction.**—The maximum amount of section 179 expense that may be apportioned and passed through to all partners has increased to $10,000 for property placed in service after December 31, 1986. Other new limits also apply. See Form 4562 and the instructions for line 9 of Schedules K and K-1 for more information.

**Installment Method.**—Generally, the use of the installment method for dealer sales of real or personal property is limited, based on the amount of the taxpayer's outstanding indebtedness. These rules also apply to casual installment sales of real property used in a business or rental activity if the sales price exceeds $150,000. See section 453C and the instructions for **Form 6252**, Computation of Installment Sale Income, for more information.

**Capitalization Rules.**—Section 263A provides uniform rules for determining which expenses must be included in

inventory costs and which expenses must be capitalized (in the case of property other than inventory). These rules apply to property produced by the partnership and, in limited cases, to property acquired for resale. The costs to be included in inventory costs or capitalized include all the direct costs and the allocable indirect costs of the property. Section 263A also contains special rules for interest paid or incurred to produce real property and certain personal property. Section 189, relating to the amortization of real property construction period interest and taxes, is repealed for costs incurred after 1986. See **Publication 538**, Accounting Periods and Methods, and **Uniform Capitalization Rules** on page 8 for more information.

**Tax Credit for Low-Income Rental Housing.**—A new credit has been provided for owners of certain low-income housing rental projects. This provision applies to buildings placed in service after 1986. See section 42 and **Form 8586**, Low-Income Housing Credit, for more information. The active participation rules of section 469 do not apply to this credit.

**At-Risk Rules.**—The at-risk rules of section 465 have been extended to cover losses incurred from the holding of real property (other than mineral property, to which the at-risk limitations applied before this change) placed in service after 1986. For partnership interests acquired by a partner after 1986, the rules also apply to real property placed in service on, before, or after January 1, 1987. See the instructions for Question B of Schedule K-1 and **Publication 925**, Passive Activity and At-Risk Rules, for more information.

**Discharge of Indebtedness.**—Generally, a discharge of indebtedness after 1986 will result in the current recognition of income if the partnership is solvent. See section 108.

**Foreign Partners.**—The Act requires partnerships to withhold U.S. tax at a 20% rate on distributions to foreign partners. This rule applies to distributions made after 1987 or, if earlier, the effective date of initial regulations issued under new section 1446.

**Travel and Entertainment Expenses.**—Generally, the amount allowable to the partnership as a deduction for meal and entertainment expenses is limited to 80% of the amount that would otherwise be allowable as a deduction. The rules for deducting luxury water travel, convention expenses, and tickets for entertainment have also been changed. See page 10 of these instructions and **Publication 463**, Travel, Entertainment, and Gift Expenses, for more information.

### Other Changes:

• Generally, the cash method of accounting will not be available to tax shelter partnerships or partnerships which have any C corporation as a partner and have average annual gross receipts greater than $5 million. See section 448 and Publication 538.

• Partnerships whose average annual gross receipts for the three prior tax years do not exceed $5 million will be able to elect a simplified method of determining dollar value LIFO inventory values. See section 474.

- Generally, the Act repealed the use of the reserve method of figuring bad debts (for other than certain financial institutions) and will require the use of the specific charge-off method. See **Publication 548**, Deduction for Bad Debts, and the instructions for line 14 of Form 1065.

- Installment sales of personal property under a revolving credit plan and installment sales of certain publicly traded property will be treated as if all payments are received in the year of sale. See section 453.

- Recently issued regulation section 1.163-8T prescribes rules for allocating interest expense for the purpose of computing passive activity limitations and investment and personal interest expense limitations. See the instructions for line 12 of Form 1065 for more information.

## Reminders

- Use the preaddressed label and envelope that comes with the tax package to help speed the processing of the partnership return.

- Do not deduct depletion on oil and gas wells on the partnership return. Instead, pass through to the partners on Schedule K-1 the information needed to compute this deduction. The partners will determine the deductible amount on their own returns.

- Special rules apply to situations in which a partner is deemed to be engaging in a transaction with a partnership other than in the partner's capacity as a member of the partnership. For additional information, see **Publication 541**, Tax Information on Partnerships.

### Registration of Tax Shelters

If the partnership is a tax shelter, is involved in a tax shelter, is considered to be the organizer of a tax shelter, or is a pass-through entity of tax shelter benefits, there are reporting requirements under section 6111 for both the partnership and its partners.

See **Form 8264**, Application for Registration of a Tax Shelter, and **Form 8271**, Investor Reporting of Tax Shelter Registration Number, and their related instructions for more information.

## Purpose of Form

Form 1065 is used to report the income, deductions, gains, losses, etc., from the operation of a partnership. Form 1065 for 1987 is an information return for the calendar year 1987 or other fiscal year beginning in 1987. However, if the partnership has a tax year of less than 12 months that begins and ends in 1988, and the 1988 Form 1065 is not available by the time the partnership is required to file its return, the partnership may use the 1987 form. The partnership must show its 1988 tax year on the 1987 Form 1065 and incorporate any tax law changes that are effective for tax years beginning after December 31, 1987.

## Who Must File

Every partnership that engages in a trade or business or has income from sources in the United States must file Form 1065. A partnership must file even if its principal place of business is outside the United States or all its members are nonresident aliens.

Religious and apostolic organizations that are exempt from income tax under section 501(d) must file Form 1065.

A syndicate, pool, joint venture, or similar organization may elect under section 761(a) not to be treated as a partnership for Federal income tax purposes and will not be required to file Form 1065 except for the year of election. See section 761(a) and Publication 541 for more information.

Real estate mortgage investment conduits (REMICs) should file new Form 1066, not Form 1065.

**Note:** If a partnership return is filed by an entity for a tax year, but it is determined that the entity is not a partnership for that tax year, sections 6221 through 6233 will apply to that entity and to persons holding an interest in that entity to the extent provided by regulations. See section 6233 for more information.

## When To File

A resident partnership must file Form 1065 by the 15th day of the 4th month following the close of its tax year. A partnership whose partners are all nonresident aliens must file its return by the 15th day of the 6th month following the close of its tax year.

However, a partnership that is required to file a return for a short period beginning in 1987 in order to comply with section 706(b), may file its short period return on or before the latest of (1) the normal due date, (2) October 15, 1987, or (3) 30 days after the date Form 1128 (if applicable) is approved. See Announcement 87-82, 1987-37 I.R.B. 30.

If you need more time to file a partnership return, file **Form 2758**, Application for Extension of Time to File, by the regular due date of the partnership return.

For information on the tax years that partnerships may adopt, see Publication 538. See also **Tax Years** on page 3 of these instructions.

## Where To File

Use the addressed envelope that came with the return. If you do not have an addressed envelope, or if the partnership moved during the year, use the Internal Revenue Service Center address for the state where the partnership's principal place of business or principal office or agency is located. No street address is necessary. See the following list of Service Centers.

A partnership without a principal office or agency or principal place of business in the United States must file its return with the Internal Revenue Service Center, Philadelphia, PA 19255.

| If the partnership's principal place of business or principal office or agency is located in ▼ | Use the following address ▼ |
|---|---|
| New Jersey, New York City and counties of Nassau, Rockland, Suffolk, and Westchester | Holtsville, NY 00501 |
| New York (all other counties), Connecticut, Maine, Massachusetts, Minnesota, New Hampshire, Rhode Island, Vermont | Andover, MA 05501 |
| Alabama, Florida, Georgia, Mississippi, South Carolina | Atlanta, GA 39901 |
| Kentucky, Michigan, Ohio, West Virginia | Cincinnati, OH 45999 |
| Kansas, Louisiana, New Mexico, Oklahoma, Texas | Austin, TX 73301 |
| Alaska, Arizona, California (counties of Alpine, Amador, Butte, Calaveras, Colusa, Contra Costa, Del Norte, El Dorado, Glenn, Humboldt, Lake, Lassen, Marin, Mendocino, Modoc, Napa, Nevada, Placer, Plumas, Sacramento, San Joaquin, Shasta, Sierra, Siskiyou, Solano, Sonoma, Sutter, Tehama, Trinity, Yolo, and Yuba), Colorado, Idaho, Montana, Nebraska, Nevada, North Dakota, Oregon, South Dakota, Utah, Washington, Wyoming | Ogden, UT 84201 |
| California (all other counties), Hawaii | Fresno, CA 93888 |
| Illinois, Iowa, Missouri, Wisconsin | Kansas City, MO 64999 |
| Arkansas, Indiana, North Carolina, Tennessee, Virginia | Memphis, TN 37501 |
| Delaware, District of Columbia, Maryland, Pennsylvania | Philadelphia, PA 19255 |

## Penalty

A penalty is assessed against the partnership if it is required to file a partnership return and it: (1) fails to file the return on time, including extensions, or (2) files a return that fails to show all the information required, unless the failure is due to reasonable cause. The amount of the penalty for each month or fraction of a month (for a maximum of 5 months) the failure continues is $50 multiplied by the total number of persons who were partners in the partnership during any part of the partnership's tax year for which the return is due. This penalty will not be imposed on certain small partnerships if they meet the required procedures under Revenue Procedure 84-35, 1984-1 C.B. 509.

Family-farm partnerships, family-owned wholesale or retail store partnerships, co-owners of investment property, etc., may not have to file Schedules L and M. See the instructions on page 6 for Question M before completing Schedules L and M.

The penalty for each failure to furnish copies of Schedule K-1 to partners is $50. In addition, if a Schedule K-1 does not include all of the information required to be shown or includes incorrect information, an additional penalty may be imposed. See sections 6722 and 6723 for more information.

## General Information

**Note:** In addition to those publications listed throughout these instructions, you may wish to get: **Publication 334**, Tax Guide for Small Business; **Publication 535**, Business Expenses; **Publication 536**, Net Operating Losses; **Publication 541**, Tax Information on Partnerships; **Publication 550**, Investment Income and Expenses; and **Publication 556**, Examination of Returns, Appeal Rights, and Claims for Refund.

For additional information on tax law changes you may also wish to get new **Publication 920**, Explanation of the Tax Reform Act of 1986 for Individuals, and new **Publication 921**, Explanation of the Tax Reform Act of 1986 for Business.

## Unresolved Tax Problems

IRS has a Problem Resolution Program for taxpayers who have been unable to resolve their problems with IRS. If the partnership has a tax problem it has been unable to resolve through normal channels, write to the partnership's local IRS District Director or call the partnership's local IRS office and ask for Problem Resolution assistance. This office will take responsibility for your problem and ensure that it receives proper attention. Although the Problem Resolution Office cannot change the tax law or make technical decisions, it can frequently clear up misunderstandings that resulted from previous contacts.

## Accounting Methods

Figure ordinary income by the accounting method regularly used in maintaining the partnership's books and records. The method generally may include the cash receipts and disbursements method, an accrual method or any other method permitted by the Internal Revenue Code. The method must clearly reflect income. See section 446. Unless allowed otherwise by law, the partnership may not change the accounting method used to report income in earlier years (for income as a whole or fo. any material item) without first getting consent on **Form 3115**, Application for Change in Accounting Method. See Publication 538 for more information.

Generally, an accrual basis taxpayer can deduct accrued expenses in the tax year that all events have occurred that determine the liability, and the amount of the liability can be figured with reasonable accuracy. However, generally, all the events that establish liability for the amount are treated as occurring only when economic performance takes place. There are exceptions for recurring items. A partnership may elect to treat the application of section 461(h) as a change of accounting method. See section 461(h).

**Caution:** *The Act contains several new accounting provisions. See the "Changes You Should Note" section of these instructions and Publication 538.*

## Tax Years

For partnership tax years beginning in 1987, section 706(b)(1)(B) generally requires partnerships to adopt, retain, or change to the same tax year as partners who own a majority interest in the partnership. If partners owning a majority interest have different tax years, the partnership must adopt the same tax year as that of its principal partners. A principal partner is a partner having an interest of 5% or more of the partnership profits and capital. If the tax year cannot be determined under either of these rules the partnership must adopt a calendar year unless another year is prescribed by regulations.

Partnerships that adopt, retain, or change to the year required by section 706(b)(1)(B) (other than calendar year partnerships that retain a calendar tax year) should type or print at the top of the Form 1065 for their first tax year beginning after 1986, "FILED UNDER SECTION 806 OF THE TAX REFORM ACT OF 1986."

Section 706(b)(1)(C) states that partnerships may have a tax year other than a tax year described in section 706(b)(1)(B) if the partnership establishes a business

purpose for that year. Revenue Ruling 87-57, 1987-28 I.R.B. 7, and Revenue Procedure 87-32, 1987-28 I.R.B. 14, provide guidance on the business purpose test.

Generally, partnerships that received permission on or after 7/1/74 to use a fiscal year that did not result in a 3-month or less deferral of income to partners may retain their tax year. Such partnerships should type or print at the top of the Form 1065 filed for their first tax year beginning after 12/31/86, "GRANDFATHERED FISCAL YEAR" and attach a copy of the ruling letter that granted the partnership permission to use its present tax year.

Revenue Procedure 87-32 also provides rules for adopting, retaining, or changing to the "natural business year" of the partnership. The natural business year of the partnership is determined by dividing gross receipts for the last 2 months of the requested fiscal year by gross receipts for the 12-month period that ends with the last month of the requested fiscal year. This computation is also made for the 2 preceding 12-month periods. Generally, if the results in each of these three computations equal or exceed 25%, then the requested fiscal year is the partnership's natural business year.

See Publication 541 for more information on the tax year that partnerships may adopt.

## Rounding Off to Whole-Dollar Amounts

You may show the money items on the return and accompanying schedules as whole-dollar amounts. To do so, drop any amount less than 50 cents and increase any amount from 50 cents through 99 cents to the next higher dollar.

## Recordkeeping

The partnership records must be kept as long as their contents may be material in the administration of any Internal Revenue law. Copies of the filed tax returns should also be kept as part of the partnership's records. Please see **Publication 583**, Information for Business Taxpayers, for more information.

## Amended Return

If, after the partnership files its return, it later becomes aware of any changes it must make to income, deductions, credits, etc., the partnership should file an amended Form 1065 and an amended Schedule K-1 for each partner to change the forms already filed. Check the box at Question H(3), page 1, Form 1065. Give a corrected Schedule K-1 (Form 1065) to each partner labeled "Amended."

**Note:** *If a partnership does not meet the small partnership exception under section 6231 or makes the election described in section 6231(a)(1)(B)(ii), the amended return will be a request for administrative adjustment and **Form 8082**, Notice of Inconsistent Treatment or Amended Return, must be filed by the Tax Matters Partner. See section 6227 for more information.*

If the partnership's Federal return is changed for any reason, it may affect its state return. This would include changes made as a result of an examination of the partnership return by the IRS. Contact the state tax agency where the state return is filed for more information.

## Information Returns That May Be Required

**Form 1096**, Annual Summary and Transmittal of U.S. Information Returns, is used to summarize and transmit information returns to the Internal Revenue Service Center.

**Form 1098**, Mortgage Interest Statement, is used to report the receipt from any individual of $600 or more of mortgage interest in the course of the partnership's trade or business.

**Forms 1099-A, B, INT, MISC, OID, and R.** You may have to file these information returns to report abandonments and acquisitions through foreclosure, proceeds from broker and barter exchange transactions, real estate transactions, interest payments, medical and dental health care payments, miscellaneous income, original issue discount, and total distributions from profit-sharing plans, retirement plans, and individual retirement arrangements. Also, use these returns to report amounts that were received as a nominee on behalf of another person.

For more information about filing these and other information returns, see **Publication 916**, Information Returns, and the Instructions for Forms 1099, 1098, 5498, 1096, and W-2G.

**Note:** *Every partnership must file information returns if, in the course of its trade or business during the calendar year, it makes payments of rents, commissions, or other fixed or determinable income (see section 6041) totaling $600 or more to any one individual, partnership, or other entity (other than a corporation, in most cases).*

**Form 5713**, International Boycott Report, is for use by persons having operations in or related to "boycotting" countries. The partnership must give each partner a copy of the Form 5713 filed by the partnership there has been participation in, or cooperation with, an international boycott.

**Form 8300**, Report of Cash Payments Over $10,000 Received in a Trade or Business, is used to report the receipt of more than $10,000 in cash or foreign currency in one transaction (or a series of related transactions).

**Form 5471**, Information Return With Respect to a Foreign Corporation. U.S. partnerships that have an interest in a foreign corporation may be required to file Form 5471.

**Form 6248**, Annual Information Return of Windfall Profit Tax.

**Form 8594**, Asset Acquisition Statement, is to be filed by both the purchaser and seller of a group of assets constituting a trade or business if goodwill or a going concern value attaches, or could attach, to such assets and if the purchaser's basis in the assets is determined only by the amount paid for the assets.

## Attachments

If you need more space on the forms or schedules, attach separate sheets. Use the same arrangement as the printed forms, and **show the totals on the printed forms**. Be sure to put the partnership's name and employer identification number on each sheet. Additionally, be sure that each separate sheet clearly indicates the line or section on the printed form relating to the information.

To assist us in processing the return, we ask that you complete every applicable entry space on Form 1065. Please do not attach statements and write "See Attached" in lieu of completing the entry spaces on this form.

## Definitions

**Partnership.** A partnership is the relationship between two or more persons who join together to carry on a trade or business, with each person contributing money, property, labor, or skill and each expecting to share in the profits and losses of the business whether or not a formal partnership agreement is made.

The term "partnership" includes a limited partnership, syndicate, group, pool, joint venture, or other unincorporated organization, through or by which any business, financial operation, or venture is carried on, that is not, within the meaning of the Internal Revenue Code, a corporation, trust, estate, or sole proprietorship. If an organization more nearly resembles a corporation than a partnership or trust, it is considered an association taxed as a corporation.

A joint undertaking merely to share expenses is not a partnership. Mere co-ownership of property that is maintained and leased or rented is not a partnership. However, if the co-owners provide services to the tenants, a partnership exists.

See Publication 541 for more information.

**General Partner.** A general partner is a member of the organization who is personally liable for obligations of the partnership.

**Limited Partner.** A limited partner is one whose potential personal liability for partnership debts is limited to the amount of money or other property that the partner contributed or is required to contribute to the partnership.

**Limited Partnership.** A limited partnership is a partnership composed of at least one general partner and one or more limited partners.

**Nonrecourse Loans.** Nonrecourse loans are those liabilities of the partnership for which none of the partners has any personal liability.

## Section 702(a) Items

Under section 702(a), the partners are required to take into account separately their distributive shares, whether or not distributed, of:

1. Gains and losses from sales or exchanges of capital assets;
2. Gains and losses from sales or exchanges of property described in section 1231;
3. Charitable contributions;
4. Dividends (passed through to corporate partners) that are eligible for a special deduction (section 241);
5. Taxes described in section 901;
6. Other items of income, gain, loss, deduction, or credit, to the extent provided by regulations. Examples of such items include nonbusiness expenses described in section 212, intangible drilling and development costs

(section 263(c)), and soil and water conservation expenditures (section 175). (See the instructions for Schedules K and K-1 later in these instructions for a more detailed list); and

7. Taxable income or loss (ordinary income or loss) other than items 1 through 6 above.

## Elections

Generally, the partnership decides how to figure taxable income from its operations. For example, it chooses the accounting method and depreciation methods it will use. The partnership also makes the elections under the following sections:

● Section 1033 provides for an election by the partnership not to recognize gain when property is compulsorily or involuntarily converted into property (other than similar property) or into money to the extent it is reinvested in similar property.

● Under section 703(b), the election for separate property treatment for oil and gas property is made by the partnership. Thus, the partnership must make the section 614 election before the partners compute their individual depletion allowances under section 613A(c)(7)(D). See Revenue Ruling 84-142, 1984-2 C.B. 117. See the instructions for Schedules K and K-1, line 18, item c., for the information on oil and gas depletion that must be supplied to the partners by the partnership.

● Section 754 provides rules under which a partnership may elect to adjust: (a) the basis of its remaining assets when assets distributed to a partner have increased or decreased in value; (b) a new partner's share of the basis of partnership assets to reflect the purchase price paid by a new partner for the new partner's interest; or (c) an estate's or other beneficiary's share of the basis of partnership assets to reflect a change in the basis of a partnership interest on the death of a partner. See regulation section 1.754-1(b). See the instructions for Question N for more information.

● Section 179 provides for an election by the partnership to expense the cost of certain depreciable property. The partnership passes this amount through to the partners. See Form 4562 for more information.

Information about other elections may be found under the applicable sections of Chapter 1 of the Code and the Income Tax Regulations.

Elections under the following Code sections are made by a partner separately on the partner's tax return and not by the partnership:

● Section 108 (income from discharge of indebtedness);

● Section 617 (deduction and recapture of certain mining exploration expenditures paid or incurred); and

● Section 901 (foreign tax credit).

In addition, individual partners (including estates and trusts) may make an election under section 59(e) to deduct ratably, over the period specified in that section, certain qualified expenditures such as intangible drilling cost, mining exploration, or research and experimental expenditures. See the instructions for Schedules K and K-1, line 18, item f., for more information.

## Distribution of Unrealized Receivables and Inventory Items

If a partnership distributes unrealized receivables or substantially appreciated inventory items for all or part of a partner's interest in other partnership property (including money), treat the transaction as a sale or exchange between the partner and the partnership. Treat the partnership gain (loss) as ordinary income (loss). Allocate it only to partners (other than the distributee partner) who will take this amount into account separately under section 702(a)(7).

If a partnership gives other property (including money) for all or part of that partner's interest in the partnership's unrealized receivables or substantially appreciated inventory items, treat the transaction as a sale or exchange of the property. See section 751 and the related regulations for definitions of unrealized receivables and substantially appreciated inventory items.

Generally, if a partner sells or exchanges a partnership interest where unrealized receivables or substantially appreciated inventory items are involved, the transferor partner must notify the partnership, in writing, within 30 days of the exchange. See **Form 8308**, Report of Sale or Exchange of Certain Partnership Interests, for the types of unrealized receivables involved. These include depreciation recapture, depletable properties, farm land, etc.

**Note:** *The transferor in a section 751(a) exchange does not have to notify the partnership of the exchange if, under section 6045, Form 1099-B is required to be filed with respect to the sale or exchange. See Form 8308 for more information.*

See Revenue Ruling 84-102, 1984-2 C.B. 119, for information when a new partner joins a partnership that has liabilities and unrealized receivables. Also, see section 6050K and Publication 541 for more information.

Furthermore, see section 751(f) for special rules in the case of tiered partnerships for section 751 exchanges.

## Net Operating Loss Deduction

A partnership is not allowed the deduction for net operating losses.

## Contributions to the Partnership

Generally, no gain (loss) is recognized to the partnership or any of the partners when property is given to the partnership in exchange for an interest in the partnership. This rule does not apply to any gain realized on a transfer of property to a partnership that would be treated as an investment company (within the meaning of section 351) if the partnership were incorporated.

The basis to the partnership of property given by a partner is the adjusted basis in the hands of the partner at the time it was given, plus any gain recognized (under section 721(b)) to the partner at that time. (See section 723 for more information.)

**Notes:** *See section 704(c) for the rules regarding partnership allocations with respect to contributed property.*

*If a partner contributed unrealized receivables, inventory items, or capital loss property to the partnership, see section 724.*

## Payments Subject to Withholding at Source

If there are any nonresident alien individuals, foreign partnerships, or foreign corporations as partners, and the partnership has items which constitute gross income from sources within the United States (see sections 638 and 861 through 864), see **Form 1042**, Annual Withholding Tax Return for U.S. Source Income of Foreign Persons.

**Form 8288**, U.S. Withholding Tax Return for Dispositions by Foreign Persons of U.S. Real Property Interests, is used by the partnership to transmit the withholding on the sale of U.S. real property by foreign persons. At the same time Form 8288 is completed, an information return, **Form 8288-A**, Statement of Withholding on Dispositions by Foreign Persons of U.S. Real Property Interests, is attached and sent to the IRS. See section 1445 and related regulations for details.

## Windfall Profit Tax

Do not enter any windfall profit tax or any overpayment of windfall profit tax on Form 1065, page 1, or on any of the numbered lines on Schedules K or K-1. Generally, the partnership will notify each partner on **Form 6248**, Annual Information Return of Windfall Profit Tax, of any income tax deduction for windfall profit tax. Generally, each partner determines if he or she is entitled to a refund of overpaid windfall profit tax. Each partner files **Form 6249**, Computation of Overpaid Windfall Profit Tax, to obtain a refund. However, if the partnership elects to be treated as authorized to act on behalf of the partners, the regulations under section 6232 will apply. Partnerships must file **Form 843**, Claim, to receive the credit or refund.

Include the partners' income tax deduction for the partnership's tax year in column (e) of Schedule M. If the partnership files on a fiscal year basis, the amount entered will not be the same as the amount shown on the Form 6248 that the partnership gives to each partner. Enter each partner's share in column (e) of Question I on Schedule K-1.

Include any overpayment of windfall profit tax the partnership received and of which you notified the partners in column (d) of Schedule M. Enter each partner's share in column (d) of Question I on Schedule K-1.

## Passive Activity Limitations

Section 469 limits the amount of losses, deductions, and credits that partners may claim from "passive activities." A passive activity generally is any activity that involves the conduct of any trade or business in which the partner does not materially participate, that is, is not involved in the activity on a regular, continuous, and substantial basis. A rental activity is also considered a passive activity regardless of how much or how little the partner participates.

Generally, losses and credits from passive activities can be used only against income and tax from passive activities, not against salary, wages, professional fees, income from a business in which the taxpayer materially participates, or certain investment income referred to in these instructions as "portfolio income."

The passive activity limitations do not apply to the partnership, but to each partner's share of any loss or credit attributable to a passive activity. Because the limitations are different for trade or business activities and because portfolio income is excluded from passive income, the partnership must report income or loss and credits separately for each of the types of activities and income defined below:

**1. Trade or business activity.**—Generally, any activity of the partnership involving the conduct of any trade or business is a passive activity for a partner if the partner does not materially participate in the activity.

A partner is treated as materially participating only if the partner is involved in the operation of the trade or business on a regular, continuous, and substantial basis.

**Except as may be provided by regulations, limited partners are treated as not materially participating in the activity.**

See the instructions for question A(2) on Schedule K-1, section 469(h), and related regulations for more information.

There is an exception to these rules, however, for oil and gas activities. The passive activity limitations do not apply to partners having an interest in a working interest in any oil or gas property which does not limit the partner's liability. See the instructions for question A(2) of Schedule K-1 for how to answer that question for oil and gas activities.

Income (loss) from a trade or business activity (including an oil and gas trade or business activity) is reported on page 1 of Form 1065.

**2. Rental real estate activity.**—Generally, a rental real estate activity is a rental activity that involves the renting or leasing of real estate. However, where significant services are provided in connection with the rental of real estate (such as in the renting of hotel rooms), the activity is treated as a trade or business and not a rental real estate activity.

Partners who actively participate in a rental real estate activity may be able to deduct up to $25,000 of these losses against income from nonpassive activities, and to use the deduction equivalent of such credits against tax on income from nonpassive activities. Generally, this $25,000 amount is reduced for high income partners.

The active participation requirement can be met without regular, continuous, and substantial involvement in operations, as long as the partner participated in making management decisions or arranging for others to provide services (such as repairs), in a significant and bona fide sense. Management decisions that are relevant in this context include approving new tenants, deciding on rental terms, approving capital or repair expenditures, and other similar decisions.

A partner does not actively participate in a rental real estate activity if his or her interest (including any interest of a spouse) in the activity at any time during the year (or shorter relevant period) is less than 10% (by value) of all interests in the activity.

**Except as may be provided by regulations, limited partners are treated as not actively participating in an activity.**

Special transitional rules apply to qualified investors in qualified low-income housing projects. See Act section 502 and the instructions for Question A(3) of Schedule K-1 for more information.

Rental real estate activity income (loss) is not reported on page 1 of Form 1065 but is instead reported on Schedule H and line 2 of Schedules K and K-1.

**3. Rental activity other than rental real estate activity.**—Generally, this term means an activity the income from which consists of payment principally for the use of tangible property other than rental real estate.

Rental activity (other than rental real estate) income (loss) is reported on line 3 of Schedules K and K-1, not on page 1 of Form 1065.

**4. Portfolio income.**—Portfolio income includes interest, dividends, royalty, and annuity income not derived in the ordinary course of a trade or business, and gain or loss on the disposition of property held for investment. Portfolio income also includes income (such as interest) earned on working capital.

Portfolio income is not reported on page 1 of Form 1065; it is reported instead on line 4 of Schedules K and K-1.

**Note:** *In the case of partnership interests acquired and activities commenced before October 23, 1986, the passive loss and credit limitations are phased in. The computation is made by the partner, not the partnership. The partnership, however, must advise partners of the amount of their passive activity income, loss, and credit, and identify whether or not these amounts qualify for the phase-in provisions of section 469. See the instructions for Questions G(1) and G(2) of Schedule K-1 for more information.*

See Publication 925 for more information on the passive activity limitations.

## Signatures

### General Partner

Form 1065 is not considered a return unless it is signed. One general partner must sign the return. If a receiver, trustee in bankruptcy, or assignee controls the organization's property or business, that person must sign the return.

### Paid Preparer's Information

If someone prepares the return and **does not charge the partnership**, that person **should not sign** the partnership return.

Generally, anyone who is paid to prepare the partnership return must sign the return and fill in the other blanks in the **Paid Preparer's Use Only** area of the return.

*The preparer required to sign the partnership's return MUST complete the required preparer information and:*

• *Sign it, by hand, in the space provided for the preparer's signature. (Signature stamps or labels are not acceptable.)*

• *Give the partnership a copy of the return in addition to the copy to be filed with the IRS.*

Tax return preparers should be familiar with their responsibilities. They should see **Publication 1045**, Information for Tax Practitioners, for more information.

## Specific Instructions

These instructions follow the line numbers on the first page of Form 1065 and on the schedules that accompany it. Specific instructions for most of the lines are provided on the pages which follow. Those lines that do not appear in the instructions are self-explanatory.

**Fill in all of the applicable lines and schedules.** Enter any items specially allocated to the partners on the appropriate line of the applicable partner's Schedule K-1 and the total amount on the appropriate line of Schedule K and not on the numbered lines on Form 1065, page 1, or in Schedules A, D, or H.

File only one return for each partnership. Mark "duplicate copy" on any copy you give to a partner.

If a syndicate, pool, joint venture, or similar group files Form 1065, a copy of the agreement and all amendments must be attached to the return, unless a copy has already been filed.

## Form 1065

### Name, Address, and Employer Identification Number

The partnership may use its legal or trade name on all tax returns and other documents filed. Use the label on the package that was mailed to the partnership and make sure it is correct. If the partnership's name, address, or employer identification number is wrong on the label, mark through it and write the correct information on the label. If the partnership does not have a package with a label, print or type the partnership's legal or trade name and address on the appropriate line.

If the post office does not deliver mail to the partnership's street address, use the partnership's P.O. Box number instead of the street address.

Show the correct employer identification number in Question D on page 1 of Form 1065. If the partnership does not have an employer identification number, it must apply for one on **Form SS-4**, Application for Employer Identification Number. See Publication 583 for more information on your employer identification number.

### Question A

#### Principal Business Activity

If, as the principal business activity, the partnership (1) purchases raw materials, (2) subcontracts out for labor to make a finished product from the raw materials, and (3) retains title to the goods, the partnership is considered to be a manufacturer and must enter "Manufacturer" in Question A and one of the codes (2000 through 3970) under "Manufacturing" on page 20 of these Instructions in Question C.

### Question F

#### Total Assets at End of Tax Year

See the instructions below for Question M before completing this question.

If you are required to complete this question, enter the total assets, as determined by the accounting method regularly used in maintaining the

**Page 6**

partnership's books and records, at the end of the partnership's tax year. If there are no assets at the end of the tax year, enter the total assets as of the beginning of the tax year.

### Question I

#### Number of Partners

Enter the number of persons who were partners at **any time** during the tax year.

### Question M

Answer Question M "Yes" if **ALL** of the following requirements are met:

1. The partnership's principal income producing activity is from one or more of the following:
   a. Co-ownership of investment property.
   b. Family-owned wholesale or retail store partnership (activity codes 5001–5996).
   c. Family farm partnership.
   d. Wholesale or retail (activity codes 5001–5996), or service (activity codes 7012–8999) partnership with **both** gross receipts and assets of less than $250,000.

   See page 20 for the list of activity codes.

2. The partnership is a domestic partnership composed of 10 or fewer partners (generally, 10 or fewer Schedules K-1 are attached to this return, except that a husband and wife (and their estates) are treated as 1 partner for this purpose) each of whom is a natural person (other than a nonresident alien) or an estate.

3. The partnership does not have any trusts or corporations as partners.

4. The partnership is not in partnership with any other partnership.

5. Each partner's interest in the capital is the same as his or her interest in the profits.

6. All of the income, deductions, and credits are allocated to each partner in proportion to that partner's pro rata interest.

7. Schedules K-1 are filed with the return and furnished to the partners on or before the due date of the partnership return including extensions.

If all of the above requirements are met and Question M is answered "Yes," the partnership is not required to complete Schedules L and M, Question F, on page 1 of Form 1065, or Question I on Schedule K-1.

### Question N

#### Section 754 Election

Under section 754, a partnership may elect to adjust the basis of partnership property when property is distributed or when a partnership interest is transferred. This election must be made in a statement that is filed with the partnership's timely filed return (including any extension) for the tax year during which the distribution or transfer occurs.

If the election is made, it applies to both distributions and transfers and to all distributions and transfers made during the tax year and in all subsequent tax years unless the election is revoked (see regulation section 1.754-1(c)).

The statement must include (1) the name and address of the partnership, (2) a declaration that the partnership elects

under section 754 to apply the provisions of section 734(b) and section 743(b), and (3) the signature of the general partner authorized to sign the partnership return.

See section 754 and the related regulations for more information.

**Note:** *If there is a distribution of property that is an interest in another partnership, see section 734(b).*

### Question O

#### Foreign Accounts

Check "Yes" if either a. **OR** b. below applies to you.

a. At any time during the year, the partnership had an interest in or signature or other authority over a bank account, securities account, or other financial account in a foreign country.

   *Exception:* Check "No" if either of the following applies to the partnership:
   • The combined value of the accounts was $10,000 or less during the whole year.
   • The accounts were with a U.S. military banking facility operated by a U.S. financial institution.

b. The partnership owns more than 50% of the stock in any corporation that would answer the question "Yes" based on item a. above.

Get Form **TD F 90-22.1**, Report of Foreign Bank and Financial Accounts, to see if the partnership is considered to have an interest in or signature or other authority over a bank account, securities account, or other financial account in a foreign country.

If you checked "Yes" for Question O, file Form TD F 90-22.1 by June 30, 1988. File it with the Department of the Treasury at the address shown on the form. Form TD F 90-22.1 is not a tax return. *Do not file it with Form 1065.*

Attach a statement that gives the name(s) of the country or countries to which Question O applies if you need additional space to write in their names.

### Question P

#### Foreign Trusts

Check "Yes" if the partnership was a grantor of, or a transferor to, a foreign trust that existed during the tax year.

A U.S. partnership that has ever transferred property to a foreign trust may have to include the income from that property in the partnership's taxable income if the trust had a U.S. beneficiary during 1987. (See section 679.)

If the partnership transfers property to a foreign corporation as paid-in surplus or as a contribution to capital, or to a foreign trust or partnership, an excise tax is imposed under section 1491 (see **Form 926**, Return by a Transferor of Property to a Foreign Corporation, Foreign Estate or Trust, or Foreign Partnership). To avoid this excise tax, the partnership may choose to treat the transfer as a taxable sale or exchange as specified in section 1057.

### Questions Q and R

Answer these questions for the calendar year 1987, even if the partnership has a fiscal tax year. For example, enter for Question R the number of months during the 12 month period from 1/1/87 to 12/31/87 the partnership was in operation without regard to when the partnership's tax year begins or ends.

## Question S

### Form 8264

See **Registration of Tax Shelters** on page 2 of these instructions.

## Question T

### Consolidated Partnership Proceedings

Generally, for tax years beginning after September 3, 1982, the tax treatment of partnership items is determined at the partnership level in a consolidated partnership proceeding, rather than in separate proceedings with individual partners.

Check the box for Question **T** if any of the following apply:
● The partnership had more than 10 partners at any time during the tax year; or
● Any partner was a nonresident alien or was other than a natural person or estate; or
● Any partner's share of any partnership item was different from his or her share of any other partnership item; or
● The partnership has elected to be subject to the rules for consolidated partnership proceedings.

"Small partnerships" as defined in section 6231(a)(1)(B) are not subject to the rules for consolidated partnership proceedings, but may make an irrevocable election to be covered by them.

For more information on the consolidated partnership proceeding rules, see **Publication 556**, Examination of Returns, Appeal Rights, and Claims for Refund, and section 6231.

## Income

### (Lines 1a–8)

**Caution:** *Report only trade or business activity income on lines 1a–8. Do not report rental activity income or portfolio income on these lines.* Rental activity income and portfolio income are separately reported on Schedules K and K-1 (rental real estate activities are also reported on Schedule H).

A rental activity is any activity of renting property where payments are primarily for the use of tangible property. Rental activities include the performance of services that are an integral part of and incidental to the activity (e.g., a laundry room in a rental apartment building). Rental activities include the lease of personal and real property.

Rental activities do not include the lease of property other than tangible property, or activities where significant services are rendered. Generally, the operation of a hotel or similar transient lodging would not be treated as a rental activity and would be reported on line 1a of Form 1065.

Portfolio income includes interest, dividends, royalty, and annuity income not derived in the ordinary course of a trade or business, and gain or loss on the disposition of property held for investment. Portfolio income also includes income (such as interest) earned on working capital. It does not include amounts derived in the ordinary course of a trade or business. For example, interest on accounts receivable earned in the ordinary course of business is not portfolio income, and is reported on page 1 of Form 1065.

Also, do not include any income that is tax exempt on lines 1a–8.

A partnership that receives any exempt income other than interest, or holds any property or engages in any activity that produces exempt income, must attach to its return an itemized statement showing the amount of each type of exempt income, and the amount of expense allocated to each type.

Tax-exempt interest income, including exempt-interest dividends received as a shareholder in a mutual fund or other regulated investment company, is reported to the partners on a statement attached to Schedule K-1 for line 18 of Schedule K-1.

Also see the instructions for **Deductions** for expenses related to tax-exempt income.

If the partnership has been involved in bankruptcy, insolvency, or similar proceedings, see section 108, **Form 982,** Reduction of Tax Attributes Due to Discharge of Indebtedness, and **Publication 908,** Bankruptcy, for more information.

## Line 1a

### Gross Receipts or Sales

Enter gross receipts or sales from all trade or business operations. Do not include rental activity or portfolio income. Also, do not include income you are required to report on lines 4 through 7. For example, do not include gross receipts from farming on this line. Instead, show net profits (losses) from farming on line 5.

## Line 2

### Cost of Goods Sold and/or Operations

If the entry on line 2 of Form 1065 is for the cost of operations, complete Schedule A, even if inventories are not used. See the instructions for Schedule A.

## Line 3

### Gross Profit

If the partnership uses the installment method for reporting gross profit under section 453A, attach a schedule showing separately the following for the current year and the 3 preceding years: (a) gross sales; (b) cost of goods sold; (c) gross profits; (d) percentage of gross profits to gross sales; (e) amounts collected; and (f) gross profit on amount collected. Enter the total reportable gross profit on line 3 and refer to the schedule attached.

Partnerships that regularly sell real or personal property and use the installment method should see section 453C.
**Note:** *The installment method may no longer be used to report the sale of personal property under a revolving credit plan.*

## Line 4

### Ordinary Income (Loss) From Other Partnerships and Fiduciaries

Enter the amount shown on Schedule K-1 (Form 1065) or Schedule K-1 (Form 1041).

Do **not** include portfolio income or rental activity income (loss) from other partnerships and fiduciaries on this line. Instead, report these amounts on the applicable lines of Schedules K and K-1, or on Schedule H if the amount is from a rental real estate activity.

Consider shares of other items separately reported on Schedule K-1 issued by the other entity as if the items were realized or incurred by this partnership.

**Note:** *Partnerships must consider the rules of section 469 when reporting items from other partnerships or fiduciaries in which they are partners or beneficiaries. For example, portfolio income from other partnerships or fiduciaries must be reported as a separately stated item to partners in this partnership and should not be reported on page 1 of Form 1065. Also, other items of income (loss) from other partnerships in which this partnership has an interest as a limited partner are generally items from a passive activity to all partners in this partnership.*

If there is a loss from another partnership, the amount of the loss that may be claimed is subject to the limitations of sections 465 and 704(d), as appropriate.

If the tax year of your partnership does not coincide with the tax year of the other partnership or fiduciary, include the ordinary income (loss) from the other entity in the tax year in which the other entity's tax year ends.

**Note:** *Be sure to show the partnership's or fiduciary's name, address, and employer identification number on a separate statement attached to this return. If the amount entered is from more than one source, identify the amount from each source.*

## Line 5

### Net Farm Profit (Loss)

Enter the partnership's net profit (loss) from **Schedule F (Form 1040),** Farm Income and Expenses. Attach Schedule F (Form 1040) to Form 1065. Do **not** include on this line any farm profit (loss) from other partnerships. Report those amounts on line 4.

Also report the partnership's fishing income on this line.

A new rule applies to farm partnerships that use the cash method of accounting, and whose prepaid expenses for feed, seed, fertilizer, other farm supplies, and the cost of poultry are more than 50% of other deductible farming expenses. Generally, any such excess may be deducted only in the year the items are actually used or consumed. See section 464(f).

Farm syndicates (section 464(c)) are required to use the accrual method of accounting. See section 448.

If a corporation is a member of a partnership engaged in farming, see section 447.

For more information, get **Publication 225,** Farmer's Tax Guide.
**Note:** *The Act provides an exception to the section 263A rules that require capitalization of production expenses by certain partnerships engaged in farming. Partners, of partnerships which are not required to use the accrual method of accounting, may elect to deduct currently the production costs of plants and animals that were deductible under prior law. Because the election to deduct these expenses is made by the partner, farm partnerships that are not required to use the accrual method should not capitalize such production expenses but should instead separately state these expenses to the partner on Schedule K-1, line 18, item k. See temporary regulation section 1.263A-1T(c) for more information.*

**Page 7**

## Line 6

### Net Gain (Loss)

**Caution:** *Include only ordinary gains or losses from the sale, exchange, or involuntary conversion of assets used in a trade or business activity. Ordinary gains or losses from the sale, exchange, or involuntary conversion of rental activity assets will be reported separately on Schedules K and K-1, generally as a part of the net income (loss) from the rental activity.*

In addition to other ordinary gains or losses from **Form 4797,** Gains and Losses From Sales or Exchanges of Assets Used in a Trade or Business and Involuntary Conversions, that are reported on this line, a partnership that is a partner in another partnership must include on Form 4797 its share of ordinary gains (losses) from sales, exchanges, or involuntary or compulsory conversions (other than casualties or thefts) of the other partnership's trade or business assets.

Do not include any recapture of expense deduction for recovery property (section 179). See the instructions for Schedule K-1, line 18, item e, and the instructions for Form 4797 for more information.

Furnish a statement to general partners reflecting any passive activity amounts that are included on line 1 of the partner's Schedule K-1. Such amounts include the ordinary gain (loss) that is passed through to this partnership from its limited interest in another partnership.

## Line 7

### Other Income (Loss)

Enter any other taxable income (loss) from a trade or business activity not included on lines 1a through 6. Include taxable income from insurance proceeds. Also include on this line the amount of credit for alcohol used as a fuel that was entered on **Form 6478,** Credit for Alcohol Used as Fuel. In the margin, next to the total amount, enter the amount of the credit and the words "Alcohol Fuel Credit." Do not include those items requiring separate computations that must be reported on Schedules K and K-1. (See the Instructions for Schedules K and K-1 later in these instructions.)

If the partnership was required to convert from the reserve method to the specific charge-off method of accounting for bad debts, use line 7 to report the ratable amount of the required adjustment. Generally, the balance in the reserve for bad debts is to be included in income ratably over a 4-year period starting with the first tax year beginning after 1986. See section 805(d)(2) of the Act and Publication 548 for more information.

The partnership must include as other income the recapture amount for section 280F if the business use of listed property drops to 50% or less. See section 280F(b)(3). To figure the recapture amount, the partnership must complete Part V of Form 4797.

Do not report portfolio or rental activity income (loss) on this line.

## Deductions

### (Lines 9a–20)

**Caution:** *Include only trade or business activity deductions on lines 9a–20.* **Do not include any expenses of a rental activity or of portfolio income on these lines.** *Rental activity deductions and deductions allocable to portfolio income are separately reported on Schedules K and K-1. See the instructions under* **Income** *on page 7 for more information on rental activities and portfolio income.*

Do not include any nondeductible amounts (such as expenses connected with the production of tax-exempt income) on lines 9a–20.

If an expense is connected with both taxable income and nontaxable income, allocate a reasonable part of the expense to each kind of income. (See section 265.)

Do not take a deduction for any qualified expenditures to which an election under section 59(e) applies. See the instructions for Schedules K and K-1, line 18, item f, for information on where to report these amounts.

**Note:** *Do not deduct in this section items which section 702 and the regulations require that the partnership state separately and which require separate computations made by the partners. An example is the section 212 expenses incurred for the production of income instead of in a trade or business. Other examples include charitable contributions, foreign taxes paid, intangible drilling and development costs, soil and water conservation expenditures, and exploration expenditures. The distributive shares of these expenses are reported as separate items to each partner on Schedule K-1. See the instructions for Schedules K and K-1 later in these instructions for more information on these and other items requiring separate computations by the partners.*

### Organization and Syndication Expenses

Amounts paid or incurred to organize a partnership or promote the sale of an interest in a partnership are capital expenditures. They are not deductible as a current expense.

Under section 709, the partnership may choose to amortize the organization expenses over a period of 60 or more months, beginning with the month in which the partnership begins business. (Include the amortization expense on line 19.) On the balance sheet (Schedule L) show the unamortized balance of organization costs and all syndication expenditures (if Schedule L is required). See the instructions for line 10 for the treatment of these amounts paid to a partner.

See section 195 for the capitalization of start-up expenditures.

Syndication costs incurred in connection with the sale of limited partnership interests are chargeable to the capital account and cannot be amortized by the partnership. See Revenue Ruling 85-32, C. B. 1985-1, 186.

### Uniform Capitalization Rules

Section 263A provides uniform rules for determining which expenses must be included in inventory costs and which expenses must be capitalized (in the case of property other than inventory). These rules apply to:

- real or tangible personal property produced by the partnership for use in its trade or business or in an activity engaged in for profit.
- real or tangible personal property produced by the partnership to be held in inventory or for sale in the ordinary course of business.
- real property acquired for resale. The rules also apply to tangible or intangible personal property acquired for resale if the partnership's average annual gross receipts for the 3 prior tax years exceed $10,000,000.

Partnerships subject to these rules are required to capitalize not only direct costs but also an allocable portion of most indirect costs (including taxes) that benefit the assets produced or acquired for resale. Generally, interest expense paid or incurred in the course of production must be capitalized and is governed by special rules.

The costs required to be capitalized under section 263A are not reported until the property to which the costs relate is sold, used, or otherwise disposed of by the partnership.

The uniform capitalization rules do not apply to timber, property produced under a long-term contract, research and experimental costs under section 174, and certain developmental and intangible costs of oil and gas or geothermal wells or other mineral property allowable as a deduction. Special rules apply to farm partnerships.

The rules do not apply to property which is produced for use by the partnership if substantial construction occurred before March 1, 1986. The uniform capitalization rules are generally effective for costs and interest paid or incurred after December 31, 1986. With respect to inventory, the rules apply to tax years beginning after 1986.

## Line 9a

### Salaries and Wages

Do not enter salaries and wages reported elsewhere, such as on Schedule A, line 3; on line 18a; or those allocable to other than a trade or business activity.

## Line 9b

### Jobs Credit

Enter the total amount of the jobs credit computed by the partnership. Subtract this from the salaries and wages shown on line 9a. See the Instructions for **Form 5884,** Jobs Credit, to figure the amount of credit to enter on line 9b.

## Line 10

### Guaranteed Payments to Partners

Deduct payments or credits to a partner for services or for the use of capital if the payments or credits are determined without regard to partnership income and are allocable to a trade or business activity. Do not do this if the payments and credits should be capitalized. Do not include distributive shares of partnership profits. Report the guaranteed payments to the appropriate partners on Schedule K-1, line 5.

Although payments or credits to a partner for services rendered in organizing a partnership may be guaranteed payments under section 707, they are not deductible on line 10. They are capital expenditures.

However, they should be separately reported on Schedule K-1, line 5.

## Line 11

### Rent

Enter rent paid on business property which is used in a trade or business activity. Do not deduct rent for a dwelling unit occupied by any partner for personal use.

## Line 12

### Interest

Include only interest incurred in the trade or business activity(ies) of the partnership that is not claimed elsewhere on the return.

Do not include interest expense on debt used to purchase rental property or debt used in a rental activity. Interest allocable to a rental real estate activity is reported on Schedule H and is used in arriving at net income (loss) from rental real estate activity(ies) on line 2 of Schedules K and K-1. Interest allocable to a rental activity other than a rental real estate activity is included on line 3b of Schedule K and is used in arriving at net income (loss) from a rental activity (other than a rental real estate activity). This net amount is reported on line 3c of Schedule K and line 3 of Schedule K-1.

Do not include interest expense on debt used to buy property held for investment. Do not include interest expense that is clearly and directly allocable to interest, dividend, royalty, or annuity income not derived in the ordinary course of a trade or business.

Interest paid or incurred on debt used to buy investment property is reported on line 16a of Schedules K and K-1. See the instructions for line 16a of Schedules K and K-1 and Form 4952 for more information on investment property.

Regulation section 1.163-8T gives rules for allocating interest expense among activities so that the passive activity limitation (section 469), investment interest limitation, and the personal interest limitation can be properly computed. Generally, interest expense is allocated in the same manner as debt is allocated. Debt is allocated by tracing disbursements of the debt proceeds to specific expenditures. These regulations give rules for tracing debt proceeds to expenditures.

The regulations also provide transitional rules. One of these transitional rules provides that interest on certain business or rental activity debt outstanding on December 31, 1986, may be allocated in the same manner as in prior years if the partnership allocates the debt in a reasonable and consistent manner. Generally, the partnership must specify how the debt is allocated by attaching a statement to its Form 1065 for the first taxable year beginning after 1986. This statement should be labeled "Transitional Allocation Statement Under Section 1.163-8T(n)(3)" and should include the following information: (1) a description of the activity; (2) the amount of debt allocated; (3) the assets among which the debt is allocated; (4) the manner in which the debt is allocated; and (5) the amount of debt allocated to each asset. The partnership may elect, however, not to use this transitional rule and instead allocate the debt based on the use of debt proceeds. The election not to apply the transitional

rule is made by attaching a statement to the Form 1065 filed for the partnership's first tax year beginning after 1986. This statement should be identified as "Election Out Under Section 1.163-8T(n)(3)."

**Note:** *Interest paid by a partnership to a partner for the use of capital should be entered on line 10. Generally, prepaid interest can only be deducted over the period to which the prepayment applies (section 461(g)). Interest incurred during contruction or improvement of real property, personal property that has a class life of 20 years or more, or other tangible property requiring more than 2 years (1 year in the case of property costing more than $1 million) to produce or construct generally must be capitalized. See section 263A for more information (section 189 is repealed). The limitations on deductions for unpaid interest are in regulation section 1.267(b)-1(b).*

## Line 13

### Taxes

Enter taxes paid or incurred on business property for carrying on a trade or business only if not included elsewhere on the return or on Schedules K and K-1. Federal import duties and Federal excise and stamp taxes are deductible only if paid or incurred in carrying on the trade or business of the partnership.

Do not deduct taxes assessed against local benefits that increase the value of the property assessed (such as for paving, etc.). Federal income taxes, estate, inheritance, legacy, succession, and gift taxes, or taxes reported elsewhere.

Do not report taxes allocable to portfolio income or to a rental activity on line 13. Taxes allocable to a rental real estate activity are reported on Schedule H. Taxes allocable to a rental activity other than a rental real estate activity are reported on line 3b of Schedule K. Taxes allocable to portfolio income are reported on line 10 of Schedules K and K-1.

See new section 263A for rules on capitalization of inventory, construction, and development costs (including taxes) incurred after 1986.

**Note:** *State and local sales tax paid or accrued in connection with the acquisition or disposition of business property must be added to the cost of the property, or, in the case of a disposition, subtracted from the amount realized. See section 164*

## Line 14

### Bad Debts

The Act generally repealed the reserve method of computing bad debts for tax years beginning after 1986, except for certain financial organizations.

As a result of the repeal of the reserve method, most partnerships will have to use the specific charge-off method of accounting for bad debts, and deduct business bad debts when they become wholly or partially worthless.

Any change from the reserve method of accounting for bad debts is treated as a change of accounting method initiated by the partnership with the consent of IRS. The balance in any reserve for bad debts is generally to be included in income ratably over a 4-year period. See the instructions for line 7 and Publication 548 for more information.

## Line 15

### Repairs

Enter the cost of incidental repairs related to a trade or business activity, such as labor and supplies, that do not add to the value of the property or appreciably prolong its life. New buildings, machinery, or permanent improvements that increase the value of the property are not deductible. They are chargeable to capital accounts and may be depreciated or amortized.

## Line 16

### Depreciation

On line 16a enter **only** the total depreciation claimed on assets used in a trade or business activity. Complete and attach Form 4562. See Form 4562 and the related instructions and **Publication 534**, Depreciation, for more information.

Do not include any expense deduction for recovery property (section 179) on this line. This amount is not deducted by the partnership because it is passed through separately to the partners on line 9 of Schedule K-1.

## Line 17

### Depletion

If the partnership claims a deduction for timber depletion, complete and attach **Form T**, Forest Industries Schedules.

Do not report depletion deductions for oil and gas properties on this line. Each partner figures depletion on these properties under section 613A(c)(7)(D). See the instructions for Schedules K and K-1, line 18, item c, for the information on oil and gas depletion that must be supplied to the partners by the partnership.

## Line 18a

### Retirement Plans, etc.

Do not deduct on this line payments for partners to retirement or deferred compensation plans including IRAs, Keoghs, and SEPs. These amounts are reported on Schedule K-1, line 11. The partners deduct these payments on their own returns.

Enter the deductible contributions made by the partnership for its common-law employees under a qualified pension, profit-sharing, annuity, or Simplified Employee Pension plan (SEP), and under any other deferred compensation plan.

If the partnership contributes to an Individual Retirement Arrangement (IRA) for employees, include the contribution in compensation on page 1, line 9a, or Schedule A, line 3, not on line 18a.

Employers who maintain a pension, profit-sharing, or other funded deferred compensation plan (other than a SEP), whether or not the plan is qualified under the Internal Revenue Code and whether or not a deduction is claimed for the current year, generally are required to file one of the following forms:

- **Form 5500**, Annual Return/Report of Employee Benefit Plan, for each plan with 100 or more participants.
- **Form 5500-C**, Return/Report of Employee Benefit Plan; or **Form 5500-R**, Registration Statement of Employee Benefit Plan, for each plan with fewer than 100 participants.

- **Form 5500EZ**, Annual Return of One-Participant (Owners and Their Spouses) Pension Benefit Plan, for each plan which covers only partners or partners and their spouses.

There are penalties for not filing these forms on time.

## Line 18b
### Employee Benefit Programs

Enter the partnership's contributions to employee benefit programs for common-law employees which are not part of the retirement plans included on line 18a, such as contributions for insurance, health, and welfare programs.

Also include the partnership's contributions to a qualified group legal services plan established for the exclusive benefit of employees (including partners) or their spouses or dependents. The plan must be a separate written plan designed to provide specified benefits of personal legal services through prepayment of, or provision in advance for, legal fees in whole or in part by the employer.

**Note:** *Section 120, which provided an exclusion for employees of contributions and legal services provided by employers, does not apply to taxable years ending after 12/31/87.*

## Line 19
### Other Deductions

Enter any other authorized deductions related to a trade or business activity for which there is no line on page 1 of Form 1065.

Do not include those items requiring separate computation that must be reported on Schedule K-1.

Do not include qualified expenditures to which an election under section 59(e) applies.

**Note for travel and entertainment expenses:** *Generally, the amount allowable to the partnership as a deduction for meal and entertainment expenses is limited to 80% of the amount that would otherwise be allowable as a deduction. This limitation (section 274(n)) generally is applied after determining the amount of the otherwise allowable deduction under section 162, which permits a deduction for ordinary and necessary expenses, and other provisions of section 274 which disallow a deduction for certain entertainment expenses. Expenditures for meals or beverages are disallowed to the extent that they are lavish or extravagant.*

*Because of the phase-in provision of section 274(l)(2), skybox rental expense will generally have to be separately stated on line 11 of Schedules K and K-1. See the instructions for line 11 of Schedules K and K-1 for more information on skybox expense.*

*The rules for deductible expenses for luxury water travel, convention expenses, and tickets for entertainment have also been changed. For example, no deduction is allowed for travel, meals, and lodging expense incurred in connection with attending an investment seminar or similar meeting. The Act repealed the deduction formerly allowable under section 212 for such expenses. The partnership cannot deduct or pass through to partners these expenses.*

**Page 10**

Also the partnership may not deduct any expense paid or incurred for a facility (such as a yacht or hunting lodge) that is used for an activity that is usually considered entertainment, amusement, or recreation. (The partnership may be able to deduct the expense if the amount is treated as compensation and reported on Form W-2 for an employee or on Form 1099-MISC for an independent contractor.)

*See **Publication 463**, Travel, Entertainment, and Gift Expenses, and **Publication 917**, Business Use of a Car, for more details.*

### Amortization

Enter the amount from Form 4562, Part II, except for section 59(e) amounts (see the instructions for Schedules K and K-1, line 18, item f). If the partnership elects the deduction for amortization of certain expenditures for research and experiments (section 174), or mine or natural deposit development (section 616), file a statement with the return.

The instructions for Form 4562 provide code section references for specific amortizable property. See also Publication 535 for more information on amortization.

**Note:** *The Act repealed the election to amortize certain expenditures related to a trademark or trade name.*

# Schedule A
## Cost of Goods Sold and/or Operations

## Line 2
### Purchases

Show withdrawals for personal use on Schedules M and K-1 (Question I) as distributions to partners, if Schedule M and Question I are required.

## Lines 8a—8c
### Valuation Methods

Your inventories can be valued at:

- cost;

- cost or market value (whichever is lower); or

- any other method approved by the Commissioner of Internal Revenue that conforms with the provisions of the applicable regulations cited below.

Taxpayers using erroneous valuation methods should request permission to change to a method permitted for Federal tax purposes. For more information regarding the change, see regulation section 1.446-1(e)(3) and Revenue Procedure 84-74, 1984-2 C.B. 738.

Check the method(s) used for valuing inventories on line 8a. Under "lower of cost or market," market generally applies to normal market conditions when there is a current bid price prevailing at the date the inventory is valued. When no regular open market exists or when quotations are nominal because of inactive market conditions, use fair market prices from the most reliable sales or purchase transactions that occurred near the date the inventory is valued. For additional requirements, see regulation section 1.471-4.

Inventory may be valued below cost when the merchandise is unsalable at normal prices or unusable in the normal way

because the goods are "subnormal" (that is, because of damage, imperfections, shop wear, etc.) within the meaning of regulation section 1.471-2(c). Such goods may be valued at a current bona fide selling price minus the direct cost of disposition (but not less than scrap value) if the taxpayer can establish such a price. See regulation section 1.471-2(c) for additional requirements.

On line 8a(iv), indicate whether you used a method of inventory valuation other than those described on line 8a(i), (ii), or (iii), and attach a statement describing the method used.

If this is the first year the "Last-in First-out" (LIFO) inventory method was either adopted or extended to inventory goods not previously valued under the LIFO method provided in section 472, attach **Form 970**, Application To Use LIFO Inventory Methods, or a statement with the information required by Form 970. Also check the LIFO box on line 8b.

If you have changed or extended your inventory method to LIFO and have had to "write up" your opening inventory to cost in the year of election, report the effect of this write up as income (line 7, page 1, Form 1065) proportionately over a 3-year period that begins in the tax year you made this election (section 472(d)).

**Section 263A Uniform Capitalization Rules.**—The uniform capitalization rules of section 263A are discussed in general on page 8. These rules apply to real and tangible personal property produced by the partnership to be held in inventory or for sale in the ordinary course of business. These rules also apply to real property acquired for resale and generally to tangible and intangible personal property acquired for resale. The rules do not apply to personal property acquired for resale unless the partnership's average annual gross receipts for the 3 preceding tax years exceeded $10 million.

Partnerships subject to section 263A will be required to make adjustments to the cost of goods sold computation on Schedule A. To the extent that section 263A costs were not included in inventory in prior years, partnerships must revalue their beginning inventory. Partnerships may elect one of the simplified methods of accounting for section 263A costs provided in the regulations for purposes of both revaluing their inventory and accounting for costs in subsequent years. Absent the election of a simplified method, partnerships are required to allocate additional costs to be included in inventory under section 263A with the same degree of specificity as was required of inventoriable costs under prior law. The following instructions are for partnerships required to use the rules of section 263A.

**Line 1.**—Beginning inventory as of the effective date must be revalued as if the section 263A rules had been in effect for all prior periods. Enter the revalued beginning inventory on line 1. An adjustment to income is required under section 481. This adjustment should be included on page 1, line 7, "Other income (loss)," and separately identified on an attached schedule. The section 481 adjustment is taken into account over a period not to exceed 4 years. In addition, since the application of section 263A is considered to be a change in accounting method, partnerships are required to complete Form 3115 to show their computation of the section 481 adjustment. Attach Form 3115 to Form 1065. Be sure to use the 1987 revision of Form 3115. See the regulations for more information on revaluing beginning inventory.

**Line 4a.**—An entry on this line is required only for partnerships electing a simplified method. In the case of partnerships electing the simplified production method, additional section 263A costs are generally those costs, other than interest, that were not capitalized or included in inventory costs under the taxpayer's method of accounting immediately prior to the effective date in regulation section 1.263A-1T but that are now required to be capitalized under section 263A. Interest is to be accounted for separately. In the case of partnerships electing the simplified resale method, additional section 263A costs are generally "those costs incurred with respect to the following categories, off-site storage or warehousing; purchasing; handling, processing, assembly, and repacking; and general and administrative costs (mixed service costs)." Enter on line 4a the balance of section 263A costs paid or incurred during the taxable year not included on lines 2 and 3. See regulation section 1.263A-1T for more information.

**Line 4b.**—Enter on line 4b any costs paid or incurred during the taxable year not entered on lines 2 through 4a.

**Line 6.**—See regulation section 1.263A-1T for more information on computing the amount of additional section 263A costs to be capitalized and added to ending inventory

## Schedule H
### Income (Loss) From Rental Real Estate Activity(ies)

Use Schedule H to report the income and deductible expenses of any rental real estate activity.

A rental real estate activity is any activity of renting real property where the payments are principally for the use of the property Rental real estate activities do not include activities where significant services are rendered. Generally, the operation of a hotel or similar transient lodging would not be treated as a rental activity and would be reported on page 1, line 1a, of Form 1065 See section 469, the related regulations, and Publication 925 for more information on rental activities.

● Do not report income or expenses on Schedule H which are reported on page 1 of Form 1065. Only trade or business activity amounts are reported on page 1.

● Do not report portfolio income or expenses on Schedule H.

● Do not report rental activity other than rental real estate activity income or expense on Schedule H

● Do not report on Schedule H expense deductions for recovery property (section 179), charitable contributions, or other items which must be reported separately to partners.

Report rental real estate activity income (loss) from other partnerships or fiduciaries on line 2 of Schedule H. Identify the other partnership or fiduciary by name, address,

and employer identification number on line 1 of Schedule H or on an attachment.

Report on line 2 ordinary gains or losses from the sale, exchange, or involuntary conversion of rental real estate activity assets. This amount comes from Form 4797, line 18.

## Schedule L
### Balance Sheets

**Note:** *Domestic partnerships with 10 or fewer partners may not have to complete Schedule L. See the instructions for Question M for the specific requirements to qualify for this exception.*

The amounts shown should agree with the partnership's primary books and records. Attach a statement explaining any differences.

Partnerships reporting to the Interstate Commerce Commission or to any national, state, municipal, or other public officer may send copies of their balance sheets prescribed by the Commission or state or municipal authorities, as of the beginning and end of the tax year, instead of completing Schedule L. However, statements filed under this procedure must contain sufficient information to enable the IRS to reconstruct a balance sheet similar to that contained on Form 1065 without contacting the partnership during processing.

**Line 17.** Nonrecourse loans are those liabilities of the partnership for which none of the partners have any personal liability.

See Revenue Ruling 84-5, 1984-1 C.B. 32, for information on partnerships that purchase timeshare units in a vacation home with a nonrecourse obligation before deducting any interest that accrues on the obligation.

See Revenue Ruling 84-118, 1984–2 C.B. 120, for information on a limited partner's basis when there is a partially nonrecourse note.

A limited partner's basis is not increased by a share of the limited partnership's liability when the general partner has personally guaranteed a nonrecourse loan to the partnership.

## Schedule M and Question I, Schedule K-1
### Reconciliation of Partners' Capital Accounts

**Note:** *Domestic partnerships with 10 or fewer partners may not have to complete Schedule M or Question I (Schedule K-1). See the instructions for Question M for the specific requirements to qualify for this exception.*

Show what caused the changes in the partners' capital accounts during the tax year.

The amounts shown should agree with the partnership's books and records and the balance sheet amounts. Attach a statement explaining any differences.

Also, the amounts on Schedule M should equal the total of the amounts reported in Question I of all the partners' Schedules K-1

Include in column (d) income reported in the partnership's books but not included in column (c). Also use column (d) to make

additions to the capital account for differences between tax accounting and book accounting. Examples of amounts to be included in column (d) include tax-exempt interest, other tax-exempt income, and allowable deductions used by the partnership to figure the amount shown in column (c) but not charged against book income this year.

Include in column (e) losses and deductions reported in the partnership's books but not included in column (c). Also use column (e) to make reductions to the capital account for differences between tax accounting and book accounting. Examples of amounts to be included in column (e) include investment interest expense, deductions related to portfolio income, expenses connected with the production of tax-exempt income, charitable contributions, and income included in column (c) but not recorded in the partnership's books this year. Do not show the amount in column (e) in parentheses.

Include in column (f) withdrawals from purchases for personal use. Do not show the amount in parentheses. Any withdrawal by a nonresident alien partner is subject to income tax withholding at the source. See **Payments Subject to Withholding at Source** for more information.

See **Windfall Profit Tax** for how to report any windfall profit tax.

**Note:** *If Schedule M and Question I are not required, see the instructions for Schedules K and K-1, line 18, item i.*

## Schedules K and K-1
### Partners' Shares of Income, Credits, Deductions, etc.

#### Purpose of Schedules

**Schedule K** (page 3 of Form 1065) is a summary schedule of all the partners' shares of the partnership's income, credits, deductions, etc. **Schedule K-1 (Form 1065)** shows each partner's separate share. One copy of each K-1 is attached to the Form 1065 filed with the Internal Revenue Service. One copy is kept with a copy of the partnership return as a part of the partnership's records. One copy is given to each partner.

**Note:** *Be sure to give each partner a copy of either the Partner's Instructions for Schedule K-1 (Form 1065) or specific instructions for each item reported on the partner's Schedule K-1 (Form 1065).*

#### General Instructions

Although the partnership is not subject to income tax, the members are liable for tax on their shares of the partnership income, whether or not distributed, and must include their share on their tax returns.

Schedules K and K-1 have the same line numbers. In addition, Schedule K-1 has Questions A through I, and line 19.

#### Substitute Forms

You do not need IRS approval to use a substitute Schedule K-1 if it is an exact facsimile of the IRS schedule, or if it contains only those lines the taxpayer is required to use, and the lines have the same

**Page 11**

numbers and titles and are in the same order as on the comparable IRS Schedule K-1. In either case, your substitute schedule must include the OMB number and the Partner's Instructions for Schedule K-1 (Form 1065) or other prepared specific instructions.

Other substitute Schedules K-1 require approval. You may apply for approval of a substitute form by writing to: Internal Revenue Service, Attention: D:R:R, 1111 Constitution Avenue, NW, Washington, DC 20224.

Each taxpayer's information must be on a separate sheet of paper. Therefore, all continuously printed substitutes must be separated before filing with the Service.

You may be subject to a penalty if you file Schedules K-1 with the Service not conforming to the specifications of Revenue Procedure 87-11, 1987-4, I.R.B. 30.

**Note:** *Separate Partner's Instructions for Schedule K-1 (Form 1065) are available at most IRS offices. This version can be attached to your substitute Schedule K-1.*

### How Income Is Shared Among Partners

Income (loss) is allocated to a partner only for the part of the year in which that person is a member of the partnership. The partnership will either allocate on a daily basis or divide the partnership year into segments and allocate income, loss, or special items in each segment among the persons who were partners during that segment. Partnerships reporting their income on the cash basis method and during the year having a change in any partner's interest in the partnership must allocate interest expense, tax expense, any payment for services or for the use of property on a daily basis. (See section 706 for more information and for the termination of a partner's interest.)

Allocate shares of income, gain, loss, deduction, or credit among the partners according to the partnership agreement for sharing income or loss generally. If the partners agree, specific items may be allocated among them in a ratio different from the ratio for sharing income or loss generally. For instance, if the net income exclusive of specially allocated items is divided evenly among three partners but some special items are allocated 50% to one, 30% to another, and 20% to the third partner, report the special items on the appropriate line of the applicable partner's Schedule K-1 and the total on the appropriate line of Schedule K instead of on the numbered lines on page 1 of Form 1065 or Schedules A or D.

If the partnership agreement does not provide for the partner's share of income, gain, loss, deduction, or credit, or if the allocation under the agreement does not have substantial economic effect, the partner's share is determined according to the partner's interest in the partnership. Regulations for section 704(b) provide rules and regulations relating to the substantial economic effect test and to the determination of a partner's interest in the partnership.

**Note:** *If a partner's interest changed during the year, see section 706(d) before determining each partner's distributive share of any item of income, gain, loss,*

deduction, etc. Also, see the regulations under sections 861 and 882 relating to the allocation and apportionment of partnership expenses for purposes of determining taxable income from specific sources or activities.

## Specific Instructions
### Schedule K Only

**Note:** *Schedule K is part of Form 1065 this year. Schedule K is required to be completed by all partnerships (including those with 10 or fewer partners). We have made this change because of the rules of new Section 469. In order for partners to comply with those rules, trade or business activity income (loss), rental activity income (loss), and portfolio income must be considered separately by the partner. Rental activity income (loss) and portfolio income are not reported on page 1 of Form 1065 so that these amounts are not combined with trade or business activity income (loss). The Schedule K is used to report the totals of these (and other) amounts.*

### Schedule K-1 Only

Prepare and give a Schedule K-1 to each person who was a partner in the partnership at any time during the year, on or before the day on which the partnership return is filed.
**Note:** *Under section 6031(c) any person who holds an interest in a partnership as a nominee for another person is required to furnish to the partnership the name, address, etc., of the other person (beneficial holder of the interest).*

If a husband and wife each had an interest in the partnership, you must prepare a separate Schedule K-1 for each of them.

If a husband and wife held an interest together, prepare one Schedule K-1 if the two of them are considered to be one partner.

On each Schedule K-1, enter the names, addresses, and identifying numbers of the partner and partnership and the partner's distributive share of each item.

For an individual partner you must enter the partner's social security number. For all other partners you must enter their employer identification number. (However, if a partner is an individual retirement arrangement (IRA), enter the identifying number of the custodian of the IRA. Do not enter the social security number of the person for whom the IRA is maintained.)
**Note:** *Space has been provided on page 2 of Schedule K-1 for you to provide information to the partners. This space may be used in lieu of attachments.*

**Special reporting requirements for passive activities.**—If items of income, loss, deduction, or credit from more than one activity are reported on Schedule K-1, the partnership must attach a statement to Schedule K-1 for each activity which is a passive activity to the partner. Rental activities are passive activities to all partners; trade or business activities are passive activities to general partners who do not materially participate in the activity and to limited partners.

The attachment must include the following information:

1. A statement that the attachment is a break down by activity of passive activity amounts included on Schedule K-1.

2. The identity of the specific activity and the type of passive activity (i.e., trade or business, rental real estate, or other rental).

3. The income, loss, deduction, or credit from the activity and the line on Schedule K-1 in which that amount is included.

4. If the statement is for a rental real estate activity and the partner is a general partner who actively participates in some but not all such activities, a statement as to whether or not the partner actively participates in this specific rental real estate activity. (See the instructions for Question A(3) of Schedule K-1).

5. If applicable, a statement that the activity commenced after October 22, 1986. (See the instructions for Question G(2) of Schedule K-1).

6. If the partner's ownership interest in the partnership increased after October 22, 1986, a statement of how much of the income, loss, deduction, or credit from the activity is attributable to that increase. This statement is only for activities commenced by the partnership before October 23, 1986. (See the instructions for Question G(1) of Schedule K-1).

7. If applicable, a statement that the partnership disposed of its interest in the activity in a fully taxable disposition to an unrelated party. See the paragraph which follows.

If the partnership disposed of its entire interest in an activity, in a fully taxable disposition to an unrelated party, the partnership must advise partners, for whom the activity was a passive activity, of the disposition and identify the activity disposed of. This notification is necessary so that the partner can apply the rules of section 469(g) which allow the partner to use losses unallowed in previous years because of the passive activity limitations. See the instructions for Form 8582 for more information on dispositions.

### Question A

Question A(1) must be answered for all partners. (If a partner holds interests as both a general and limited partner attach a schedule for each activity which shows the amounts from the partner's interest as a limited partner).

Questions A(2) and A(3) are to be answered only for partners who hold an interest as a general partner. These questions are asked to enable the partner to apply the passive activity rules of section 469. Questions A(2) and A(3) apply only to general partners because limited partners are not considered to materially or actively participate in the activities of the partnership. However, see "Exception for qualified low-income housing projects" on page 13.

**Question A(2).**—Check "Yes" if the partner materially participates in ALL trade or business activities of the partnership. (See "Exception for working interests in oil and gas properties" below). In general, a partner is treated as materially participating in an activity only if the partner is involved in the operations of the activity on a regular, continuous, and substantial basis. The participation of a partner's spouse is taken into consideration in applying the material participation standard. See section 469, the related regulations, and the instructions for Form 8582 for more information. Also see section 469 for the definition of material participation regarding partners that are closely held corporations or personal service corporations.

Check "No" if the partner did not materially participate in all trade or business activities. It is possible for a partner to materially participate in some business activities of the partnership and not in others. If the partner materially participated in some but not all trade or business activities, see **Special reporting requirements for passive activities,** above.

*Exception for working interests in oil and gas property.* — *The passive activity rules of section 469 do not apply to certain working interests in oil or gas property. A partner whose liabilities are not limited with regard to oil or gas property is considered to have a working interest. Therefore, if the activity to which Question A(2) applies is a working interest in oil or gas property, check the "Yes" block for Question A(2).*

**Question A(3).** — Check "Yes" if the partner actively participates in ALL rental real estate activities of the partnership. (See "Exception for qualified low-income housing projects," below.) Generally, a partner is not considered to actively participate in a rental real estate activity, if at any time during the year (or shorter relevant period), the value of the partner's (including any interest of the spouse of the partner) interest in the activity is less than 10% of all interests in the activity.

If the partner meets the 10% test, the partner will be considered to actively participate so long as he or she participates, for example, in the making of management decisions or arranging for others to provide services (such as repairs), in a significant and bona fide sense.

Check "No" if the partner did not actively participate in all rental real estate activities. If the partnership has more than one rental real estate activity see **Special reporting requirements for passive activities,** on page 12.

*Exception for qualified low-income housing projects.* — *The passive activity rules of section 469 do not apply to losses from a qualified low-income housing project for any tax year in the relief period. See section 502 of the Act for a definition of a qualified low-income housing project and the relief period. Attach a statement to Schedule K-1 (or use the information space provided on page 2 of Schedule K-1) to identify any line 2 loss that is attributable to a qualified low-income housing project. Check the "Yes" box if the activity to which Question A(3) relates is a qualified low-income housing project.*

## Question B
### Partner's Share of Liabilities

Enter each partner's share of nonrecourse liabilities and other liabilities. **Nonrecourse liabilities** are those liabilities of the partnership for which none of the partners has any personal liability. See the **Note** below for the special rule for qualified nonrecourse financing. If the partner terminated his or her interest in the partnership during the year, enter the share that existed immediately before the total disposition. In all other cases, enter it as of the end of the year.

If the partnership is engaged in two or more different types of at-risk activities, or a combination of at-risk activities and any other activity, attach a statement showing the partner's share of nonrecourse liabilities and other liabilities for **each** activity. See sections 465(c)(2) and (3) and Publication 925 to determine if the partnership is engaged in more than one at-risk activity.

If a partnership is engaged in an activity subject to the limitations of section 465(c)(1) (i.e., films or video tapes, leasing section 1245 property, farming, or oil and gas property), give each partner his or her share of the total pre-1976 loss(es) from that activity for which there existed a corresponding amount of nonrecourse liability at the end of each year in which the loss(es) occurred. See **Form 6198,** Computation of Deductible Loss From an Activity Described in Section 465(c), and related instructions for more information.
**Note:** The Act extended the at-risk rules to real property (see **Changes You Should Note**). The Act also provided an exception for "qualified" nonrecourse financing that is secured by real property used in an activity of holding real property. The partner is considered at-risk for "qualified" nonrecourse amounts.

Qualified nonrecourse financing generally includes financing that is secured by real property and that is loaned or guaranteed by a Federal, state or local government or borrowed from a "qualified" person. Qualified persons include any person actively and regularly engaged in the business of lending money, such as a bank or savings and loan association. Qualified persons generally do not include related parties (unless the nonrecourse financing is commercially reasonable and on substantially the same terms as loans involving unrelated persons), the seller of the property, or a person who receives a fee because of the investment in the real property. See section 465 and Publication 925 for more information on qualified nonrecourse financing.

Enter the partner's share of partnership-level qualified nonrecourse financing on the **other** line of Question B. The partner as well as the partnership must meet the qualified nonrecourse rules. Therefore, the partnership must attach a statement to Schedule K-1 (or use the space provided on page 2 of Schedule K-1) to identify partnership-level qualified nonrecourse financing included in Question B. The statement must include the information the partner needs to determine if the qualified nonrecourse rules are also met at the partner level.

## Question C
### What Type of Entity Is This Partner?

State on this line whether the partner is an individual, a corporation, a fiduciary, a partnership, an exempt organization, or a nominee (custodian). If a nominee indicate the type of entity the nominee represents:
I—Individual; C—Corporation;
F—Fiduciary; P—Partnership;
E—Exempt Organization; or
IRA—Individual Retirement Arrangement.

## Question D
### Partner's Profit, Loss, and Capital Sharing Percentages

Enter in Question D, column (ii), the percentages existing at the end of the year.

However, if a partner's interest terminated during the year, enter in column (i) the percentages that existed immediately before the termination. When the profit or loss sharing percentage has changed during the year, show the prechange percentage in column (i) and the end of year percentage in column (ii). If there are multiple changes in the profit and loss sharing percentage during the year, attach a statement giving the date and percentage before each change. "Ownership of capital" means the portion of the capital that the partner would receive if the partnership was liquidated at year end by the distribution of undivided interests in partnership assets and liabilities.

## Question F
### Tax Shelter Registration Number

The partnership must complete this line for all partners, if applicable. If the partnership invested in a registration-required shelter, the partnership must also attach a copy of its Form 8271 to Schedule K-1. If the partnership itself is a tax shelter, it must identify the type of tax shelter on an attachment to Schedule K-1 or the space provided on page 2 of Schedule K-1. See Form 8271 for a list of the types of tax shelters and for more information.

## Question G

These questions should be answered only for partners to whom passive activity income, loss, deduction, or credit is passed through. The information is needed by partners to apply the phase-in relief provisions of section 469. Interests in passive activities acquired by the partner on or before October 22, 1986, are eligible for phase-in relief of the passive loss rules. Interests acquired after October 22, 1986, do not qualify for phase-in relief (unless there was a contractual obligation on October 22, 1986, to purchase the interest).

Therefore, if a partner first acquires an interest in the partnership after October 22, 1986, or a partner's ownership interest is increased after October 22, 1986, the portion of his or her interest attributable to that new interest or increase does not qualify for phase-in relief. For example, if after that date a partner increases his or her ownership interest from 25% to 50%, only the losses and credits attributable to the 25% interest held prior to October 23, 1986, will qualify for the phase-in relief.

Generally, to qualify for the phase-in relief, the interest held by the partner must be in an activity which had commenced by October 22, 1986. If the partnership commences a new activity after that date, the new activity does not qualify for phase-in relief (unless on or before August 16, 1986, the partnership entered into a binding contract to acquire assets used to conduct the activity, or construction of the property used in the activity began).
**Question G(1).** — Check "Yes" if a partner's percentage of ownership interest in the partnership increased after October 22, 1986. Phase-in relief applies only with respect to the percentage of ownership interest held by the partner on 10/22/86 and at all times thereafter. For example, if a partner reduces his or her ownership interest after 10/22/86 from 20% to 10%,

and subsequently purchased additional interests restoring his or her share to 20%, then Question G(1) should be checked "Yes," and only the 10% interest held throughout qualifies for phase-in relief.

If Question G(1) is checked "Yes," also attach a statement to Schedule K-1, for Question G(1), that identifies, for each activity started or acquired by the partnership **before** 10/23/86, the amount of passive activity income, loss, deduction, and credit that is attributable to the partner's increase in ownership interest after October 22, 1986. The space provided on page 2 of Schedule K-1 may be used in lieu of an attachment.

**Example:** Assume that the tax year of ABC Partnership is a calendar year running from 1/1/87 to 12/31/87. Partner A held a 25% ownership interest in the partnership from 1985 to 11/30/87. On 12/1/87 partner A's ownership interest increased to 50%. Partner A's distributive share of the ordinary loss of the partnership is $325, all of which is a passive loss to partner A. $275 of that loss was allocable to the 11 months that A held a 25% ownership interest in the partnership. $50 of the loss was allocable to the one month that A held a 50% ownership interest.

Since A held only a 25% ownership interest in the partnership on 10/22/86, one half ($25) of this $50 loss is attributable to A's increase in ownership interest after 10/22/86.

**Question G(2).**—Check "Yes" if the partnership started or acquired a new activity after October 22, 1986 (unless the binding contract or construction exceptions of section 469 apply). If the "Yes" block is checked, attach a statement to Schedule K-1, identify the income (loss), credit, etc., attributable to the activity and state that the activity was commenced after October 22, 1986. Losses and credits from such activities do not qualify for phase-in relief.

**Note:** *The increase in ownership or acquisition (or start) of a new activity does not have to occur in 1987 for Questions G(1) and G(2) to apply. These questions should be checked "Yes" if the increase in ownership or acquisition of a new activity occurred at any time after 10/22/86.*

### Question H

Check this box if the partnership is required to change tax years because of section 706(b) and this Schedule K-1 is for the partnership's resulting short tax year.

### Question I

**Reconciliation of Partner's Capital Account**

See the instructions for Question M and Schedule M of Form 1065.

### Schedules K and K-1 (unless otherwise noted)

An item is specially allocated if it is allocated to a partner in a ratio that is different from the ratio for sharing income or loss generally. Report specially allocated items as follows:

● Specially allocated **short-term** capital gain (loss), enter on line 4d of the applicable partner's Schedule K-1. Enter the total amount on line 4d of Schedule K.

● Specially allocated **long-term** capital gain (loss), enter on line 4e of the applicable partner's Schedule K-1. Enter the total amount on line 4e of Schedule K.

● Specially allocated ordinary gain (loss), enter on line 7 of the applicable partner's Schedule K-1. Enter the total amount on line 7 of Schedule K.

● Other specially allocated items should be reported on the applicable line(s) of the applicable partner's Schedule K-1 and the total amount on the applicable line of Schedule K. For example, specially allocated contributions would be included on line 8 along with any other contributions.

## Income (Loss)

### Line 1

**Ordinary Income (Loss) From Trade or Business Activity(ies)**

Enter the partner's share of the ordinary trade or business income (loss) reported on Form 1065, page 1, line 21. If line 21 is a loss, enter the partner's full share of the loss. If the partner holds interests in the partnership both as a general partner and as a limited partner, enter the total loss for all interests held in the partnership. Enter the loss without reference to the adjusted basis of the partner's interest in the partnership or the partner's amount at risk.

If the partnership has more than one trade or business activity, and one or more of these activities is a passive activity to the partner, identify on an attachment to Schedule K-1 the amount from each passive activity. See **Special reporting requirements for passive activities** on page 12.

Line 1 should not include rental activity or portfolio income (loss).

### Line 2

**Rental Real Estate Income (Loss)**

Enter income or loss from rental real estate activities of the partnership from line 17 of Schedule H (Form 1065). If a loss from a qualified low-income housing project is reported on line 2, identify this loss on a statement attached to the Schedule K-1 of each partner who is a qualified investor in the qualified project.

Section 502 of the Act provides that any loss sustained by a qualified investor in a qualified low-income housing project for any tax year in the relief period is not subject to limitation under section 469. See section 502 of the Act and Publication 925 for definitions and other details. Section 502 of the Act also provides that the low-income housing credit (section 42) may not be taken for any qualified low-income housing project for which any person has been allowed any benefit under the exception provided in Act section 502.

If the partnership has more than one rental real estate activity, identify on an attachment to Schedule K-1 the amount from each of these activities. See **Special reporting requirements for passive activities** on page 12.

### Line 3

**Other Rental Income (Loss)**

On Schedule K, line 3a, enter gross income from rental activities other than rental real estate activities. See page 7 of these instructions, section 469, and Publication 925 for the definition of rental activities. Include on line 3a, the gain (loss) from line 18 of Form 4797 that is attributable to the sale, exchange, or involuntary conversion of an asset used in a rental activity other than a rental real estate activity.

On line 3b of Schedule K enter the deductible expenses of the activity, and attach a schedule of these expenses to Form 1065.

Enter the net income (loss) on line 3c of Schedule K; enter each partner's share on line 3 of Schedule K-1.

If the partnership has more than one rental activity reported on line 3, identify on an attachment to Schedule K-1 the amount from each of these activities. See **Special reporting requirements for passive activities** on page 12.

### Line 4

**Portfolio Income**

See page 5 of these instructions for a definition of portfolio income. Do not reduce portfolio income by expenses allocable to it. Such expenses (other than interest expense) are reported on line 10 of Schedules K and K-1 and are generally subject to separate computation by partners. Interest expense allocable to portfolio income is generally investment interest expense and is reported on line 16a of Schedules K and K-1.

**Lines 4a and 4b.**—Enter only taxable interest and dividends on these lines.

Taxable interest is interest that is included in ordinary income from all sources except interest exempt from tax, and interest on tax-free covenant bonds.

**Caution:** *Be sure to give each payer of interest and dividend income the partnership's correct identification number. Otherwise, the payer may withhold 20% of the interest or dividend income. You may also be subject to penalties.*

**Lines 4d and 4e.**—The amount reported for line 4d of Schedule K comes from line 4 of Schedule D (Form 1065) plus any short-term capital gain (loss) that is specially allocated to partners. Report each partner's share on line 4d of Schedule K-1. The amount reported for line 4e of Schedule K comes from line 9 of Schedule D (Form 1065) plus any long-term capital gain (loss) that is specially allocated to partners. Report each partner's share on line 4e of Schedule K-1.

**Caution:** *Generally, amounts reported on Schedule D (Form 1065) are gain or loss attributable to the disposition of property held for investment and are, therefore, classified as portfolio income (loss). If, however, an amount reported on line 4d or 4e is a passive activity amount to the partner, the amount must be identified on an attachment to Schedule K-1 (or the space provided on page 2 of Schedule K-1).*

**Line 4f.**—Report and identify other portfolio income on an attachment for line 4f (or use the space provided on page 2 of Schedule K-1). For example, income reported to the partnership from a real estate mortgage investment conduit (REMIC), in which the partnership is a residual interest holder, would be reported on an attachment for line 4f.

if the partnership holds a residual interest in a REMIC, report on the attachment for line 4f the partner's share of taxable income (net loss) from the REMIC (line 1b of Schedules Q (Form 1066)), "excess inclusion" (line 2c of Schedules Q (Form 1066)), and section 212 expenses (line 3b of Schedules Q (Form 1066)). Do not report these section 212 expenses on line 10 of Schedules K and K-1. Because Schedule Q (Form 1066) is a quarterly statement, the partnership must follow the Schedule Q instructions to figure the amounts to report to the partner for the partnership's tax year.

## Line 5

### Guaranteed Payments

Enter: (1) the guaranteed payments to partners for salaries and interest deducted by the partnership and reported on Form 1065, page 1, line 10; and (2) the guaranteed payments to partners that the partnership is required to capitalize. (See the instructions for Form 1065, line 10.)

Generally, amounts reported on line 5 are not considered to be related to a passive activity. For example, guaranteed payments for personal services paid to a partner would not be passive activity income. Likewise, interest paid to any partner is not passive activity income. If, however, any amount reported on this line is subject to the passive activity rules of section 469, attach a statement to Schedule K-1 identifying the amounts. The information space on page 2 of Schedule K-1 can be used in lieu of an attachment.

## Line 6

### Net Gain (Loss) Under Section 1231 (other than due to casualty or theft)

Do not include specially allocated ordinary gains and losses or net gains or losses from involuntary conversions due to casualties or thefts on this line. Instead, report them on line 7. The amount for this line comes from line 7 of Form 4797. If the partnership has more than one activity and the amount on line 6 is a passive activity amount to the partner, attach a statement to Schedule K-1 (or use the space provided on page 2 of Schedule K-1) that identifies to which activity the section 1231 gain (loss) relates.

## Line 7

### Other Income (Loss)

Use line 7 to report other items of income, gain, or loss not included on lines 1-6. On an attachment (or the space provided on page 2 of Schedule K-1) identify the amount and the activity (if the activity is a passive activity to the partner and the partnership has more than one activity) to which the amount relates.

Items to be reported on line 7 include.
- Gains from the disposition of farm recapture property (see Form 4797) and other items to which section 1252 applies.
- Recoveries of bad debts, prior taxes, and delinquency amounts (section 111)
- Gains and losses from wagers (section 165(d))
- Any income, gain, or loss to the partnership under section 751(b)
- Specially allocated ordinary gain (loss)
- Net gain (loss) from involuntary conversions due to casualty or theft. The

amount for this line is shown on **Form 4684**, Casualties and Thefts, Section B, line 20a, 20b, or 21.

Each partner's share must be entered on Schedule K-1. Also give each partner a schedule that shows the amounts to be reported on the partner's Form 4684, Section B, line 16, columns (b)(i), (b)(ii), and (c).

**Note:** *If there was a gain (loss) from a casualty or theft to property not used in a trade or business or for income-producing purposes, notify the partner. The partnership should not complete Form 4684 for this type of casualty or theft. Instead, the partner will complete his or her own Form 4684.*

## Deductions

**Note:** *Do not include in the amounts shown on lines 8-11 qualified expenditures to which an election under section 59(e) applies. See the instructions for line 18, item f, for more information on where to report these amounts.*

## Line 8

### Charitable Contributions

Enter the total amount of charitable contributions made by the partnership during its tax year on Schedule K and each partner's distributive share on Schedule K-1. Attach an itemized list to both schedules that shows the amount subject to the 50%, 30%, and 20% limitations.

If the partnership made a qualified conservation contribution under section 170(h), also include the fair market value of the underlying property before and after the donation, and describe the conservation purpose furthered by the donation. Give a copy of this information to each partner.

If the partnership contributes property and the aggregate amount of the claimed value exceeds $500, **Form 8283**, Noncash Charitable Contributions, must be completed and attached to the Form 1065. The partnership must give a copy of its Form 8283 to every partner if the value of an item or group of similar items of contributed property exceeds $5,000 even though the amount allocated to each partner is $5,000 or less. For property that does not meet the $5,000 filing requirement, the partnership does not have to furnish the partners with its Form 8283. It should pass through the fair market value showing the partner's share of contributed property so the partners will be able to complete their Forms 8283. See the **Instructions for Form 8283** for additional information.

## Line 9

### Expense Deduction for Recovery Property

A partnership may elect to expense part of the cost of certain property that the partnership purchased this year for use in its trade or business. See Publication 534 for a definition of what kind of property qualifies for the section 179 deduction. Because this expense is separately reported on Schedule K-1 to the partners, the partnership itself should not deduct the section 179 expense. Show the total section 179 expense on Schedule K, line 9, and allocate it to each partner on Schedule K-1

(Form 1065), line 9. However, do not complete this line for any partner that is an estate or trust.

The partnership must specify the item(s) of section 179 property which it elects to treat as an expense, the portion of the cost of each item which is being treated as an expense, and the partner's allocable share of the cost of section 179 property placed in service during the taxable year. If the section 179 amount is a passive activity amount to the partner, and the partnership has more than one activity, the partnership must also specify the activity to which the property relates. Do this on a schedule attached to Schedule K-1 or on the space provided on page 2 of Schedule K-1. The partnership must also complete Part I of Form 4562 and attach it to Form 1065. See Form 4562 for more information.

See the instructions for line 18, item e, for any recapture of section 179 amount.

**Note:** *Generally, for section 179 property placed in service after 1986, the amount the partnership may elect to expense is $10,000. The $10,000 limit is reduced by the amount of section 179 property placed in service during the taxable year which exceeds $200,000.*

## Line 10

### Deductions Related to Portfolio Income

Enter on this line expenses allocable to portfolio income other than interest expense and section 212 expenses reported to the partnership from its interest in a REMIC. Generally, expenses related to portfolio income are miscellaneous itemized deductions to the partner and are subject to the 2% limitation of section 67. If, however, any of the expenses reported on line 10 are not subject to the 2% limitation, identify those expenses on an attachment to Schedule K-1 (or the space provided on page 2 of Schedule K-1).

Generally, interest expense related to portfolio income is investment interest expense and should be reported as a separate item on line 16a of Schedules K and K-1, instead of line 10. Section 212 expenses from the partnership's interest in a REMIC are reported on line 4f of Schedules K and K-1.

**Note:** *The Act repealed the deduction allowed under section 212 for expenses allocable to a convention, seminar, or similar meeting. Because these expenses are not deductible by partners, partnerships should not report them on Form 1065, page 1, or on Schedule K-1.*

## Line 11

### Other Deductions

Use line 11 to report deductions not included on lines 8-10. On an attachment (or the space provided on page 2 of Schedule K-1) identify the amount and the activity (if the activity is a passive activity to the partner and the partnership has more than one activity) to which the amount relates.

Items to be reported on line 11 include
a. Amounts paid by the partnership that would be itemized deductions on any of the partners' income tax returns if they were paid directly by a partner for the same purpose. Do not, however, enter expenses related to portfolio income or investment interest expense on this line.

**Page 15**

If there was a loss from an involuntary conversion due to casualty or theft from income-producing property, include in the total amount for this line the amount from Form 4684, Section B, line 14.

b. Any penalty on early withdrawal of savings.

c. Soil and water conservation expenditures (section 175).

d. Expenditures for the removal of architectural and transportation barriers to the elderly and handicapped which the partnership has elected to treat as a current expense (section 190).

e. Payments for a partner to an IRA, Keogh, or SEP.

If there is a defined benefit plan (Keogh), attach to the Schedule K-1 for each partner a statement showing the amount of benefit accrued for the tax year.

f Skybox or other private luxury box seat rental expenses subject to limitation under section 274(l)(2). If the partnership leases a skybox or other private luxury box for more than one event, the rental expense is limited under section 274(l)(2) to the face value of nonluxury seat tickets generally held for sale to the public multiplied by the number of seats in such box. The 80% limit of section 274(n) then applies to this reduced amount. The restriction of section 274(l)(2) is phased in over a 3 year period.

Unless the partnership knows the beginning date of a partner's tax year, the attachment for line 11, item f, must show each partner's share of the deductible amount under tax law provisions effective for tax years beginning in 1987 and the deductible amount under tax law provisions effective for tax years beginning in 1988. If a partner's tax year is known, it is only necessary to report the deductible amount for the partner's tax year.

## Credits

**Lines 12b, 12c, 12d, 12e, and 13.**—Lines 12b, 12c, 12d, and 12e have been added to Schedule K-1 to help partners apply the passive activity limitations of section 469. These lines relate to rental activities. Use line 13 to report credits related to trade or business activities.

Do not enter an amount on Schedule K-1 for lines 12c, 12d, 12e, and 13. Instead, report the required information to the partner on an attached schedule and write "see attached" in column (b) of the applicable line of Schedule K-1. Provide on the attachment the line number of Schedule K-1 (12c, 12d, 12e, or 13) to which the information relates. If the partnership has more than one activity, and one or more of these is a passive activity to the partner, identify the amount for lines 12b-13 from each passive activity. See **Special reporting requirements for passive activities,** on page 12.

**Line 12b. Low-income housing credit.**— Section 42 provides a credit that may be claimed by owners of residential rental projects providing low-income housing. The credit is generally effective for buildings placed in service after 1986. If the partners are eligible to compute the low-income housing credit, complete and attach **Form 8586,** Low-Income Housing Credit, to Form 1065. **Note:** No low-income housing credit can be determined with respect to any project for which any person has been allowed any benefit under Act section 502 (relating to the transitional exception rule for low-income housing).

**Line 12c. Qualified rehabilitation expenditures related to rental real estate activity(ies).**— Attach to each partner's Schedule K-1 a schedule showing the amount to be reported on Form 3468.

**Line 12d. Credits related to rental real estate activity(ies) other than 12b and 12c.**— Report any information which the partners need to figure credits related to a rental real estate activity, other than the low-income housing credit and the rehabilitation tax credit. Attach to each partner's Schedule K-1 a schedule showing the amount to be reported and the form on which the amount should be reported.

**Line 12e. Credits related to other rental activity(ies).**— Use this line to report information which the partners need to figure credits related to a rental activity other than a rental real estate activity. Attach to each partner's Schedule K-1 a schedule showing the amount to be reported and the form on which the amount should be reported.

**Line 13. Other credits.**—Enter on an attached schedule each partner's allocable share of any credit or credit information which is related to a trade or business activity.

Examples of credits that can be reported on lines 12(d), 12(e), and 13 (depending on the activity to which they relate) are the following:

**a.** Credits which are figured at the partnership level and then apportioned to partners. These include:

● Jobs Credit. Complete and attach Form 5884 to Form 1065. This credit is apportioned among the partners according to their interest in the partnership at the time the wages on which the credit is computed were paid or accrued.

● Credit for Alcohol Used as Fuel. Complete and attach Form 6478 to Form 1065. This credit is apportioned to persons who were partners on the last day of the partnership's tax year. The credit must be included on page 1, line 7, of Form 1065. See section 40 for an election the partnership can make not to have the credit apply.

● Nonconventional source fuel credit. The credit is figured at the partnership level and then is apportioned to persons who are partners in the partnership on the last day of the partnership's tax year. Attach a separate schedule to the return to show the computation of the credit. See section 29 for more information.

| Worksheet for Figuring Net Earnings (Loss) From Self-Employment | | |
|---|---|---|
| 1 a Ordinary income (loss) (Form 1065, page 1, line 21) | **1a** | |
| b Part allocated to partners who are estates, trusts, corporations, exempt organizations, IRAs, or limited partners | **1b** | |
| c Subtract line 1b from line 1a. (If line 1a is a loss, reduce line 1a by the amount on line 1b.) | **1c** | |
| 2 Guaranteed payments to partners included on Schedules K-1, line 5 | **2** | |
| 3 Net loss from Form 4797 (Form 1065, page 1, line 6) | **3** | |
| 4 a Total (add lines 2 and 3). | **4a** | |
| b Part allocated to partners who are estates, trusts, corporations, exempt organizations, IRAs, or limited partners | **4b** | |
| c Subtract line 4b from line 4a | **4c** | |
| 5 Add lines 1c and 4c. (If line 1c is a loss, reduce line 1c by the amount on line 4c.) | **5** | |
| 6 a Net gain from Form 4797 (Form 1065, page 1, line 6) | **6a** | |
| b Part allocated to partners who are estates, trusts, corporations, exempt organizations, IRAs, or limited partners | **6b** | |
| c Subtract line 6b from line 6a | **6c** | |
| 7 a Subtract line 6c from line 5. (If line 5 is a loss, increase the loss on line 5 by the amount on line 6c.) | **7a** | |
| b Guaranteed payments to individual general partners included on line 2 above. Include on line 14a of the applicable individual general partner's Schedule K-1 | **7b** | |
| c Subtract line 7b from line 7a. (If line 7a is a loss, increase the loss on line 7a by the amount on line 7b.) Include each individual general partner's share on line 14a of Schedule K-1. Add this amount to any amount from line 7b of this worksheet | **7c** | |
| 8 Guaranteed payments to individual limited partners included on line 2 above. Enter here and on the applicable partner's Schedule K-1, line 14a | **8** | |
| 9 Net earnings (loss) from self-employment. Add lines 7b, 7c, and 8. (If line 7c is a loss, reduce the loss on line 7c by the total of the amounts on lines 7b and 8.) Enter here and on Schedule K, line 14a | **9** | |

• Unused credits from cooperatives. The unused credits are apportioned to persons who are partners in the partnership on the last day of the partnership's tax year. Attach a statement to Schedule K-1 to show each partner's share of each unused credit.

• Orphan drug credit and credit for increasing research activities. Complete and attach **Form 6765**, Credit for Increasing Research Activities.

**b.** Credits which are figured by the partner rather than by the partnership. These include:

• Investment Tax Credit. Complete and attach Form 3468 to Form 1065. See Form 3468 and the related instructions for information on eligible property and the lines on Form 3468 to complete. Do not include that part of the cost of the property the partnership has elected to expense under section 179. Attach to each Schedule K-1 a separate schedule showing each partner's share of the partnership's investment in qualified energy property, qualified rehabilitation expenditures , and any regular investment credit property. Also indicate the lines of Form 3468 on which the partners should report these amounts.

## Self-Employment

**Note:** If the partnership is an options dealer or a commodities dealer, see section 1402(i) before completing lines 14a, b, and c, to determine the amount of any adjustment that may have to be made to the amounts shown on the Worksheet for Figuring Net Earnings (Loss) From Self-Employment. If the partnership is engaged solely in the operation of a group investment program, earnings from the operation are not self-employment earnings for either the general or limited partners.

### Worksheet Instructions

Lines 1b, 4b, and 6b.—Allocate the amounts on these lines in the same way Form 1065, page 1, line 21, is allocated to these particular partners.

Line 2.—Include in the amount on line 2 any guaranteed payments to partners reported on Schedules K and K-1, line 5 Also include other ordinary income and expense items reported on Schedules K and K-1 that are used to compute self-employment earnings under section 1402.

Line 3.—For purposes of this line only, do not enter an amount in parentheses.

### Line 14a

#### Net Earnings (Loss) From Self-Employment

**Schedule K.** Enter on line 14a the amount from line 9 of the worksheet.

**Schedule K-1.** Do not complete this line for any partner that is an estate, trust, corporation, exempt organization, or Individual Retirement Arrangement (IRA).

Enter on line 14a of Schedule K-1 each individual general partner's share of the amount shown on line 7c of the worksheet. To figure each individual general partner's share of the amount on line 7c, multiply the amount on line 7c by the percentage you get when you divide each individual general partner's share of the partnership's ordinary income (loss) (line 1 of Schedule K-1) by the total partnership ordinary

income (loss) (line 1 of Schedule K-1) for all the individual general partners. Enter the amount shown on line 7b of the worksheet on the applicable individual general partner's Schedule K-1, line 14a. Add it to the partner's share of the amount on line 7c of the worksheet.

If a partner is both a general and a limited partner, add that partner's share of the amount on lines 7b and 7c to that partner's share of the amount on line 8 and enter the total on line 14a of that partner's Schedule K-1.

**Limited partners.**—A limited partner's share of partnership ordinary income (loss) shown on line 1 of Schedules K and K-1 is not self-employment income. Limited partners may treat as self-employment income only guaranteed payments for services they actually rendered to, or on behalf of, the partnership to the extent that those payments are established as payment for those services (line 8 of the worksheet). Show only these amounts on line 14a of Schedule K-1 for a limited partner.

**General partners.**—General partners' net earnings (loss) from self-employment do not include:

• Dividends on any share(s) of stock and interest on any bonds, debentures, notes, etc., unless the dividends or interest are received in the course of a trade or business, such as a dealer in stocks or securities or interest on notes or accounts receivable.

• Rentals from real estate, except rentals received in the course of a trade or business as a real estate dealer or payments for rooms or space when substantial services are provided.

• Royalty income, except royalty income received in the course of a trade or business

See the instructions for Schedule SE (Form 1040) for more information

### Line 14b

#### Gross Farming or Fishing Income

Enter the gross farming or fishing income that is used by an individual partner to figure self-employment income under the optional method.

### Line 14c

#### Gross Nonfarm Income

Enter the gross nonfarm income that is used by an individual partner to figure self-employment income under the optional method.

## Tax Preference Items

### Lines 15a through 15f

Lines 15a–15f must be completed whether or not a partner is subject to the alternative minimum tax.

Enter items of income and deductions that are tax preference items. See **Form 6251**, Alternative Minimum Tax—Individuals, **Form 4626**, Alternative Minimum Tax—Corporations, **Form 8656**, Alternative Minimum Tax—Fiduciaries, and **Publication 909**, Alternative Minimum Tax, to determine the amounts to enter and for other information

Do not include as a tax preference item any qualified expenditures to which an election under section 59(e) may apply.

If a partnership elected to use the new depreciation system for property placed in service after 7/31/86 and before 1/1/87, it

should use line 15c to report the preference amount for that property. See Form 4562 for an explanation of the new depreciation system.

**Line 15c. Depreciation Adjustment on Property Placed in Service After 12/31/86.**—Refigure depreciation as follows: For property other than real property and property on which the straight line method was used, use the 150 percent declining balance method, switching to straight line for the 1st tax year when that method gives a better result. Use the class life (instead of the recovery period) and the same conventions as you used on Form 4562. For personal property having no class life, use 12 years. For residential rental and nonresidential real property, use the straight line method over 40 years. Determine the depreciation adjustment by subtracting the recomputed depreciation from the depreciation claimed on Form 4562. See Form 6251 for more information.

**Line 15d. Depletion.**—Do not include any depletion on oil and gas wells. The partners must compute their depletion deduction separately under section 613A.

In the case of mines, wells, and other natural deposits, other than oil and gas wells, enter the amount by which the deduction for depletion under section 611 (including percentage depletion for geothermal deposits) is more than the adjusted basis of such property at the end of the tax year. Figure the adjusted basis without regard to the depletion deduction and figure the excess separately for each property

**Lines 15e(1) and 15e(2).**—Enter only the income and deductions for oil, gas, and geothermal properties that are used to figure the partnership's ordinary income or loss (line 21 of Form 1065). If there are items of income or deduction for oil, gas, and geothermal properties included in the amounts that are required to be passed through separately to the partners on Schedule K-1 (items not reported in line 1 of Schedule K-1), give each partner a schedule identifying these amounts.

Figure the amount for lines 15e(1) and (2) separately for oil and gas properties which are not geothermal deposits and for all properties which are geothermal deposits.

Give the partners a schedule that shows the separate amounts that are included in the computation of the amounts on lines 15e(1) and (2).

**Line 15e(1). Gross Income From Oil, Gas, and Geothermal Properties.**—Enter the aggregate amount of gross income (within the meaning of section 613(a)) from all oil, gas, and geothermal properties received or accrued during the tax year that was included on page 1, Form 1065.

**Line 15e(2). Deductions Allocable to Oil, Gas, and Geothermal Properties.**—Enter the amount of any deductions allocable to oil, gas, and geothermal properties reduced by the excess intangible drilling costs that were included on page 1, Form 1065, on properties for which the partnership made the election to expense intangible drilling costs in tax years beginning before January 1, 1983. Do not include on line 15e nonproductive well costs or the amount shown on line 16b, page 1, Form 1065. Instead, use any applicable amount on line 16c, page 1, Form 1065.

See Form 6251 for information on how to compute excess intangible drilling costs.

**Line 15f. Other.**—Attach a schedule which shows each partner's share of other items not shown on lines 15a through 15e(2) that are tax preference items or that the partner needs to complete Form 6251, Form 4626, or Form 8656. See these forms and their instructions to determine the amount to enter.

The Act revised certain tax preference items and added new ones.

New or revised tax preference items or adjustments include the following:
● Completed contract method of accounting for long-term contracts entered into after February 28, 1986.
● Installment sales of inventory or stock in trade after 3/1/86 and sales of business or rental real property where the sales price exceeds $150,000.
● Losses from passive activities. Passive activity losses are not allowed in computing alternative minimum taxable income. In order to compute alternative minimum tax, partners adjust their passive activity income or loss by other preference items included in that passive activity amount. The partnership, therefore, must identify for each passive activity, the amount of any other preference items included in the partner's passive activity income or loss.
● Losses from passive farming activities. No loss from any tax shelter farm activity is allowed for alternative minimum tax purposes.
● Charitable contributions of appreciated property. Provide the partners with the amount of difference between their allocable share of the fair market value of capital gain property donated to a charitable organization, and their allocable share of the partnership's adjusted basis in the donated property.

## Investment Interest

### Lines 16a through 16b(2)

Lines 16a–16b(2) must be completed whether or not a partner is subject to the investment interest rules.

**Line 16a. Investment Interest Expense.**— Include on this line interest paid or accrued to purchase or carry property held for investment. Property held for investment includes property that produces portfolio income (interest, dividends, annuities, royalties, etc.). Therefore, interest expense allocable to portfolio income should be reported on line 16a of Schedule K-1 (rather than line 10 of Schedule K-1).

Property held for investment includes a partner's interest in a trade or business activity that is not a passive activity to the partner and in which the partner does not materially participate. An example would be a partner's working interest in oil and gas property (i.e., the partner's interest is not limited) if the partner does not materially participate in the oil and gas activity.

Investment interest does not include interest expense allocable to a passive activity.

The amount on line 16a will be deducted (after applying the investment interest expense limitations of section 163(d)) by individual partners on their Form 1040.

For more information, see **Form 4952,** Investment Interest Expense Deduction.

**Lines 16b(1) and 16b(2). Investment Income and Expenses.**—Enter on line 16b(1) only the investment income included on line 4 of Schedule K-1. Enter on line 16b(2) only the investment expense included on line 10 of Schedule K-1.

If there are items of investment income or expense included in the amounts that are required to be passed through separately to the partner on Schedule K-1 (items other than the amounts included in lines 4 and 10 of Schedule K-1), give each partner a schedule identifying these amounts.

Investment income includes gross income from property held for investment, gain attributable to the disposition of property held for investment, and other amounts that are gross portfolio income. Investment income and investment expenses do not include any income or expenses from a passive activity.

Property subject to a net lease is not treated as investment property because it is subject to the passive loss rules. Do not reduce investment income by losses from passive activities.

Investment expenses are deductible expenses (other than interest) directly connected with the production of investment income. See the instructions for Form 4952 for more information on investment income and expenses.

## Foreign Taxes

### Lines 17a through 17g

Lines 17c–17g must be completed whether or not a partner is eligible for the foreign tax credit.

In addition to the instructions below, see the following for more information:
● **Form 1116,** Computation of Foreign Tax Credit—Individual, Fiduciary, or Nonresident Alien Individual, and the related instructions.
● **Form 1118,** Computation of Foreign Tax Credit—Corporations, and the related instructions.
● **Publication 514,** Foreign Tax Credit for U.S. Citizens and Resident Aliens.

**Line 17a. Type of Income.**—Enter the type of income as follows:
● Passive income
● High withholding tax interest
● Financial services income
● Shipping income
● Dividends from an IC-DISC or former DISC
● Distributions from a foreign sales corporation (FSC) or former FSC
● General limitation income— all other income from sources outside the United States (including income from sources within U.S. possessions)

If, for the country or U.S. possession shown on line 17b, the partnership had **more than one** type of income, enter "**More than one type**" and attach a schedule for each type of income for lines 17b through 17g.

**Line 17b. Name of Foreign Country or U.S. Possession.**—Enter the name of the

foreign country or U.S. possession. If, for the type of income shown on line 17a, the partnership had income from, or paid taxes to, **more than one** foreign country or U.S. possession, enter "**More than one foreign country or U.S. possession**" and attach a schedule for each country for lines 17a and 17c through 17g.

**Line 17c. Gross Income From Sources Outside the United States.**—Enter in U.S. dollars the total gross income from sources outside the United States. Attach a schedule that shows type of income such as the following:
● Passive income
● High withholding tax interest
● Financial services income
● Shipping income
● Dividends from an IC-DISC or former DISC
● Distributions from a foreign sales corporation (FSC) or former FSC
● General limitation income— all other income from sources outside the United States (including income from sources within U.S. possessions)

See section 904(d) for types of income that must be reported to partners for figuring their foreign tax credit.

**Line 17d. Applicable Deductions and Losses.**—Enter in U.S. dollars the total applicable deductions and losses. Attach a schedule that shows each type of deduction or loss as follows:
● expenses directly allocable to each type of income;
● pro rata share of all other deductions not directly allocable to specific items of income; and
● pro rata share of losses from other separate limitation categories.

**Line 17e. Foreign Taxes Paid or Accrued.**—Enter in U.S. dollars the total foreign taxes (described in section 901) that were paid or accrued by the partnership to foreign countries or U.S. possessions. Attach a schedule that shows the date(s) the taxes were paid or accrued, and the amount in both foreign currency and in U.S. dollars, as follows:
● taxes withheld at source on dividends;
● taxes withheld at source on rents and royalties; and
● other foreign taxes paid or accrued.

**Line 17f. Reduction in Taxes Available for Credit.**—Enter in U.S. dollars, the total reduction in taxes available for credit. Attach a schedule that shows separately the:
● reduction for foreign mineral income (section 901(e));
● reduction for failure to furnish returns required under section 6038;
● reduction for taxes attributable to boycott operations (section 908);
● reduction for foreign oil and gas extraction income (section 907(a)); and
● reduction for any other items (specify).

**Line 17g. Other.**—Enter in U.S. dollars any items not covered on lines 17c, 17d, 17e, and 17f, such as taxable income (loss) of foreign branches from sources outside the United States for corporate partners (Form 1118, Schedule A, column 15).

## Other
### Line 18

Do not put an amount on this line. Instead, enter on an attached statement the description and amount of each partner's share of each of the items listed in a through l. Also identify the activity to which the amount relates if the activity is a passive activity to the partner and the partnership has more than one activity. Show income or gains as a positive number. Show losses with the number in parentheses.

a. Taxes paid on undistributed capital gains by a regulated investment company. As a shareholder of a regulated investment company, the partnership will receive notice on **Form 2439**, Notice to Shareholder of Undistributed Long-Term Capital Gains, that the company paid tax on undistributed capital gains.

b. The number of gallons of the fuels used during the tax year and the appropriate tax rate for each type of use identified on **Form 4136**, Computation of Credit for Federal Tax on Gasoline and Special Fuels, and in the related instructions. Each partner's share of the credit for qualified diesel-powered highway vehicles as shown on Form 4136.

c. The partner's share of gross income from the property, share of production for the tax year, etc., needed to figure the partner's depletion deduction for oil and gas wells. The partnership should also allocate to each partner a proportionate share of the adjusted basis of each partnership oil or gas property. The allocation of the basis of each property is made as specified in section 613A(c)(7)(D).

  The partnership cannot deduct depletion on oil and gas wells. The partner must determine the allowable amount to report on his or her return. See Publication 535 for more information.

d. Tax-exempt interest income, including exempt-interest dividends received as a shareholder in a mutual fund or other regulated investment company.

e. Recapture of expense deduction for recovery property (section 179). For property placed in service after 1986, the section 179 deduction is recaptured at any time the business use of the property drops to 50% or less. Enter the amount that was originally passed through to the partners and the partnership's tax year in which the amount was passed through. Tell the partner if the recapture amount was caused by the disposition of the recovery property. Do not include this amount in the partnership's income.

f. Total qualified expenditures (and the applicable period) paid or incurred during the tax year to which an election under section 59(e) may be applicable. Enter this amount for all partners whether or not a partner is permitted to make an election under section 59(e). Generally, section 59(e) allows partners to deduct ratably over 10 years (3 years in the case of circulation expenditures) otherwise deductible circulation expenses, research and experimental expenditures, intangible drilling and development costs, development expenses, and mining exploration expenditures. If a partner makes this election, these items are not treated as tax preference items.

  Because partners are generally allowed this election, the partnership cannot deduct these amounts or include them as tax preference items on Schedule K-1. The partnership, instead, passes through the information that partners need to compute their separate deduction.

  Do not include amounts paid or incurred in prior tax years.

g. Intangible drilling costs (IDCs) under section 263. See Publication 535 to determine the amount to pass through to each partner. Individual partners (including estates and trusts) may choose to deduct IDCs under section 263 or under section 59(e) but not both

h. Deduction and recapture of certain mining exploration expenditures paid or incurred under section 617. Individual partners (including estates and trusts) may choose to deduct these expenditures under section 617 or under section 59(e).

i. Any items the partners need to determine the basis of their interest for purposes of section 704(d) because Schedule M and Question I on Schedule K-1 are not completed; or any items (other than those shown on Question B) the partners need to figure their amount at risk.

j. Any information or statements the partners need to comply with section 6111, and section 6661.

k. The partner's share of farm production expenses, if the partnership is not required to use the accrual method of accounting. See temporary regulation section 1.263-1T(c).

l. Any other information a partner may need to file his or her return that is not shown anywhere else on Schedule K-1. For example, if there is a pension plan that is a partner, special information may be needed by that partner to properly file its tax return.

## Property Subject to Recapture of Investment Credit
### Lines 19a–19e (Schedule K-1 only)

Lines 19a–19e must be completed whether or not a partner is subject to the recapture of investment credit.

Complete line 19 when regular or energy investment credit property is disposed of, ceases to qualify, or there is a decrease in the percentage of business use before the end of the "life-years category" or "recovery period" assigned. For more information, see **Form 4255**, Recapture of Investment Credit, and Publication 572.

B - 23

# Codes for Principal Business Activity and Principal Product or Service

These codes for the Principal Business Activity are designed to classify enterprises by the type of activity in which they are engaged to facilitate the administration of the Internal Revenue Code. Though similar in format and structure to the Standard Industrial Classification Codes (SIC), they should not be used as SIC codes.

Using the list below, enter on page 1, Question C, the code for the specific industry group for which the largest percentage of "total assets (Schedule L, line 13, column D)" is used.

In Question A, state the principal business activity. In Question B, state the principal product or service which accounts for the largest percentage of total assets. For example, if the principal business activity is "Retail food store," the principal product or service may be "dairy products."

## Agriculture, Forestry, and Fishing

Code

**Farms:**
- 0120 Field crop.
- 0160 Vegetable and melon farms.
- 0170 Fruit and nut tree farms.
- 0180 Horticultural specialty.
- 0211 Beef cattle feedlots.
- 0212 Beef cattle, except feedlots.
- 0215 Hogs, sheep, and goats.
- 0240 Dairy farms.
- 0250 Poultry and eggs.
- 0260 General livestock (except animal specialty).
- 0270 Animal specialty.

**Agricultural services and forestry:**
- 0740 Veterinary services.
- 0753 Livestock breeding.
- 0754 Animal services, except livestock breeding and veterinary.
- 0780 Landscape and horticultural services.
- 0790 Other agricultural services.
- 0800 Forestry, except logging.
- 0400 Logging.

**Fishing, hunting, and trapping:**
- 0930 Commercial fishing, hatcheries, and preserves.
- 0970 Hunting, trapping, and game propagation.

## Mining
- 1000 Metal mining.
- 1200 Coal mining.
- 1300 Oil and gas extraction.
- 1400 Nonmetallic minerals except fuel.

## Construction

**General building contractors and operative builders:**
- 1510 General building contractors.
- 1531 Operative builders.

**Heavy construction contractors:**
- 1611 Highway and street construction.
- 1620 Heavy construction, except highway.

**Special trade contractors:**
- 1711 Plumbing, heating, and air conditioning.
- 1721 Painting, paperhanging, and decorating.
- 1731 Electrical work.
- 1740 Masonry, drywall, stone, tile.
- 1750 Carpentering and flooring.
- 1761 Roofing, siding, and sheet metal.
- 1771 Concrete work.
- 1781 Water well drilling.
- 1790 Other building trade contractors (excavation, glazing, etc.)

## Manufacturing
- 2000 Food and kindred products.
- 2200 Textile mill products.
- 2300 Apparel and other textile products.
- 2400 Lumber and wood products, except furniture.
- 2500 Furniture and fixtures.
- 2700 Printing, publishing, and allied industries.
- 2800 Chemicals and allied products.
- 3000 Rubber and plastic products.
- 3100 Leather and leather products.
- 3200 Stone, clay, and glass products.
- 3300 Primary metal industries.
- 3400 Fabricated metal products.
- 3500 Machinery, except electrical.
- 3600 Electrical and electronic equipment.
- 3700 Transportation equipment
- 3970 Other manufacturing industries.

Code

## Transportation, Communication, Electric, Gas, and Sanitary Services

**Local and interurban passenger transit:**
- 4121 Taxicabs.
- 4189 Other passenger transportation.

**Trucking and warehousing:**
- 4210 Trucking (local and long distance), except trash collection.
- 4216 Trash collection without own dump.
- 4220 Public warehousing.

**Other transportation including transportation services:**
- 4400 Water transportation.
- 4540 Transportation by air.
- 4722 Passenger transportation arrangement.
- 4799 Other transportation services.
- 4800 Communication.
- 4900 Utilities, including dumps, snowplowing, etc.

## Wholesale Trade—Selling Goods to Other Businesses, Government, or Institutions, etc.

**Durable goods, including machinery, equipment, wood, metals, etc.**
- 5001 Selling for your own account.
- 5002 Agent or broker for other firms—more than 50% of gross sales on commission.

**Nondurable goods, including food, fiber, chemicals, etc.**
- 5101 Selling for your own account.
- 5102 Agent or broker for other firms—more than 50% of gross sales on commission.

## Retail Trade

**Building materials, hardware, garden supply, and mobile home dealers:**
- 5211 Lumber and other building materials dealers.
- 5231 Paint, glass, and wallpaper stores.
- 5251 Hardware stores.
- 5261 Retail nurseries and garden stores.
- 5271 Mobile home dealers.

**General merchandise:**
- 5331 Variety stores.
- 5398 Other general merchandise stores.

**Food stores:**
- 5411 Grocery stores.
- 5420 Meat and fish markets, freezer provisioners.
- 5431 Fruit stores and vegetable markets.
- 5441 Candy, nut, and confectionery stores.
- 5451 Dairy products stores.
- 5460 Retail bakeries.
- 5490 Other food stores.

**Automotive dealers and service stations:**
- 5511 New car dealers (franchised).
- 5521 Used car dealers.
- 5531 Auto and home supply stores.
- 5541 Gasoline service stations.
- 5551 Boat dealers.
- 5561 Recreational vehicle dealers.
- 5571 Motorcycle dealers.
- 5599 Aircraft, and other automotive dealers.

**Apparel and accessory stores:**
- 5611 Men's and boys' clothing and furnishings.
- 5621 Women's ready-to-wear stores.
- 5631 Women's accessory and specialty stores.
- 5641 Children's and infants' wear stores.
- 5651 Family clothing stores.
- 5661 Shoe stores.
- 5681 Furriers and fur shops.
- 5699 Other apparel and accessory stores.

Code

## Furniture, home furnishings, and equipment stores:
- 5712 Furniture stores.
- 5713 Floor covering stores.
- 5714 Drapery, curtain, and upholstery stores.
- 5719 Home furnishings, except appliances.
- 5722 Household appliance stores.
- 5732 Radio and television stores.
- 5733 Music stores.
- 5734 Computer and software stores.

**Eating and drinking places:**
- 5812 Eating places.
- 5813 Drinking places.

**Miscellaneous retail stores:**
- 5912 Drug stores and proprietary stores.
- 5921 Liquor stores.
- 5932 Used merchandise and antique stores (except motor vehicle parts).
- 5941 Sporting goods stores and bicycle shops.
- 5942 Book stores.
- 5943 Stationery stores.
- 5944 Jewelry stores.
- 5945 Hobby, toy, and game shops.
- 5946 Camera and photographic supply stores.
- 5947 Gift, novelty, and souvenir shops.
- 5948 Luggage and leather goods stores.
- 5949 Sewing, needlework, and piece goods stores.
- 5961 Mail order houses.
- 5962 Merchandising machine operators.
- 5963 Direct selling organizations.
- 5983 Fuel oil dealers.
- 5984 Liquefied petroleum gas (bottled gas) dealers.
- 5989 Other fuel dealers (except gasoline)
- 5992 Florists.
- 5996 Other miscellaneous retail stores.

## Finance, Insurance, and Real Estate
- 6000 Banking.
- 6100 Credit agencies other than banks.

**Security and commodity brokers, dealers, exchanges, and services:**
- 6212 Security underwriting syndicates.
- 6218 Security brokers and dealers, except underwriting syndicates.
- 6299 Commodity contracts brokers and dealers; security and commodity exchanges; and allied services.

**Real estate:**
- 6411 Insurance agents, brokers, and services.
- 6511 Real estate operators (except developers) and lessors of buildings.
- 6520 Lessors of real property other than buildings.
- 6531 Real estate agents, brokers, and managers.
- 6541 Title abstract offices.
- 6552 Subdividers and developers, except cemeteries.
- 6553 Cemetery subdividers and developers.

**Holding and other investment companies:**
- 6746 Investment clubs.
- 6747 Common trust funds.
- 6748 Other holding and investment companies.

## Services

**Hotels and other lodging places:**
- 7012 Hotels.
- 7013 Motels, motor hotels, and tourist courts.
- 7021 Rooming and boarding houses.
- 7032 Sporting and recreational camps.
- 7033 Trailer parks and camp sites.

Code

**Personal services:**
- 7215 Coin-operated laundries and dry cleaning.
- 7219 Other laundry, cleaning, and garment services.
- 7221 Photographic studios and portrait studios.
- 7231 Beauty shops.
- 7241 Barber shops.
- 7251 Shoe repair and hat cleaning shops.
- 7261 Funeral services and crematories.
- 7291 Income tax preparation.
- 7299 Miscellaneous personal services.

**Business services:**
- 7310 Advertising.
- 7340 Janitorial and window cleaning.
- 7350 Equipment rental and leasing.
- 7370 Computer and data processing services.
- 7398 Other business services.

**Automotive repair and services:**
- 7510 Automotive rentals and leasing, without drivers.
- 7520 Automobile parking.
- 7538 General automobile repair shops.
- 7539 Other automotive repair shops.
- 7540 Automotive services, except repair.

**Miscellaneous repair services:**
- 7622 Radio and TV repair shops.
- 7628 Electrical repair shops, except radio and TV.
- 7641 Reupholstery and furniture repair.
- 7680 Other miscellaneous repair shops.

**Motion picture:**
- 7812 Other motion picture and TV film and tape activities.
- 7830 Motion picture theaters.
- 7840 Video tape rental stores.

**Amusement and recreation services:**
- 7920 Producers, orchestras, and entertainers.
- 7933 Bowling alleys.
- 7941 Professional sports clubs and promoters.
- 7948 Racing, including track operation.
- 7980 Other amusement and recreation services.
- 7991 Physical fitness facilities.

**Medical and health services:**
- 8011 Offices and clinics of medical doctors (MD's).
- 8021 Offices and clinics of dentists.
- 8031 Offices of osteopathic physicians.
- 8041 Offices of chiropractors.
- 8042 Offices of optometrists.
- 8047 Other licensed health practitioners.
- 8048 Registered and practical nurses.
- 8050 Nursing and personal care facilities.
- 8060 Hospitals.
- 8072 Dental laboratories.
- 8098 Other medical and health services.

**Other services:**
- 8111 Legal services.
- 8200 Educational services.
- 8351 Child day care.
- 8722 Certified public accountants.
- 8723 Other accounting, auditing, and bookkeeping services.
- 8740 Management, consulting, and public relations services.
- 8911 Engineering and architectural services.
- 8999 Other services, not elsewhere classified.

# SCHEDULE K-1
## (Form 1065)
Department of the Treasury
Internal Revenue Service

# Partner's Share of Income, Credits, Deductions, etc.

For calendar year 1987 or fiscal year
beginning ........................., 1987, and ending ........................., 19.....

OMB No. 1545-0099

## 1987

Partner's identifying number ▶

Partner's name, address, and ZIP code

Partnership's identifying number ▶

Partnership's name, address, and ZIP code

---

**A(1)** Is this partner a general partner? . . . ☐ Yes ☐ No

If "yes" to Question A(1):

(2) Did this partner materially participate in the trade or business activity(ies) of the partnership? (See page 12 of the Form 1065 Instructions. Leave blank if no trade or business activities.). . . . ☐ Yes ☐ No

(3) Did this partner actively participate in the rental real estate activity(ies) of the partnership? (See page 13 of the Form 1065 Instructions. Leave blank if no rental real estate activities.). . . ☐ Yes ☐ No

**B** Partner's share of liabilities

Nonrecourse. . . . . . . . . $ ........................

Other . . . . . . . . . . . $ ........................

**C** What type of entity is this partner? ▶

| **D** Enter partner's percentage of: | (I) Before decrease or termination | (II) End of year |
|---|---|---|
| Profit sharing . . . . . . . | ..........% | ..........% |
| Loss sharing . . . . . . . | ..........% | ..........% |
| Ownership of capital . . . | ..........% | ..........% |

**E** IRS Center where partnership filed return ▶ ....................

**F** Tax Shelter Registration Number ▶ ....................

**G(1)** Did the partner's ownership interest in the partnership increase after Oct. 22, 1986? . . . . . ☐ Yes ☐ No

If yes, attach statement. (See page 13 of the Form 1065 Instructions.)

(2) Did the partnership start or acquire a new activity after Oct. 22, 1986? . . . . . . . . ☐ Yes ☐ No

If yes, attach statement. (See page 14 of the Form 1065 Instructions.)

**H** Check here ▶ ☐ if this Schedule K-1 is for a short tax year required by section 706(b).

**I** Reconciliation of partner's capital account:

| (a) Capital account at beginning of year | (b) Capital contributed during year | (c) Income (loss) from lines 1, 2, 3, and 4 below | (d) Income not included in column (c), plus nontaxable income | (e) Losses not included in column (c), plus unallowable deductions | (f) Withdrawals and distributions | (g) Capital account at end of year |
|---|---|---|---|---|---|---|
| | | | | | | |

---

**Caution:** *Refer to attached Partner's Instructions for Schedule K-1 (Form 1065) before entering information from this schedule on your tax return.*

| | | (a) Distributive share item | (b) Amount | (c) 1040 filers enter the amount in column (b) on: |
|---|---|---|---|---|
| **Income (Loss)** | 1 | Ordinary income (loss) from trade or business activity(ies) . . . . . | | ⎱ See Partner's Instructions for Schedule K-1 (Form 1065) |
| | 2 | Income or loss from rental real estate activity(ies) . . . . . . | | |
| | 3 | Income or loss from other rental activity(ies) . . . . . . . | ///////// | |
| | 4 | Portfolio income (loss): | | |
| | a | Interest . . . . . . . . . . . . . | | Sch. B, Part I, line 2 |
| | b | Dividends . . . . . . . . . . . . | | Sch. B, Part II, line 4 |
| | c | Royalties . . . . . . . . . . . . | | Sch. E, Part I, line 5 |
| | d | Net short-term capital gain (loss) . . . . . . . . . | | Sch. D, line 5, col. (f) or (g) |
| | e | Net long-term capital gain (loss) . . . . . . . . | | Sch. D, line 12, col. (f) or (g) |
| | f | Other portfolio income (loss) (attach schedule) . . . . . | | (Enter on applicable lines of your return) |
| | 5 | Guaranteed payments . . . . . . . . . . . | | ⎱ See Partner's Instructions for Schedule K-1 (Form 1065) |
| | 6 | Net gain (loss) under section 1231 (other than due to casualty or theft) | | |
| | 7 | Other (attach schedule) . . . . . . . . . | | (Enter on applicable lines of your return) |
| **Deductions** | 8 | Charitable contributions . . . . . . . . . . | | See Form 1040 Instructions |
| | 9 | Expense deduction for recovery property (section 179) . . . . | | ⎱ See Partner's Instructions for Schedule K-1 (Form 1065) |
| | 10 | Deductions related to portfolio income . . . . . . . | | |
| | 11 | Other (attach schedule) . . . . . . . . | | |
| **Credits** | 12a | Credit for income tax withheld . . . . . . . . | | See Form 1040 Instructions |
| | b | Low-income housing credit . . . . . . . . . | | Form 8586, line 8 |
| | c | Qualified rehabilitation expenditures related to rental real estate activity(ies) (attach schedule) | ///////// | |
| | d | Credit(s) related to rental real estate activity(ies) other than 12b and 12c (attach schedule) | ///////// | ⎱ See Partner's Instructions for Schedule K-1 (Form 1065) |
| | e | Credit(s) related to rental activity(ies) other than 12b, 12c, and 12d (attach schedule) | ///////// | |
| | 13 | Other credits (attach schedule) . . . . . . . | | |

**For Paperwork Reduction Act Notice, see Form 1065 Instructions.**

Schedule K-1 (Form 1065) 1987

☆ U. S. GOVERNMENT PRINTING OFFICE: 1987—183-170

| | | (a) Distributive share item | (b) Amount | (c) 1040 filers enter the amount in column (b) on: |
|---|---|---|---|---|
| **Self-employment** | 14a | Net earnings (loss) from self-employment . . . . . . . . | | Sch. SE, Part I |
| | b | Gross farming or fishing income . . . . . . . . . . | | } ( See Partner's Instructions for Schedule K-1 (Form 1065) ) |
| | c | Gross nonfarm income . . . . . . . . . . . . | | |
| **Tax Preference Items** | 15a | Accelerated depreciation of real property placed in service before 1/1/87 . . . . . . . . . . . . . . . . . | | Form 6251, line 5a |
| | b | Accelerated depreciation of leased personal property placed in service before 1/1/87 . . . . . . . . . . . . . . . | | Form 6251, line 5b |
| | c | Depreciation adjustment on property placed in service after 12/31/86 | | Form 6251, line 4g |
| | d | Depletion (other than oil and gas) . . . . . . . . . | | Form 6251, line 5h |
| | e | (1) Gross income from oil, gas, and geothermal properties . . . | | See Form 6251 Instructions |
| | | (2) Deductions allocable to oil, gas, and geothermal properties . . | | See Form 6251 Instructions |
| | f | Other (attach schedule) . . . . . . . . . . . . | | ( See Partner's Instructions for Schedule K-1 (Form 1065) ) |
| **Investment Interest** | 16a | Interest expense on investment debts . . . . . . . . | | Form 4952, line 1 |
| | b | (1) Investment income included in Schedule K-1, lines 4a through 4f . | | } ( See Partner's Instructions for Schedule K-1 (Form 1065) ) |
| | | (2) Investment expenses included in Schedule K-1, line 10 . . . | | |
| **Foreign Taxes** | 17a | Type of income _____ | | Form 1116, Check boxes |
| | b | Name of foreign country or U.S. possession _____ | | Form 1116, Part I |
| | c | Total gross income from sources outside the U.S. (attach schedule) . | | Form 1116, Part I |
| | d | Total applicable deductions and losses (attach schedule) . . . | | Form 1116, Part I |
| | e | Total foreign taxes (check one): ▶ ☐ Paid ☐ Accrued . . . | | Form 1116, Part II |
| | f | Reduction in taxes available for credit (attach schedule) . . . | | Form 1116, Part III |
| | g | Other (attach schedule) . . . . . . . . . . . . | | See Form 1116 Instructions |
| **Other** | 18 | Other items and amounts not included in lines 1 through 17g and 19 that are required to be reported separately to you . . . . . | | (See Partner's Instructions for Schedule K-1 (Form 1065)) |

| | 19 | Properties: | A | B | C | |
|---|---|---|---|---|---|---|
| **Property Subject to Recapture of Investment Credit** | a | Description of property (State whether recovery or nonrecovery property. If recovery property, state whether regular percentage method or section 48(q) election used.) | | | | Form 4255, top |
| | b | Date placed in service . | | | | Form 4255, line 2 |
| | c | Cost or other basis . | | | | Form 4255, line 3 |
| | d | Class of recovery property or original estimated useful life . | | | | Form 4255, line 4 |
| | e | Date item ceased to be investment credit property | | | | Form 4255, line 8 |

**Other Information Provided by Partnership:**

_____

_____

_____

_____

_____

_____

# 1987

**Department of the Treasury**
**Internal Revenue Service**

# Partner's Instructions for Schedule K-1 (Form 1065)

## (For Partner's Use Only)

*(Section references are to the Internal Revenue Code unless otherwise noted.)*

## Changes You Should Note

The Tax Reform Act of 1986 made many changes that affect the partnership and its partners. Among the changes made to Schedule K-1 to help partners comply with the new law are the following:

● Line 1 reports only income (loss) from any trade or business activity of the partnership.

● Line 2 reports income (loss) from any rental real estate activity of the partnership.

● Line 3 reports income (loss) from any rental activity of the partnership other than a rental real estate activity.

● Lines 4a–4f report the "portfolio income" of the partnership. Portfolio income includes interest, dividends, royalties, and gain (loss) on the disposition of assets held for investment.

These changes were made because of new section 469. Section 469 provides limitations on losses and credits from "passive activities." Generally, a passive activity is a trade or business activity in which the partner does not materially participate. A rental activity is also considered a passive activity. See **Passive Activity Limitations** on page 3 for more information.

These instructions also provide information on other changes that may affect you. In addition to reading these instructions, you may wish to get new **Publication 920**, Explanation of the Tax Reform Act of 1986 for Individuals, and new **Publication 921**, Explanation of the Tax Reform Act of 1986 for Business.

## Purpose of Schedule K-1

The partnership uses Schedule K-1 to report to you your share of the partnership's income, credits, deductions, etc. **Please keep it for your records. Do not file it with your tax return.** A copy has been filed with the IRS.

Although the partnership is not subject to income tax, you are liable for tax on your share of the partnership income, whether or not distributed, and you must include your share on your tax return.

The amount of loss and deduction that you may claim on your tax return may be less than the amount reported on Schedule K-1. Generally, the amount of loss and deduction you may claim is limited to your basis in the partnership and the amount for which you are considered at risk. If you have losses, deductions, or credits from a passive activity, you must also apply the passive activity rules. **It is the partner's responsibility to consider and apply any applicable limitations. See Limitations on Losses, Deductions, and Credits,** on page 3, for more information.

Use these instructions to help you report the items shown on Schedule K-1 on your tax return.

Where "(attach schedule)" appears beside a line item, it means you should see the schedule that the partnership has attached for that line or the space provided on page 2 of Schedule K-1.

Where "(see instructions for Form 1065)" appears beside an item or line, it means the partnership should see the Instructions for Form 1065 before completing these lines. You may ignore this notation.

## General Information

**New rule for partnership tax years.—** Section 706(b) generally requires partnerships to change to the same taxable year as the tax year of partners who own a majority (more than 50%) interest in the partnership's profits and capital. Partnerships will accomplish this change, if required, by filing a short year partnership return.

If you are a partner in a partnership that is required under section 706(b) to change to a new tax year, your partnership should identify the Schedule K-1 issued to you for its short tax year by checking Question H. Generally, you may prorate and report ratably your share of the partnership's excess of income over expenses for the short tax year over 4 years (beginning with 1987). You may, however, elect to report your share of the short year's income in the year in which the partnership's short tax year ends; usually this would be 1987. See **Publication 541**, Tax Information on Partnerships, for more information.

**Inconsistent treatment of items.—** Generally, you must report partnership items shown on your Schedule K-1 (and any attached schedules) or similar statement, consistent with the way the partnership treated the items on its filed return. This rule does not apply if your partnership is within the "small partnership" exception and does not elect to have the section 6231(a)(1)(B)(ii) election apply. See section 6222 for the inconsistent treatment rules.

If your treatment on your original or amended return is (or may be) inconsistent with the partnership's treatment, or if the partnership was required to, but has not filed a return, you must file **Form 8082**, Notice of Inconsistent Treatment or Amended Return (Administrative Adjustment Request (AAR)), with your original or amended return to identify and explain the inconsistency (or to note that a partnership return has not been filed).

**Errors.—**If you believe the partnership has made an error on your Schedule K-1, notify the partnership and ask for a corrected Schedule K-1. Do not change any items on your copy. Be sure that the partnership sends a copy of the corrected Schedule K-1 to the Internal Revenue Service. However, see **Inconsistent treatment of items.**

**Sale or exchange of partnership interest.—**Generally, if a partner sells or exchanges a partnership interest where unrealized receivables or substantially appreciated inventory items are involved, the partner must notify the partnership, in writing, within 30 days of the exchange. An exception to this rule is made in the case of sales or exchanges of publicly traded partnership interests for which a broker is required to file Form 1099-B. See Form 8308 for the types of unrealized receivables involved.

**Nominee reporting.—**Any person who holds an interest in a partnership as a nominee for another person is required to furnish to the partnership the name, address, etc., of the other person (i.e., the beneficial holder of the interest). See section 6031(b) and (c), and the related regulations for more information.

**United States persons with interests in foreign partnerships.—**If you are a U.S. person in a foreign partnership that does not file a partnership return, you may be required to furnish information necessary to determine your correct income (loss) from the partnership. See regulation section 1.6031. See also section 6046A for other information you may be required to report.

**Windfall profit tax.—**Generally, if you are a producer of domestic crude oil, your partnership will inform you on **Form 6248**, Annual Information Return of Windfall Profit Tax, of your income tax deduction for the windfall profit tax rather than on Schedule K-1. You will have to determine if you are entitled to a refund of overpaid windfall profit tax. File **Form 6249**, Computation of Overpaid Windfall Profit Tax, to obtain a refund.

**Note:** *If your partnership elects to be treated as authorized to act on behalf of the partners, the regulations under section 6232 will apply.*

**International boycotts.—**Every partnership that had operations in, or related to, a boycotting country, company, or a national of a country, must file **Form 5713**, International Boycott Report.

If the partnership cooperated with an international boycott, it must give you a copy of the form. You also must file Form 5713 to report the activities of the partnership and any other boycott operations of your own. Please see Form 5713 and the instructions for more information.

## Definitions

*General partner.* —A general partner is a member of the organization who is personally liable for obligations of the partnership.

*Limited partner.* —A limited partner is one whose potential personal liability for partnership debts is limited to the amount of money or other property that the partner contributed or is required to contribute to the partnership.

*Nonrecourse loans.* —Nonrecourse loans are those liabilities of the partnership for which none of the partners has any personal liability.

*Elections.* —Generally, the partnership decides how to figure taxable income from its operations. For example, it chooses the accounting method and depreciation methods it will use.

However, certain elections are made by you separately on your income tax return and not by the partnership. These elections are made under the following code sections:

● Section 108(b)(5) (income from discharge of indebtedness);

● Section 617 (deduction and recapture of certain mining exploration expenditures, paid or incurred); and

● Section 901 (foreign tax credit).

If you are an individual partner (including estates and trusts), you may make an election under section 59(e) to deduct ratably over the period of time specified in that section, certain qualified expenditures. For more information, see the instructions for line 18, items f, g, and h.

*Additional information.* —For more information on the treatment of partnership income, credits, deductions, etc., see: **Publication 541**, Tax Information on Partnerships; **Publication 535**, Business Expenses; and **Publication 556**, Examination of Returns, Appeal Rights, and Claims for Refund.

## Specific Instructions

**Name, address, and identifying number.** —Your name, address, and identifying number, as well as the partnership's name, address, and identifying number, should be entered.

**Question A.** —Question A(1) is answered by the partnership for all partners. Questions A(2) and A(3) are answered by the partnership only for partners who hold an interest as a general partner.

Questions A(2) and A(3) are answered to help partners who hold an interest as a general partner apply the passive activity rules.

**Question B.** —Question B should show your share of the partnership's nonrecourse liabilities and other liabilities as of the end of the partnership's tax year. If you terminated your interest in the partnership during the tax year, Question B should show the share that existed immediately before the total disposition. A partner's "other liability" is, generally, any partnership liability for which a partner is personally liable (but see **Note** below).

Use the total of the two amounts for computing the adjusted basis of your partnership interest. Generally, you may use the amount shown next to "Other" to compute your amount at risk. Do not include any amounts that are not at risk that may be included in "Other."

If your partnership is engaged in two or more different types of at-risk activities, or a combination of at-risk activities and any other activity, the partnership should give you a statement showing your share of nonrecourse liabilities and other liabilities for each activity.

**Note:** *The Act extended the at-risk rules to real property. The Act also provided an exception for "qualified" nonrecourse financing that is secured by real property used in an activity of holding real property. You are considered at-risk for "qualified" nonrecourse amounts.*

*Qualified nonrecourse financing generally includes financing that is secured by real property and that is loaned or guaranteed by a Federal, state, or local government or borrowed from a "qualified" person. Qualified persons include any person actively and regularly engaged in the business of lending money, such as a bank or savings and loan association. Qualified persons generally do not include related parties, the seller of the property, or a person who receives a fee because of the investment in the real property. See* **Publication 925**, *Passive Activity and At-Risk Rules, for more information on qualified nonrecourse financing.*

*If the partnership had a liability that qualified as qualified nonrecourse financing at the partnership level, it included your share of such liability in the* **Other** *line of Question B. The partnership should also have identified such amounts on an attachment to Schedule K-1 (or the space provided on page 2 of Schedule K-1). You, as well as the partnership, must meet the qualified nonrecourse rules on this debt before you can include these amounts in your at-risk computation.*

See **Limitations on Losses, Deductions, and Credits** for more information on the at-risk limitations.

**Question F.** —If the partnership is a registration-required tax shelter itself or if the partnership has invested in a registration-required tax shelter, it should have completed Question F. If you claim or report income, loss, deduction, or credit from a tax shelter, you are required to attach **Form 8271**, Investor Reporting of Tax Shelter Registration Number, to your tax return. If the partnership has invested in a tax shelter, it is required to give you a copy of its Form 8271 with Schedule K-1. You should use the information on this Form 8271 to complete Part I of your Form 8271.

If the partnership itself is a registration-required tax shelter, use the information on Schedule K-1 (name of the partnership, partnership identifying number, tax shelter registration number) to complete Part I of Form 8271. The partnership will also identify the type of tax shelter on an attachment to Schedule K-1 or in the space provided on page 2 of Schedule K-1.

**Questions G(1) and G(2).** —These questions are answered only for partners to whom passive activity amounts are passed through from the partnership. These questions are asked to enable partners, for whom the passive activity rules of section 469 are applicable, to apply the phase-in relief provisions of those rules. See **Passive Activity Limitations** on page 3 for information on the phase-in relief provisions.

If Questions G(1) and G(2) are checked "No," phase-in relief provisions apply to the entire passive activity amounts from this partnership.

**Question G(1).** —The phase-in relief provisions do not apply to passive activity losses and credits from interests in the partnership acquired after October 22, 1986, unless the partner had a contractual obligation on that date to purchase the interest.

If Question G(1) is checked "Yes," the partnership should have attached a statement to Schedule K-1, for each passive activity commenced by the partnership prior to 10/23/86, identifying your share of income, loss, deduction, and credit attributable to a new or increased ownership interest in the partnership that you acquired after 10/22/86.

**Question G(2).** —If Question G(2) is checked "Yes," the partnership should have attached a statement to your Schedule K-1 to identify your share of amounts from activities commenced by the partnership after 10/22/86. If these amounts are passive activity losses or credits to you, the phase-in relief provisions will not apply to them.

See the instructions for **Form 8582**, Passive Activity Loss Limitations, for information on how to use Questions G(1) and G(2) to figure the phase-in relief provisions of section 469.

**Question H.** —See **New rule for partnership tax years** on page 1 of these instructions.

## Lines 1a–19

If you are an individual partner, take the amounts shown in column (b) and enter them on the lines on your tax return as indicated in column (c). If you are not an individual partner, report the amounts in column (b) as instructed on your tax return.

The line numbers in column (c) are references to forms in use for calendar year 1987. If you file your tax return on a calendar year basis, but your partnership files a fiscal year 1987/1988 partnership return, enter these amounts on the corresponding lines of the tax forms in use for 1988.

If you have losses, deductions, credits, etc., from a prior year that were not deductible or usable because of certain limitations, such as the at-risk rules, they may be taken into account in determining your net income, loss, etc., for this year. However, do not combine the prior-year amounts with any amounts shown on this Schedule K-1 to get a net figure to report on any supporting schedules, statements, or forms (such as **Schedule E (Form 1040)**, Supplemental Income Schedule) attached to your return. Instead, report the amounts on the attached schedule, statement, or form on a year-by-year basis.

If you have amounts, other than those shown on Schedule K-1, to report on Schedule E (Form 1040), enter each item on a separate line of Part II of Schedule E.

## Lines 1–3

The amounts shown on lines 1 through 3 reflect your share of income or loss from partnership business or rental operations without reference to limitations on losses or adjustments that may be required of you because of (1) the adjusted basis of your partnership interest, (2) the amount for which you are at-risk as determined under section 465, or (3) the passive activity limitations of section 469. Information on these provisions is given below.

## Limitations on Losses, Deductions, and Credits

### Basis Rules

Generally, you may not claim your share of a partnership loss (including capital loss) that is greater than the adjusted basis of your partnership interest at the end of the partnership's tax year.

Items which increase your basis are:
- Money and your adjusted basis in property contributed to the partnership.
- Your share of the partnership's income.
- Your share of the increase in the liabilities of the partnership (or your individual liabilities caused by your assumption of partnership liabilities).

Items which decrease your basis are:
- Money and the adjusted basis of property distributed to you.
- Your share of the partnership's losses.
- Your share of the decrease in the liabilities of the partnership (or your individual liabilities assumed by the partnership).

The above is not a complete list of items and factors which determine basis. See Publication 541 for a more complete discussion of how to determine the adjusted basis of your partnership interest.

### At-Risk Rules

Generally, if you have (1) a loss or other deduction from an activity carried on as a trade or business or for the production of income by the partnership, and (2) amounts in the activity for which you are not at risk, you will have to complete **Form 6198,** Computation of Deductible Loss From an Activity Described in Section 465(c), to figure the allowable loss to report on your return.

**Note:** *The at-risk rules have been extended to cover the holding of real property (other than mineral property) placed in service after 12/31/86. For partnership interests acquired after 1986, the rules also apply to real property placed in service on, before, or after 1/1/86.*

The at-risk rules generally limit the amount of loss (including loss on disposition of assets) and other deductions (such as the section 179 deduction) that you can claim to the amount you could actually lose in the activity.

Generally, you are not at risk for amounts such as the following:
- Nonrecourse loans used to finance the activity, to acquire property used in the activity, or to acquire your interest in the activity, that are not secured by your own property (other than that used in the activity). See **Question B,** on page 2, for the exception for qualified nonrecourse financing secured by real property.

- Cash, property, or borrowed amounts used in the activity (or contributed to the activity, or used to acquire your interest in the activity) that are protected against loss by a guarantee, stop-loss agreement, or other similar arrangement (excluding casualty insurance and insurance against tort liability).
- Amounts borrowed for use in the activity from a person who has an interest in the activity, other than as a creditor, or who is related, under section 465(b)(3), to a person (other than yourself) having such an interest.

To help you complete Form 6198, the partnership should give you your share of the total pre-1976 loss(es) from a section 465(c)(1) activity for which there existed a corresponding amount of nonrecourse liability at the end of the year in which this loss(es) occurred. In addition, you should get a separate statement of income, expenses, etc., for each activity from the partnership.

### Passive Activity Limitations

New section 469 provides rules that limit the deduction of certain losses and credits.

These rules apply to partners who:
- Are individuals, estates, trusts, closely held corporations, or personal service corporations, and
- Have a loss or credit from a passive activity.

A passive activity is generally a trade or business activity in which the partner does not materially participate or a rental activity. **Except as may be provided by regulations, limited partners are not considered to materially participate in the trade or business activities of the partnership.**

If you have a loss or deduction from a passive activity, you will need to complete Form 8582 to figure the allowable amount to report on your return. You will also need to complete Form 8582 if you have passive activity income from this partnership and passive activity loss or deduction from another source.

The amounts reported on lines 1 and 13 of Schedule K-1 are passive activity income (loss) or credits from the trade or business of the partnership if you are a limited partner or if question A(2) is checked "No" and you are a general partner. (See, however, the caution to general partners on page 4.) The amounts reported on lines 2, 3, and 12b through 12e of Schedule K-1 are from rental activities of the partnership and are passive activity income (loss) or credits to all partners. There is an exception to this rule for losses incurred by qualified investors in qualified low-income housing projects. The partnership will identify any of these qualified amounts on an attachment for line 2.

Section 469 also provides a special rule for rental real estate activities in which the partner actively participates. Generally, such partners are allowed to deduct up to $25,000 of these losses (and credits in a deduction equivalent sense) against non-passive income. Generally, the $25,000 allowance is phased out when a partner's adjusted gross income exceeds $100,000 ($200,000 in the case of the low-income housing and rehabilitation credits). **Except as may be provided by regulations, limited partners are not considered to**

**actively participate in the rental real estate activities of the partnership.** You will be allowed this special allowance for amounts reported on lines 2 and 12d only if you are a general partner and Question A(3) is checked "Yes." (See, however, the caution to general partners on page 4.) Active participation is not required, however, for the low-income housing credit or for the rehabilitation investment credit. Therefore, all partners are generally allowed the special $25,000 deduction equivalent allowance for credits reported on lines 12b and 12c. The $25,000 allowance does not apply to losses on line 3 or credits on line 12e.

The limitations of section 469 are figured at the partner level after combining passive activity amounts from this partnership with passive activity amounts from other sources. An overall loss from passive activities generally may not offset income such as salary, interest, dividends, and active business income. Credits from a passive activity generally are limited to tax attributable to passive activities. The instructions for Form 8582 will give you directions on how to combine passive activity amounts, how to apply the passive loss rules if you have an overall passive activity loss, and how to compute the amount of any passive activity loss you can claim.

Phase-in relief provisions apply to losses and credits attributable to partnership interests acquired before October 23, 1986, provided the passive activity commenced before that date. The phase-in provisions are computed by the partner, not the partnership. The partnership, however, advises you of the amount of any passive activity income, loss, or credit and the amount of those losses and credits that do not qualify for phase-in relief. See the instructions for Questions G(1) and G(2) on page 2.

If the partnership disposed of its entire interest in an activity, in a fully taxable disposition to an unrelated party, the partnership must advise you of the disposition if the activity was a passive activity to you. This notification is necessary so that you can apply the rules of section 469(g) which allow you to use losses unallowed in previous years because of the passive activity limitations.

See the instructions for Form 8582 and Publication 925 for more information on the passive activity limitations.

**Note:** *If the partnership reports amounts from more than one activity on your Schedule K-1 and one or more of these activities is a passive activity to you, the partnership should have attached a statement to tell you your share of income, loss, deduction, and credit from each passive activity and the line on Schedule K-1 in which that amount is included. If applicable, the statement will indicate if the amount does not qualify for phase-in relief.*

*If you are a general partner and you materially participate in some trade or business activities and not in others, the attachment will show which trade or business amounts are passive activity amounts to you. If you are a general partner and you actively participate in some rental real estate activities and not in others, the attachment will show which amounts qualify for the special $25,000 allowance and which do not.*

*The passive activity limitations do not apply to partners having a working interest in any oil and gas property in which the partner does not hold a limited interest. Therefore, the partnership should check "Yes" to Question A(2) for oil and gas activities if you are a general partner whose liabilities are not limited with regard to the oil and gas property (whether or not you materially participate in the oil and gas activity).*

**Caution to general partners for whom Questions A(2) or A(3) are checked "No":** *If your partnership has more than one trade or business activity or more than one rental real estate activity and you materially (actively) participate in some but not all activities, the partnership should have checked "No" for Question A(2) or A(3). If so, you must see the attachment for each passive activity as you follow the line-by-line instructions.*

*Treat Question A(2) as being checked "No" for trade or business amounts reported as passive activity amounts on the attachment. Treat trade or business amounts included on Schedule K-1 but not included on the passive activity attachment as though Question A(2) were checked "Yes" for those amounts.*

*See the attachment for each rental real estate activity to see if you actively participated in the activity. Treat amounts from such activities in which you did actively participate as though Question A(3) were checked "Yes." Treat amounts from such activities in which you did not actively participate as though Question A(3) were checked "No."*

## Line-by-Line Instructions

### Income

**Line 1. Ordinary income (loss) from trade or business activity(ies).**—The amount reported for line 1 is your share of the ordinary income (loss) from the trade or business activity(ies) of the partnership. Generally, where you report this amount on Form 1040 depends on whether or not the amount is from an activity which is a passive activity to you. If you are an individual partner filing your 1987 Form 1040, find your situation in the following guide and report your line 1 income (loss) as instructed, after applying the basis and at-risk limitations on losses.

• Questions A(1) and A(2) of your Schedule K-1 are checked "Yes." Report line 1 income (loss) on Schedule E (Form 1040), Part II, column (h) or (j).

• Question A(1) is checked "No" or Question A(1) is checked "Yes" but Question A(2) is checked "No." If income is reported on line 1, report the income on Schedule E, Part II, column (g). If, in addition to this passive activity income, you have a passive activity loss from this partnership or from any other source, also report the line 1 income on Form 8582. If a loss is reported on line 1, report the loss on the applicable line of Form 8582, to determine how much of the loss can be reported on Schedule E, Part II, column (f).

**Line 2. Income or loss from rental real estate activity(ies).**—Generally, the income (loss) reported on line 2 is a passive activity amount to all partners. There is an

exception, however, for losses from a qualified low-income housing project. The loss limitations of section 469 do not apply to qualified investors in qualified low-income housing projects. The partnership will have attached a schedule for line 2 to identify such amounts, if applicable.

Use the following instructions to determine where to enter a line 2 amount.

• If you have a loss on line 2 (other than a qualified low-income housing project loss), enter the loss on the applicable line of Form 8582 to determine how much of the loss can be reported on Schedule E (Form 1040), Part II, column (f). If Questions A(1) and A(3) of Schedule K-1 are checked "Yes," your share of the loss will be eligible for the special $25,000 allowance for rental real estate losses. See the instructions for Form 8582 for more information.

**Note:** *If you are a qualified investor reporting a qualified low-income housing project loss, report the loss on Schedule E, Part II, column (h).*

• If you have income on line 2, enter the income on Schedule E, Part II, column (g). If, in addition to this passive activity income, you have a passive activity loss from this partnership or from any other source, also report the line 2 income on Form 8582.

**Line 3. Income or loss from other rental activity(ies).**—The amount on line 3 is a passive activity amount for all partners.

• If line 3 is a loss, report the loss on the applicable line of Form 8582.

• If income is reported on line 3, report the income on Schedule E (Form 1040), Part II, column (g). If, in addition to this passive activity income, you have a passive activity loss from this partnership or from any other source, also report the line 3 income on Form 8582.

**Line 4. Portfolio income (loss).**—Income or loss referred to as "portfolio" income or loss in these instructions is not part of a passive activity subject to the rules of section 469. Portfolio income includes interest, dividend, and royalty income, and gain or loss on the sale of property held for investment. Column (c) of Schedule K-1 tells individual partners where to report this income on Form 1040.

**Caution:** *Generally, amounts reported on lines 4d and 4e are gain or loss attributable to the disposition of property held for investment and are therefore classified as portfolio income (loss). If, however, an amount reported on line 4d or 4e is a passive activity amount, the partnership will identify the amount.*

The partnership uses line 4(f) to report portfolio income other than interest, dividend, royalty, and capital gain (loss) income. It will attach a statement or use the space provided on page 2 of Schedule K-1 to tell you what kind of portfolio income is reported on line 4(f). An example of portfolio income that could be reported for line 4(f) is income from a real estate mortgage investment conduit (REMIC) in which the partnership is a residual interest holder.

If the partnership has a residual interest in a REMIC, it will report on the statement your share of REMIC taxable income (net loss) which you report on Schedule E (Form 1040), Part IV, column (d). The statement will also report your share of "excess inclusion" which you report on Schedule E,

Part IV, column (c), and your share of section 212 expenses which you report on Schedule E, Part IV, column (e). If you itemize your deductions on Schedule A (Form 1040), you may deduct these section 212 expenses as a miscellaneous deduction subject to the 2% adjusted gross income limit.

**Line 5. Guaranteed payments.**—Generally, amounts on this line are not part of a passive activity and should be reported on Schedule E (Form 1040), Part II, column (j). For example, guaranteed payments for personal services paid to any partner are not passive activity income. If, however, any amount reported on this line is subject to the passive activity rules of section 469, the partnership should have attached a statement to Schedule K-1 to identify that amount.

**Line 6. Net gain (loss) under section 1231 (other than due to casualty or theft).**—If the amount on line 6 relates to a rental activity, the section 1231 gain (loss) is a passive activity amount. If the amount relates to a trade or business activity and you are a limited partner (or you are a general partner for whom Question A(2) of Schedule K-1 is checked "No"), the section 1231 gain (loss) is a passive activity amount.

• If the amount is not a passive activity amount to you, report it on line 2, column (g) or (h), whichever is applicable, of Form 4797, Gains and Losses From Sales or Exchanges of Assets Used in a Trade or Business and Involuntary Conversions. You do not have to complete the information called for on columns (b) through (f). Write "From Schedule K-1 (Form 1065)" across these columns.

• If gain is reported on line 6 and it is a passive activity amount to you, report the gain on line 2, column (h), of Form 4797 and be sure to see "Passive Loss Limitations" on page 1 of the instructions for Form 4797.

• If a loss is reported on line 6 and it is a passive activity amount to you, see "Passive Loss Limitation" on page 1 of the instructions for Form 4797. You will need to use Form 8582 to determine how much of the loss is allowed on Form 4797.

**Line 7. Other income (loss).**—Amounts on this line are other items of income, gain, or loss not included on lines 1–6. The partnership should give you a description and the amount of your share for each of these items.

The instructions given below tell you where to report line 7 items if such items are not passive activity amounts.

Report loss items which are passive activity amounts to you on Form 8582.

Report income or gain items which are passive activity amounts to you as instructed below. If, in addition to this passive activity income or gain, you have passive activity losses from any source, also report the passive activity income or gain on Form 8582.

Line 7 items may include the following:

• Partnership gains from disposition of farm recapture property (see Form 4797) and other items to which section 1252 applies.

• Recoveries of bad debts, prior taxes, and delinquency amounts (section 111). Report on line 21, Form 1040.

**Page 4**

- Gains and losses from wagers (section 165(d)).
- Any income, gain, or loss to the partnership under section 751(b). Report this amount on line 10, Form 4797.
- Specially allocated ordinary gain (loss). Report this amount on Form 4797, line 10.
- Net gain (loss) from involuntary conversions due to casualty or theft. The partnership will give you a schedule that shows the amounts to be entered on **Form 4684**, Casualties and Thefts, Section B, Part II, line 16, columns (b)(i), (b)(ii), and (c).

## Deductions

**Line 8. Charitable contributions.**—The partnership will give you a schedule that shows which contributions were subject to the 50%, 30%, and 20% limitations. For further information, see the Form 1040 instructions.

If contributions of property other than cash are made and if the fair market value of one item or group of similar items of property exceeds $5,000, the partnership is required to give you a copy of **Form 8283**, Noncash Charitable Contributions, to attach to your tax return. Do not deduct the amount shown on this form. It is the partnership's contribution. You should deduct the amount shown on line 8 of your Schedule K-1 (Form 1065).

If the partnership provides you with information that the contribution was property other than cash and does not give you a Form 8283, see the Instructions for Form 8283 for filing requirements. A Form 8283 does not need to be filed unless the total claimed value of all contributed items of property exceeds $500.

**Line 9. Expense deduction for recovery property.**—The maximum amount of expense deduction for recovery property (section 179 deduction) that you can claim from all sources is $10,000. The $10,000 limit is reduced if the total cost of section 179 property placed in service during the year exceeds $200,000. The partnership will give you information on your share of the cost of the partnership's section 179 property so that you can compute this limitation. Your section 179 deduction is also limited to your taxable income from all of your trades or businesses. See **Form 4562**, Depreciation and Amortization, and Publication 534 for more information.

If the section 179 deduction is a passive activity amount, report it on Form 8582. If it is not a passive activity amount, report it on Schedule E (1040), Part II, column (i).

**Line 10. Deductions related to portfolio income.**—Amounts entered on this line are the expenses (other than investment interest expense and expenses from a REMIC) paid or incurred to produce portfolio income. Generally, you should enter line 10 amounts on **Schedule A (Form 1040)**, line 21. If, however, any line 10 amount should not be entered on line 21 of Schedule A, the partnership will have identified that amount for you.

**Line 11. Other deductions.**—Amounts on this line are other deductions not included on lines 8, 9, and 10, such as:

- Itemized deductions other than those reported on line 10 (1040 filers enter on Schedule A (Form 1040)).

**Note:** If there was a gain (loss) from a casualty or theft to property not used in a trade or business or for income-producing purposes, you will be notified by the partnerships. You will have to complete your own Form 4684.

- Any penalty on early withdrawal of savings.
- Soil and water conservation expenditures (section 175).
- Expenditures for the removal of architectural and transportation barriers to the elderly and handicapped which the partnership has elected to treat as a current expense (section 190).
- Payments for a partner to an IRA, Keogh, or a Simplified Employee Pension (SEP) plan. See Form 1040 Instructions for line 24 of Form 1040 in order to figure your IRA deduction. Payments made to a Keogh or SEP plan will be entered on Form 1040, line 26. If the payments to a Keogh plan were to a defined benefit plan, the partnership should give you a statement showing the amount of the benefit accrued for the tax year.
- Skybox or other private luxury box rental expense subject to limitation under section 274(l)(2). The restrictions of section 274(l)(2) are phased in over a 3 year period. The amount allowed as a deduction depends on when the partner's tax year begins. Therefore, unless the partnership knows the beginning date of your tax year, it will attach a statement to show your share of the deductible amount for tax years beginning in 1987 and 1988. Report the amount that corresponds with your tax year. If the partnership knows your tax year, it will report only the deductible amount for that year.

The partnership should give you a description and the amount of your share for each of these items.

## Credits

**Line 12b. Low-income housing credit.**— Your share of the partnership's low-income housing credit is shown on line 12b. Any allowable credit is entered on **Form 8586**, Low-Income Housing Credit.

**Caution:** You cannot claim the low-income housing credit on any qualified low-income housing project for which any person was allowed any benefit under section 502 of the Tax Reform Act of 1986.

**Line 12c. Rehabilitation expenditures related to a rental real estate activity.**— The partnership should attach a statement to Schedule K-1 that shows your share of the partnership's rehabilitation expenditures that are related to each rental real estate activity. Any allowable credit is claimed on **Form 3468**, Computation of Investment Credit.

**Line 12d. Other credits related to rental real estate activities.**—If applicable, the partnership will use this line, through an attached statement, to give you the information you need to compute credits related to rental real estate activities other than the low-income housing credit and the rehabilitation investment credit.

**Line 12e. Credits related to other rental activities.**—If applicable, the partnership will use this line, through an attached statement, to give you the information you need to compute credits related to rental activities other than rental real estate activities.

**Line 13. Other credits.**—If applicable, the partnership will use this line, through an attached statement, to give the information you need to compute credits related to a trade or business activity.

Credits that may be reported on lines 12d, 12e, or 13 (depending on the type of activity they relate to) include the following:

- Nonconventional source fuel credit.
- Unused credits from cooperatives.
- The credit for increasing research activities and orphan drug credit (enter these credits on **Form 6765**, Credit for Increasing Research Activities).
- Jobs credit. Complete **Form 5884**, Jobs Credit, and attach it to your return. See the form for definitions, special rules, and limitations.
- Credit for alcohol used as fuel. Complete **Form 6478**, Credit for Alcohol Used as Fuel, and attach it to your return.
- Investment tax credit. If applicable, the partnership will, through an attached statement, show your share of the partnership's qualified rehabilitation expenditures, energy property qualifying for the credit, and any regular investment credit property that qualifies for the credit. Generally, you can claim a tax credit based on these amounts by filing Form 3468.

The partnership should give you a description and the amount of your share for each of these items.

**Note:** The passive activity limitations of section 469 may limit the amount of credits on lines 12b, 12c, 12d, 12e, and 13 that you may take. Lines 12b, 12c, 12d, and 12e credits are related to the rental activities of the partnership and are passive activity credits to all partners. Line 13 credits are related to the trade or business activities of the partnership and are passive activity credits to all limited partners (and to general partners for whom Question A(2) is checked "No"). In general, except to the extent phase-in relief is available, credits from passive activities are limited to tax attributable to passive activities.

However, partners for whom Questions A(1) and A(3) are checked "Yes" may be able to use line 12d credits against tax on other income. The amount of these credits so usable is limited to their deduction equivalent up to $25,000 (net of losses from rental real estate activities deductible against up to $25,000 of other income).

The lines 12b and 12c credits may be taken against tax on other income, subject to the same $25,000 limitation, regardless of whether questions A(1) and A(3) are checked "Yes." Line 12e credits are limited to tax attributable to passive activities. The $25,000 deduction equivalent does not apply to line 12e and line 13 credits.

## Self-Employment

**Lines 14a, 14b, and 14c.**—If you and your spouse are both partners, each of you must complete and file your own **Schedule SE (Form 1040)**, Computation of Social Security Self-Employment Tax, to report your partnership earnings (loss) from self-employment. Do not report the self-employment amounts for both of you on one Schedule SE (Form 1040).

**Line 14a. Net earnings (loss) from self-employment.**—Before entering this amount on Schedule SE (Form 1040), you must adjust it by any section 179 expense

**Page 5**

claimed, unreimbursed partnership expenses claimed, and depletion claimed on oil and gas properties.

If the amount on this line is a loss, enter only the deductible amount on Schedule SE (Form 1040). See **Limitations on Losses, Deductions, and Credits** on page 3.

If your partnership is an options dealer or a commodities dealer, see section 1402(i).

If your partnership is an investment club, see Revenue Ruling 75-525, 1975-2 C.B. 350.

**Line 14b. Gross farming or fishing income.**—If you are an individual partner, enter the amount from this line on Schedule E (Form 1040), Part VI, line 43. You may also use this amount to figure self-employment income under the optional method on Schedule SE (Form 1040), Part II.

**Line 14c. Gross nonfarm income.**—If you are an individual partner, use this amount to figure self-employment income under the optional method on Schedule SE (Form 1040), Part II.

## Tax Preference Items

Use the information reported on lines 15a through 15f (as well as your preference items from other sources) to prepare your **Form 6251,** Alternative Minimum Tax—Individuals, **Form 4626,** Alternative Minimum Tax—Corporations, or **Form 8656,** Alternative Minimum Tax—Fiduciaries.

**Lines 15e(1) and 15e(2). Gross income from, and deductions allocable to, oil, gas, and geothermal properties.**—The amounts reported on these lines include only the gross income from, and deductions allocable to, oil, gas, and geothermal properties that are included on line 1 of Schedule K-1. The partnership should attach a schedule that shows any income from or deductions allocable to such properties that are included on lines 2 through 11 and line 18 of Schedule K-1. Use the amounts reported on lines 15e(1) and 15e(2) and the amounts on the attached schedule to help you determine the net amount to enter on line 5g of Form 6251.

**Line 15f. Other.**—Enter the information on the schedule attached by the partnership for line 15f on the applicable lines of Form 6251.

**Note:** *The Act made many changes to the alternative minimum tax provisions. One of the new preference items is passed through to you, if applicable, on line 15c. Other new or revised preference items and information are passed through to you on a schedule for line 15f. Among these preference items are use of the completed contract method, installment sales of certain property, losses from passive farming activities, charitable contributions of appreciated property, and passive activity losses (as adjusted). To help you adjust your passive activity amount the partnership, if it has more than one activity, will identify for each passive activity the amount of other preference items included in your passive activity income or loss. Enter these items on the appropriate line of Form 6251.*

## Investment Interest

If the partnership paid or accrued interest on debts it incurred to buy or hold investment property, the amount of interest you can deduct may be limited.

**Page 6**

For more information and the special provisions that apply to investment interest expense, see **Form 4952,** Investment Interest Expense Deduction, and **Publication 550,** Investment Income and Expenses.

**Line 16a. Interest expense on investment debts.**—Enter this amount on Form 4952 along with your investment interest expense from other sources. Form 4952 will help you determine how much of your total investment interest is deductible.

**Lines 16b(1) and (2). Investment income and investment expenses.**—Use the amounts on these lines to determine the amount to enter on line 6 of Form 4952.

**Caution:** *The amount shown on lines 16b(1) and (2) includes only investment income and expenses included on lines 4 and 10 of this Schedule K-1. The partnership should attach a schedule which shows the amount of any investment income and expenses included in any other lines of this Schedule K-1. Use these amounts, if any, to adjust lines 16b(1) and 16b(2) to determine your total investment income and total investment expenses from this partnership. Combine these totals with investment income and expenses from all other sources to determine the amount to enter on line 6 of Form 4952.*

## Foreign Taxes

**Lines 17a–17g.**—Use the information on lines 17a through 17g, and on any attached schedules, to figure your foreign tax credit. For more information, see: **Form 1116,** Computation of Foreign Tax Credit—Individual, Fiduciary, or Nonresident Alien Individual, and the related instructions; **Form 1118,** Computation of Foreign Tax Credit—Corporations, and the related instructions; and **Publication 514,** Foreign Tax Credit for U.S. Citizens and Resident Aliens.

## Other

**Line 18.**—Amounts included on the statement for this line are other amounts not included elsewhere such as:

**a.** Taxes paid on undistributed capital gains by a regulated investment company. (Form 1040 filers enter your share of these taxes on line 60, and add the words "Form 1065.")

**b.** Number of gallons of the fuels used during the tax year and the appropriate tax rate for each type of use identified on **Form 4136,** Computation of Credit for Federal Tax on Gasoline and Special Fuels, and in the related instructions. Also your share of the credit allowed for qualified diesel-powered highway vehicles as shown on Form 4136.

**c.** Your share of gross income from the property, share of production for the tax year, etc., needed to figure your depletion deduction for oil and gas wells. The partnership should also allocate to you a share of the adjusted basis of each partnership oil or gas property. See Publication 535 for how to figure your depletion deduction.

**d.** Tax-exempt interest income earned by the partnership. You must report on your return, as an item of information, the amount of tax-exempt interest received or accrued during the year. Individual partners should report this amount on line 9 of Form 1040.

**e.** Recapture of expense deduction under section 179. If the recapture was caused by a disposition of the property, include the amount on Form 4797, line 16.

The amount to be recaptured will be limited to the amount you deducted in the prior year.

**f.** Total qualified expenditures (and the applicable period) paid or incurred during the tax year to which an election under section 59(e) applies and 59(e) type expenditures for corporate partners.

If you are an individual partner (including an estate or trust), you may either deduct the total amount of these expenditures or you may make an election under section 59(e) to deduct them ratably over the period of time specified in section 59(e). If a partner makes this election, these items are not treated as tax preference items. See section 59(e) and make the election on **Form 4562,** Depreciation and Amortization.

If intangible drilling costs or certain mining expenditures are passed through to you, see items g and h, which follow, before deducting them under section 59(e).

**g.** Intangible drilling costs (IDCs) under section 263. See Publication 535 for more information. If you are an individual partner (including an estate or trust), you may choose to deduct IDCs under section 263 or under section section 59(e), but not both.

**h.** Deduction and recapture of certain mining exploration expenditures paid or incurred. You may choose to deduct these expenditures under section 617 or under section 59(e), but not both.

**i.** Any items you need to determine the basis of your partnership interest for purposes of section 704(d) because Question I on Schedule K-1 is not completed; or any items (other than those shown in Question B) you need to figure your amount at risk.

**j.** Any information or statements you need to comply with section 6661 (regarding substantial understatement of tax liability) or section 6111 (regarding tax shelters).

**k.** Farm production expenses. You may be eligible to elect to deduct these expenses currently or capitalize them under section 263A. See Publication 225 and temporary regulation section 1.263A-1T(c).

**l.** Any other information you may need to file your return that is not shown elsewhere on Schedule K-1.

The partnership should give you a description and the amount of your share for each of these items.

### Recapture of Investment Credit

**Line 19.**—When investment credit property is disposed of or ceases to qualify, or there is a decrease in the percentage of business use before the "life-years category" or "recovery period" assigned, you will be notified. You may have to recapture (pay back) the investment credit taken in prior years. Use the information on line 19 to figure your recapture tax on **Form 4255,** Recapture of Investment Credit. See the Form 3468 on which you took the original credit for other information you need to complete Form 4255.

You may also need Form 4255 if you disposed of more than one-third of your interest in a partnership. See Publication 572, for more information.

☉ U S GOVERNMENT PRINTING OFFICE 1987 183-171

# *More Books from the Successful Business Library*

Career Builder: A Plan For Career Success . . . . . . . . . . . . . . . . . . $34.95
Controlling Your Company's Freight Costs . . . . . . . . . . . . . . . . . . $34.95
Cost-Effective Market Analysis . . . . . . . . . . . . . . . . . . . . . . . . . $34.95
Debt Collection: Successful Strategies for the Small Business . . . . . . . $34.95
The Loan Package . . . . . . . . . . . . . . . . . . . . . . . . . . . . . . . $34.95
Mail Order Legal Manual . . . . . . . . . . . . . . . . . . . . . . . . . . . $45.00
Managing People . . . . . . . . . . . . . . . . . . . . . . . . . . . . . . . $34.95
Marketing Your Products and Services Successfully . . . . . . . . . . . . $34.95
Negotiating the Purchase or Sale of a Business . . . . . . . . . . . . . . . $34.95
Publicity and Public Relations Guide for Business . . . . . . . . . . . . . $34.95
Risk Analysis: How to Reduce Insurance Costs . . . . . . . . . . . . . . . $34.95
Surviving and Prospering in a Business Partnership . . . . . . . . . . . . $34.95
Staffing a Small Business: Hiring, Compensating and Evaluating . . . . $34.95
Tax Tips for Small Business, 1989-90 (paperback) . . . . . . . . . . . . . $15.95
Venture Capital Proposal Package . . . . . . . . . . . . . . . . . . . . . . $34.95

**Corporation Formation Package & Minute Book.** A step-by-step workbook which guides you through the incorporation and maintenance of your business as a close corporation. Converts into a legal corporate minute book. *[Companion software available. See software list.]*

(Please specify which state: **California, Florida, or Texas**) . . . . . . . . . . $34.95

---

## Starting and Operating a Business in . . . . . . . . . . . . . . . $29.95

*Author Michael D. Jenkins, a Harvard-educated attorney and accountant, and his state co-authors (most of whom are associated with the accounting firm of Ernst & Young) have put together a step-by-step guide for starting and operating a business for the states listed below. A "one-stop" resource guide which takes you through current federal and state laws and regulations.*

| | | | |
|---|---|---|---|
| Alabama | Iowa | Nebraska | Rhode Island |
| Arizona | Kansas | Nevada | S. Carolina |
| Arkansas | Kentucky | N. Hampshire | Tennessee |
| California | Louisiana | New Jersey | Texas |
| Colorado | Maine | New Mexico | Utah |
| Connecticut | Maryland | New York | Vermont |
| Delaware | Massachusetts | N. Carolina | Virginia |
| Georgia | Michigan | Ohio | Washington |
| Florida | Minnesota | Oklahoma | W. Virginia |
| Hawaii | Mississippi | Oregon | Wisconsin |
| Illinois | Missouri | Pennsylvania | Wyoming |
| Indiana | | | |

---

# From PSI Research and Oasis Press

*"When it comes to business, we help you do the job right."*

**PSI RESEARCH/THE OASIS PRESS**
300 North Valley Drive
Grants Pass, OR 97526
(503/479-9464)
(FAX 503/476-1479)

*Order Toll-Free 1-800/228-2275 or use the order form*

# *Easy-To-Use Software by PSI*

**Save valuable time and money . . .**
**Increase your productivity . . .**

Whether you're preparing a loan request, developing a company policy manual, writing an entire business plan, or creating a customer database, PSI Software will give you pre-written forms, charts, graphs, policies, letters, or spreadsheets to help improve your business' operation.

*Note: Unless otherwise specified, all software listed below are for an IBM-PC or compatible with a minimum of 512K (Macintosh versions are available for some products). Disks are available for both 3 1/2" and 5 1/4" disk drives. Companion workbooks and manuals from the Successful Business Library can be purchased with the software as part of the package.*

### UNIQUE STAND ALONE SOFTWARE (WITH BUILT-IN WORD PROCESSING)

*The "Stand Alone" software programs listed below are integrated packages, which require no additional software to run the program. The wordprocessing program is built-in; the text is automatically formatted, so all you have to do is type in the words. If you already have the Oasis Press book, you can purchase the software alone—We do not advise you to purchase the software without the workbook.*

- **Develop Your Business Plan** — Easy-to-Use Stand Alone software helps you create a complete, professional business plan. Just type in the words, and input the numbers. The word processor helps you to write the plan with ease, while the templates allow you to do the necessary "number crunching" to easily compute your company's figures—all this in one package.
  *Workbook and software* . . . . . . . . . . . . . . . . . . . . . . . . . . . . . . . . . *$79.95*
  *Software only* . . . . . . . . . . . . . . . . . . . . . . . . . . . . . . . . . . . . . . . *$49.95*

- **Company Policy Manual** — An integrated package with over 50 possible policies to choose from, so you can customize your own company policy manual. Just type in once your company's specific information (such as company name, etc.), and it will appear throughout the text. All you need to do then is tell the computer which policies you wish to use and print those policies as they are; or you can tailor the model policies to fit your company's needs.
  *Workbook and software* . . . . . . . . . . . . . . . . . . . . . . . . . . . . . . . . . *$79.95*
  *Software only* . . . . . . . . . . . . . . . . . . . . . . . . . . . . . . . . . . . . . . . *$49.95*

### TEXTFILES

*"Textfiles" listed below are in ASCII format, which allows use with virtually any wordprocessing program (i.e. for the IBM PC or compatible: WordPerfect, WordStar, Galaxy, and many other wordprocessing programs which utilize ASCII files; and for the Apple Macintosh or compatible: MacWrite, WordPerfect-Mac, Quark Express, etc.).*

- **Company Policy Manual** — Textfiles with over 50 model policies for creating a company policy manual. Separate wordprocessing program is required for the Mac version; however, a complimentary wordprocessing program is included with the IBM version of the textfiles. Print the policies as is, or use a wordprocessing program to tailor the model policies to your company's specific needs.
  *Workbook and disk with ASCII Textfiles* . . . . . . . . . . . . . . . . . . . . . . *$69.95*
  *Disk alone with ASCII Textfiles* . . . . . . . . . . . . . . . . . . . . . . . . . . . *$39.95*

*(Continued on Back Page)*

- **Corporation Package** — Textfiles for generating bylaws, minutes, and other necessary forms originating from Oasis Press' *Corporation Formation Packages*. The complimentary wordprocessor helps you access those forms and documents with ease to assist you in forming a close corporation in the following states:

**California**          **Florida**          **Texas**

*(Please specify which state when ordering. Note: Not currently available for the Mac.)*
*Manual and disk with ASCII Textfiles* . . . . . . . . . . . . . . . . . . . . . . . . *$69.95*
*Disk alone with ASCII Textfiles* . . . . . . . . . . . . . . . . . . . . . . . . . . . *$39.95*

## OTHER SOFTWARE PROGRAMS FOR IBM PCs OR COMPATIBLES

- **The Small Business Expert** — Software which answers basic business questions quickly and easily, providing up-to-date information on over 125 business topics. Features a unique checklist and overview of requirements for any state you choose. Also includes information on federal regulations, taxes, and much more. *(For IBM-PC or compatible with 256K plus hard disk or two 360K floppy disks or one 720K floppy.)*
*Software & Manual* . . . . . . . . . . . . . . . . . . . . . . . . . . . . . . *$39.95*

- **Word Processing Program** — PSI Research's preferred word processing program, practical and user-friendly for beginners and sophisticated and feature-packed for advanced users. *(For IBM-PC or compatible with 192K.)*
*Software & Instruction Manual* . . . . . . . . . . . . . . . . . . . . . . . *$59.95*

- **CashPlan** — Ready-to-Go Program to computerize the spreadsheets in the Starting and Operating a Business books. Helps estimate personal or business expenses to help project how much cash you will need and when. *(For IBM-PC or compatible with 256K.)*
*Booklet and Disk* . . . . . . . . . . . . . . . . . . . . . . . . . . . . . . . *$39.95*

- **CPR: Customer Profile and Retrieval** — Easy-to-use customer database program, easily modified to suit your business needs. You can customize even further through dBase III+, dBase IV, Foxbase, or Clipper. Features flexibility to store as many customers as your hard disk storage space allows. Also allows printing of mailing labels or Rolodex cards.
*Manual and Disk* . . . . . . . . . . . . . . . . . . . . . . . . . . . . . . . *$69.95*

- **Spreadsheet Program** — Spreadsheet program, which can be used to create spreadsheets from scratch or run the spreadsheet template from *Financial Templates for Small Business* or *Financial Tools for Managing a Small Business*. Features include a 2048 row x 256 column format, graphics and macro capabilities, pop-up menu design, and on-screen help. (Lotus 1-2-3 compatible.)
*Spreadsheet Manual and Disk* . . . . . . . . . . . . . . . . . . . . . . . *$79.95*
*Spreadsheet plus Financial Templates for Small Business manual and disk* . . . *$99.50*

- **Financial Templates for Small Business** — Multi-purpose templates to computerize financial calculations featured in The Oasis Press' Successful Business Library books. Ready to use with the spreadsheet program above or with other spreadsheet programs, such as Microsoft's Excel for the Mac or Lotus 1-2-3 for IBM.
*Financial Templates for Small Business* . . . . . . . . . . . . . . . . . . . *$49.95*

- **Financial Tools for Managing a Small Business** — Software program designed to make use of information generated from sales and changes in inventory to help you manage your cash flow more effectively. Ready to use with Oasis' Spreadsheet Program above. *(640K Ram, Lotus 1-2-3 or Oasis Spreadsheet Program is required.)*
*Financial Tools for Managing a Small Business* . . . . . . . . . . . . . . . *$69.95*

**TO ORDER, USE THE ATTACHED ORDER FORM, OR CALL 1-800/228-2275.**

# PSI Research
## Order Form

**Toll-free order number  - 1-800-228-2275**

### *Items Ordered*

| Title | Qty | Price | Total |
|-------|-----|-------|-------|
| _____ | ____ | ____ | ____ |
| _____ | ____ | ____ | ____ |
| _____ | ____ | ____ | ____ |
| _____ | ____ | ____ | ____ |
| _____ | ____ | ____ | ____ |
| _____ | ____ | ____ | ____ |
| _____ | ____ | ____ | ____ |

**Subtotal** _____
**\*Shipping** _____
**Total** _____

\* *Please see other side for information on shipping costs and method of payment. (Call for shipping charges when ordering more than one item.)*

### *Shipping Address*

Name _____

Company _____

Address _____ Ste./Flr. _____

City _____ State _____ Zip _____

Daytime Phone _____ Date _____

## PSI Research
### 300 North Valley Drive
### Grants Pass, Oregon 97526
### 503/479-9464

# Shipping and Method of Payment Information

____ **Check enclosed, payable to PSI Research.** PSI Research will pay shipping charges for UPS Ground Service for destinations in continental U.S.

For other destinations, include shipping for desired method of delivery.

If you want shipping other than UPS Ground, check which of the following you prefer and add the additional charges indicated for weekday delivery. (Includes a handling charge for expediting.)

     ____ UPS Next Day Air, $16.40

     ____ UPS Second Day Air, $7.50

     ____ Federal Express, $7.50


_____ **Charge** to my VISA __ Mastercard __ American Express __ (shipping added)

Check which of the following you prefer and the additional charges will be added for weekday delivery (Includes a charge for expediting.)

     ____ UPS Next Day Air, $20.00

     ____ UPS Second Day Air, $11.00

     ____ Federal Express, $9.00

     ____ UPS Ground, $3.50
        (no additional charge for expediting)


Card number _____

Expiration date of card _____

Name on card _____
          (include middle initial or company name if on card)

Daytime telephone number (_____)_____-_____


**PSI Research**
300 North Valley Drive
Grants Pass, Oregon 97526
503/479-9464
FAX: 503/476-1479